STRANGE WONDERS

Searching for My Youth
in America's National Parks

To Desmond,

I hope your boys
develop a love for
the parks as I did

Whit Thornton

STRANGE WONDERS

Searching for My Youth
in America's National Parks

Whit Thornton

On the Road
PRESS

ISBN 978-0-9908149-0-0 (Hardcover)
ISBN 978-0-9908149-1-7 (Paperback)
ISBN 978-0-9908149-2-4 (ebook)

Library of Congress Control Number 2014953927

First Printing November 2014
Printed in the United States of America
by On The Road Press

Book design by Rebecca Byrd Bretz Arthur

To Jane

If thou be'st born to strange sights,
Things invisible to see,
Ride ten thousand days and nights,
Till age snow white hairs on thee,
Thou, when thou return'st, wilt tell me,
All strange wonders that befell thee.

—from "Song," by John Donne

Contents

Preface

In the summer of 1962, when I was fifteen, having just completed my sophomore year in high school, my parents and I took a seven week camping trip through the Northwest National Parks. This was the second time in three summers that we had embarked on an extended national parks tour. In 1960, we had covered the Southwest National Parks from Big Bend in Texas to Yosemite in California and all the major parks in between.

These were not so much vacation excursions as business trips for my father, Dade, who was a professional photographer. His work was on par with that of the best of his craft, including Ansel Adams. Dad intended to compile his work into a photographic essay on the national parks, something that at the time had not been done.

In 1960, I embraced the trip with enthusiasm. It was a great adventure. Two years later, however, the thought of spending seven weeks alone with my parents on an extended road trip was decidedly less appealing. I was in that awkward period of adolescence where I was not yet an adult but had left childhood behind. I was starting to question my father as a role model but did not yet know who I was or what I wanted to become. I envied my classmates who were spending their summers playing ball in the scorching heat of the tropical Miami sun, swimming in the tepid, turquoise waters off South Beach and Key Biscayne or making spending money cutting grass, washing cars—performing any odd job for a dollar. But I had no choice, so I went on the trip, determined to make another adventure of it.

One of my assigned tasks was to keep a daily journal of our activities. Each night by the dancing light of the campfire, I dutifully scribbled a short narrative account of the day, writing in a small black leather-bound record book with a red spine and lined pages. Years later, the journal would be one of my most prized possessions, bringing back memories of places visited, things seen, and emotions felt, that made me feel as if I were there, still fifteen. Yet, my life took me on a path unlike my father's. I became a person very different from him.

The trip had been a rite of passage, something I was drawn back to over the years. As if I were a salmon with an urge to return to spawn in the rivers of my youth, I had a desire to retrace the 1962 trip and repeat its highlight accomplishment, climbing the Grand Teton, a granite pinnacle 13,770 feet high.

Ken Burns' documentary *The National Parks: America's Best Idea*, further whetted my appetite for the trip, demonstrating that the Thorntons had not been the only family to make extended pilgrimages to the parks in the early 1960s. I wondered if others like me yearned to repeat the journeys of their youth.

While I never lost my love of the outdoors or my thirst for adventure, my career as a lawyer with its unceasing demands on my time did not afford me the opportunity to accomplish that vision. Finally, with retirement approaching, I decided that 2012, the 50th anniversary of the trip, would be the fitting time to make the journey and see if the years had truly separated me from the youth I felt so close to in reading my journal and studying my father's photographs of the trip.

The 2012 reprise trip was to be a journey of discovery to try to recapture my youth. Although I was 65, and a cancer survivor, I was in good shape. I could still see the boy in my father's photographs, running away from me, the distance between us slowly increasing, but he was still in sight. I felt that I had enough kick left that, with a good burst, I could catch him.

It was also a mission to complete the book that my father had envisioned but had never started. To my surprise it also became an unintended journey of reconciliation to bridge a chasm between father and son that had existed for nigh onto fifty years.

Route of the 2012 Journey

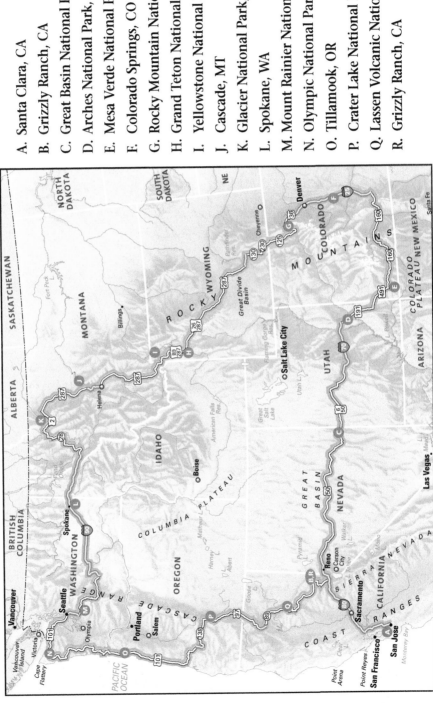

A. Santa Clara, CA
B. Grizzly Ranch, CA
C. Great Basin National Park, NV
D. Arches National Park, UT
E. Mesa Verde National Park, CO
F. Colorado Springs, CO
G. Rocky Mountain National Park, CO
H. Grand Teton National Park, WY
I. Yellowstone National Park, WY
J. Cascade, MT
K. Glacier National Park, MT
L. Spokane, WA
M. Mount Rainier National Park, WA
N. Olympic National Park, WA
O. Tillamook, OR
P. Crater Lake National Park, OR
Q. Lassen Volcanic National Park, CA
R. Grizzly Ranch, CA

ONE

Return to the Mountain

The beam from my headlight penetrated the blackness, illuminating the loose scree in front of me. I struggled to keep up with Anneka, our Exum guide, as we trudged up the steep rock-strewn slope from the Lower Saddle towards the decision point at the Crack of Doom. The night was cold but the air was calm, in sharp contrast to the howling west wind from Idaho on that night fifty years earlier when I was last on this mountain, an eager fifteen-year-old outfitted in Boy Scout hiking boots, thin jeans, a hooded sweatshirt, and a nylon windbreaker.

Exum Guides now provides a five-page list of mandatory and suggested equipment and apparel to prepare climbers for the ever changing weather on the Grand Teton. With the remembrance of how I nearly froze on my first climb, I followed the instructions to the letter. I was ready for any weather, although the weight of my pack was a constant reminder that preparation carried a cost. Nonetheless, a heavy pack was a small price compared to being caught at 13,770 feet with the wrong clothes. While the forecast was for good weather, the Grand Teton can be fickle and unforgiving.

I have always been intrigued by mountains and views from high points that extend off into the horizon. As a child growing up on the flat sea level sands of South Florida, the horizon was always no farther than a stretch of my arm. I climbed trees for a better view. On the seemingly interminable drives north up the long spine of Florida on Route 27, and later the Sunshine State Parkway, I would strain at the crest of every hill past Apopka to spot the thin blue line on the horizon that marked the southern terminus of the Smoky Mountains. The first sightings would always be false greetings that shortly dissolved into wispy clouds separating above the horizon until we entered Georgia, where the light blue line would hold and gradually become substance instead of a fading mirage. Finally, the Smokies were in sight. It never failed to thrill me.

I first climbed the Grand Teton in July 1962, the summer after my sophomore year in high school, one of eleven climbers led by two young guides in their twenties from Exum Mountain Guide Service. I made the climb on a lark, an adventure, something to express my independence on a seven week camping trip with my parents. In retrospect perhaps it was my Vision Quest, marking a rite of passage from my youth.

I wanted to see the view from the summit but we made the entire climb and descent enveloped in cold, damp clouds with visibility limited to the granite ledges and outcroppings within our grasp. At the summit there was no panoramic view of the valley or the adjacent mountain ranges; beyond our huddled climbing group there was only grey white cold. Our stay at the summit was brief.

We hurried down the mountain to avoid any further deterioration in the weather. At the Headwall below the Lower Saddle, we passed a group of ten climbers from the Appalachian Mountain Club who were headed towards the summit. Several days later I learned that the group had been caught on the Grand Teton in a freak July snow storm. One climber died of exposure and the remainder of the party was airlifted off the mountain by helicopter in what *Sports Illustrated* in a 1965 article termed "one of most difficult mountain rescues ever attempted."

Our guides, Jake Breitenbach and Peter Lev, brought our group safely down the mountain then immediately went back up as part of the rescue party for the stranded Appalachian Mountain Club group. Both Jake and Peter were extraordinary individuals and in the prism of my adolescent eyes were what I aspired to be— strong, independent, confident men who loved life and who life loved back. But life gives and it also takes.

Grand Teton gave me my first taste of mortality. The fact that I had shared the Headwall rope with the ill-fated Appalachian Mountain Club climbers, had looked at the face of the doomed climber, and could have suffered a like fate if the weather had turned earlier or Jake and Pete were less skillful, made me more aware of my vulnerability, although no more risk averse. The lesson was compounded the next year when I learned that Jake Breitenbach, who had seemed invincible, god-like, was killed in the Khumbu Icefall on the first American expedition to Mount Everest.

As years passed, the details of the Grand Teton climb remained vivid in my memory: the hike in darkness along the Saddle to the rope-in point; the climb along the narrow ledge, ironically called "Wall Street;" the friction pitch where we pushed away from the refuge of the slick rock face to gain traction; the spider-like scramble up the chimney with hands and feet wedged against the sharp-edged cornice as we climbed to the summit. They were scenes I could recall in Technicolor, unfaded by the years, yet there was a gnawing sense of incompleteness. I had made the climb yet had been denied the view from the summit, the same feeling I would have had if the landing on the moon had been staged in a studio. My accomplishment seemed unreal, almost fake. I had been there, touched the Geodetic summit marker, rappelled over a rock face 100 feet into a grey void, had a certificate of ascent signed by Jake and Peter, but I had not been able to actually see the thousand foot exposure as I had inched along Wall Street, nor had I felt the adrenaline rush of the panoramic view from the Teton summit and experienced the visual affirmation of my accomplishment.

Except for some rock climbing later on the 1962 trip near the summit of Mount Lassen, and scaling the sea cliffs of Acadia National Park in the summer of 1963, the Grand Teton climb was my first and last technical rock climb. My desire to complete the experience and repeat the climb grew as I aged. I also wanted to repeat the climb as my own small personal tribute to Jake Breitenbach's memory.

Now, fifty years later, I was back on the Mountain.

I prepared for the climb by working out for six months at Planet Granite, a rock climbing gym in the San Francisco Bay Area. The outside of the gym's tall pre-fab steel building gave no hint of the incredible scene inside: towering faux granite faces pocked with artificial hand and footholds with dozens of climbing ropes dangling from the top, most attached to spider-like climbers making ascents along routes color coded by difficulty. I was awed by the sight.

Without a climbing buddy to hold one end of the rope on what climbers call a "belay" to break a fall if a climber loses footing on an ascent, my workouts were limited to the "bouldering" area, a vertical wall approximately 12 foot in height with hand and footholds, similar to the big wall but not as high and without the safety ropes. The floor around the bouldering area was a thick mat that cushioned any fall. I had my share of tumbles off the wall at the beginning but my bouldering skills improved to the point where I could easily climb the 12 foot vertical wall by the novice routes. I thought I was ready for the challenge of the Grand Teton.

In 1962, we had summited by the Exum Ridge route. The route was pioneered by Glen Exum in 1931 when, as a young college student, he made a solo ascent of the Grand Teton wearing leather cleated football shoes, making a blind leap at the end of the Wall Street ledge to discover a new route to the summit. Owen-Spaulding is the other most popular route, which, while still a technical climb, is somewhat derisively referred by some climbers as the "walk-up" route.

I wanted very much to repeat the climb by the Exum Ridge route, savoring the memories from my previous climb and testing age against the recollections of my youth. However, after climbing school I had been exhausted and my instructor, Peter, suggested the Owens-Spaulding route would be the better choice.

Peter injured his knee at some point during climbing school and was unable to make the Grand Teton climb. I was fortunate that another climber, Greg, offered to share his guide. Greg had been an avid climber. He had planned on the Exum Ridge but was agreeable to any route.

That had been two days ago. The exertion of climbing school, yesterday's eight-mile hike to the Lower Saddle, with the 5,000-foot elevation gain, my sleep in the Exum Hut at 11,500 feet cut short after two hours when one of the twelve climbers packed into the 10x10 hut started snoring, the four a.m. wakeup, all were now taking a toll on my body and psyche.

I fought to keep pace with Anneka and I tried to listen for Greg behind me to see if he was struggling, but my labored breathing was so loud I could not hear whether Greg was also winded. My muscles already ached from the rigors of the two previous days and the actual climb had not yet begun. We would soon be at the decision point for which route to take, Owen-Spaulding or Exum Ridge. I was conflicted as to what to do. I wanted to suggest that we take the Exum Ridge route because I knew I would forever regret being the cause of holding Greg back from his goal, which was mine also, but I was tired and knew that the mountain could be unforgiving of any misstep or misjudgment. I was 65 years old, a prostate cancer survivor, and while I felt I was in excellent shape, had I deluded myself? In my quest to recapture my youth had I pushed myself too far?

TWO

My Most Unforgettable Character

For many years *Reader's Digest* ran a series of articles called, "My Most Unforgettable Character." I have no doubt that if this statement were posed as a question, a great number, if not the majority, of the people whose path brought them in contact with my father would quickly name him. By profession, Dade Thornton was a self-described third-generation artist/photo-grapher; by avocation, he was a writer, collector, amateur herpetologist, naturalist, folk musician, wood carver, conservationist, culinary chef, latter-day Beau Brummel, civic leader, party planner extraordinaire, and cutthroat croquet player who was not above improving his position with a surreptitious foot nudge when an opponent's back was turned.

Dade Thornton
Photographer

A handsome man, he was of medium height with thick wavy black hair that he tried to tame by combing it straight back, but an unruly lock usually fell free and curled across his forehead adding an apostrophe to his mustache and distinctive goatee. He smoked a pipe filled with his special blend of Bond Street, Half and Half, and Holiday tobacco. This semi-permanent facial protrusion, clamped firmly between his teeth, cloaked him in a perpetual hazy aura of fragrant translucent blue-gray smoke. When he talked, and even when he sang, his lips moved but the pipe remained still except for the puffs of smoke that curled upward from the bowl with each exhaled breath. Overall, he had a rakish look that he accentuated with a wild wardrobe of multi-colored jackets, ascot ties and trousers worn sockless with loafers even on formal occasions. Dade stood out in a crowd.

Born in Northport, New York, he would forever be considered a Yankee by my mother's family who were from Wellborn, a small town in North Florida near the Georgia line. My mother, Hilda, was born there in a small split-timber cabin that I visited as a child. Shortly after my visit, federal revenue agents demolished the cabin and the moonshine still operating on the premises.

Farming was a difficult life in Wellborn. Shortly before the Great Depression, my grandfather, Barney Bryan, moved his family to Miami where he took a steady job as a patrolman on the police force. The Bryans were a large family of nine siblings, six boys and three girls, with my mother the fourth oldest. There was always room for one more hungry mouth at the Bryan table during the hard times of the Depression and no one from the neighborhood was turned away.

Dade's father, Lawrence Thornton, was a photographer for Chase Bank in New York City. The reasons are murky, but when Dade was a young teenager his mother, Eleanor, and his father divorced. She moved to Maitland, Florida with Dade, his sister and his brother. Maitland was a sleepy suburb of Orlando before the Disney boom.

I remember my grandmother's house as dark inside, smelling of wood smoke and age. It stood on a large lot with massive live oak trees festooned with gray garlands of Spanish moss hanging from ponderous limbs that defied gravity, seemingly destined to become an unlimited source of prime firewood with the next big wind. The house was bordered on one side by an orange grove. It fronted on an uneven brick cobblestone road. On the other side was a rutted sand lane that led to Lake Minnehaha, one of a string of beautiful small bodies of water in the area that served first as Dade's playground, later as a laboratory for his interest in herpetology, then as a commuter path for his canoe to Rollins College, where he studied for a year.

My grandmother, Eleanor, was a character in her own right but in a more conventional sense. Her story is strikingly similar to that of Marjorie Kinnan Rawlings, whose autobiographical work, *Cross Creek,* describes a strong-willed woman who single handedly created a life for herself in Central Florida during the 1930s. I have no knowledge that they ever met but Cross Creek is only 95 miles from Maitland.

Eleanor Hadsell was educated at Barnard College, the women's affiliate of Columbia University in New York City. She played sports and studied fine arts in Paris, France. After the divorce and her move to Maitland, she supported the family by becoming a professional photographer, covering weddings and creating memorable family portraits. To supplement her income and perhaps to satisfy her adventurous nature she obtained a boat pilot license and captained tourists on scenic boat excursions from Mt. Dora to Silver Springs.

To her family she was known as Camera, a play on her professional calling. She was as stylish in her dress as my father but in a classic way. Camera always wore a colorful Hermes scarf around her neck, a cap or hat set at a jaunty angle, with matching shoes, purse and gloves. She was tall and thin with short gray hair that flipped up on the ends. She lived alone and never remarried.

After his first year at Rollins College, my father left to join the service to fight in World War II. He was rejected for duty based on an asthmatic condition, which he passed on to me. Disappointed and feeling he could not return to Rollins after his heroic departure, he moved to Miami to start his own life as a photographer, leaving behind his ambition of becoming a professional herpetologist. Dade was a fierce independent spirit, ambitious, motivated, and fueled with energy that bordered on the manic. He was one of the rare individuals who never worked for anyone but himself. During his entire life he was self-employed, the master of his own fortune.

In Miami, Dade transformed himself from a solitary individual, spending his time alone exploring the woods and hunting snakes, to an outgoing personality, growing his photography business through contacts made in social and civic organizations. He joined the Lions Club, the Optimist Club, became a Boy Scout leader, and started a youth organization called the Jr. Conservation Club. He had a charismatic personality and a touch of eccentricity that attracted a following. He reveled in the attention, receiving the approval from his new friends that had been withheld by his mother who may have seen a reflection of her ex-husband in her eldest son.

Dade frequently visited Harrison Photo Supply in the course of his photography business to purchase film, photographic paper, chemicals and equipment. There he met my mother, Hilda, a pretty, outgoing sales clerk. They fell in love and were soon married over the objection of Hilda's father and brothers who distrusted the Yankee who spent his free time in the swamps of the Everglades hunting snakes and other reptiles. He was twenty and she was twenty-three. From the time they met their lives seemed to take different arcs as Dade grew more social and outgoing while Hilda, as she aged, became increasingly withdrawn, and much like Dade's mother she quietly, yet clearly, expressed her disapproval of his eccentricities.

I was born three years after they were married, their one and only child. During my early years we lived in the first floor of an apartment building behind a furniture store on 36th Street in the Allapattah section of Miami. The apartment housed my father's portrait studio, a darkroom for processing photographs, a living room, one bedroom, and a combination kitchen/dining room. I slept on the top of a bunk bed in the bedroom and my parents slept on a rollaway bed in the kitchen/dining room. The apartment was small but the yard was spacious and my parents entertained large groups there frequently.

The studio could not be seen from the street, so to mark the location my father carved an ornate ten-foot tall totem pole with "Photography by Thornton" painted across the wings of an owl at the top. The totem pole was placed at the head of the driveway next to the street. It was periodically pilfered by pledges from the University of Miami on fraternity scavenger hunts. The contraband would be returned anonymously in the dark of night several days or a week after it had disappeared. Eventually the thefts stopped when the location of the totem pole became so well known that it no longer presented a sufficient challenge for the scavenger list.

A unique business sign

At the Lion's Club my father met two neighborhood dentists, Al Akers and Bud Lund, who shared his love of the outdoors and became his lifelong friends. The three frequently went camping together along the Ocklawaha River in North Florida, wearing fringed chamois shirts and leggings with moccasins and wide-brimmed safari hats with zebra skin bands. They each had impressive looking bowie knives with ornate handles molded of dental plastic. My father's knife had a cobra head handle with needle sharp fangs and fitted into a snakeskin sheath. The three outdoorsmen would set trotlines to catch catfish and hunted for frogs at night, wearing headlights whose yellow beams would reflect back the eyes of frogs and frequently alligators that always shared the river.

On one trip to the Ocklawaha, the three campers decided to enliven their experience, printing wanted posters for Deadeye Dade, Al the Assassin, and Bobo the Butcher, describing a series of heinous crimes attributed to the three with photographs in their camp regalia, offering a reward of $10,000, stating in microscopic print that it was payable in Confederate money. They plastered the Ocklawaha region with the posters and thought it was fine fun.

The joke turned serious when the county sheriff confronted the men for their fictitious crimes in a local bar decorated with a print of Custer's Last Stand on the wall. The tableau seemed on the verge of springing to life but they eventually were able to convince him it was a harmless prank. Fortunately, he had a sense of humor or it could have been the end for Deadeye Dade, Al the Assassin, and Bobo the Butcher. They were each armed and certainly looked dangerous.

When I was six years old I received my own chamois outfit and went along on the trips. I learned that frog legs are delicious fried, particularly cooked fresh in a cast iron skillet on a campfire with the smell of pines and wood smoke; the palate is aroused and the taste of everything is improved.

My father's interests in snakes and reptiles continued unabated. On weekends he would frequently take members of his scout troop or a few friends on snake hunting trips in the Everglades. He favored cruising slowly the back roads in the Glades at night during the winter with a spotter perched on the hood of the car looking for snakes, which, being coldblooded, seek the warmth

The Thorntons and Akers on the Ocklawaha

of the road surface. When a snake was located, the spotter would give a hand signal and try not to get run over as the driver hit the brake and the forward momentum would launch the spotter towards the usually docile quarry. The snake was quickly captured by hand, or if poisonous, pinned with a curved snake hook and then grabbed safely behind its triangular head, and placed in a snake sack, which was nothing more than a recycled flour bag.

Another favorite place to look for snakes on these outings was under wooden bridges. Yellow rat snakes frequently were found in the dark crevices under the bridges, but they could be aggressive. Getting bit at least once was the price for reaching into the lair of the rat snakes, who not surprisingly were reluctant to leave the dark confines of the bridge girders.

Dade's interest in snakes introduced him to another kindred soul, Bill Haast, the owner of the Miami Serpentarium, a combination laboratory and tourist attraction where visitors could view the most deadly snakes from around the world, including the king cobra and bushmaster, and also watch Haast extract venom from the snakes for scientific and medical purposes.

Dade and Bill Haast with a Bushmaster

Haast and Dade had a common bond in that they had both been bitten numerous times by poisonous serpents and survived. In Haast's case, he had gradually developed an immunity by injecting himself with small quantities of various serpent venom; his blood eventually becoming a serum for snakebite victims. Dade claimed to have been bitten eight times by water moccasins and rattlesnakes. Fortunately, they are serpents whose venom is not always lethal to healthy adults. The irony is that he survived snake bites, boar attacks, and the perils of a lifetime in the wilderness only to die ravaged by his own body, a victim of cancer.

Dade took advantage of the fact that snakes are cold-blooded and their metabolism slows when the temperature falls. He would build elaborate sets in his studio replicating the natural habitat of the snake he was photographing. He would then, over my mother's

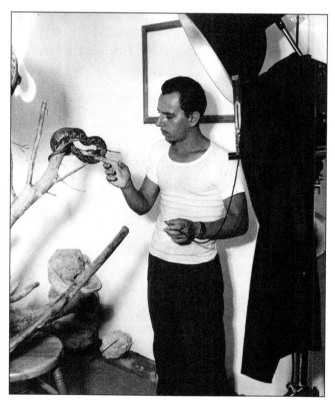

Posing a brown water snake

strong objection, place the subject in our home refrigerator, chilling the snake until it was practically comatose. The docile snake would be carefully placed in the set and Dade would move it around into a natural pose, much like placing a fashion model in a photo shoot. He followed the same process with poisonous snakes. The results were extraordinary. Some of his best work can be found in the Encyclopedia Britannica.

Dade and Haast had a theory that the fear of snakes is not a natural instinct but is a learned response fostered by society's almost universal disdain of serpents. To prove their hypothesis they had a perfect subject—me. I have a newspaper article with a photograph of me as a baby, less than a year old, a large Indigo snake coiled around my neck, the weight of the snake bending me forward. Yet I'm flashing a two tooth grin, unafraid, obviously enjoying the experience.

The newspaper story accurately reported the experiment behind the photograph but proving the theory almost resulted in a family schism. My mother was furious and social services initiated an investigation into whether a snake-handling photographer was providing a proper home for a baby. The hysteria died down quickly, my mother was pacified, and social services dropped its interest.

The innate fear experiment

In the late 1950s, my father took a group from the Jr. Conservation Club on a trip to the small Bahamian island of Bimini, 60 miles east of Miami; a jaunt that would change his professional career. The youth group sailed to Bimini on the Little Whale, a 30-foot schooner, to experience the island culture and to fish. On the trip my father met Neville Stuart, the founder and owner of the Bimini Big Game Fishing Club. Stuart invited Dade to return to Bimini to photograph the fishing tournaments hosted by the Club for world class tuna and marlin anglers. Dade shot the anglers, their fish, activities of the tournament, and sold them as albums of 8x10 black and white photographs. His clients included some of the most successful and powerful men in business. Their passion outside of work was the competition of big game fishing, and they traveled around the world to tournaments in the Bahamas, South America, Australia, Hawaii, Hatteras, Palm Beach, and points in between.

Dade was a flamboyant promoter who realized early that in order to sell albums each tournament had to offer something different. There had to be opportunities to take photographs of the anglers in situations other than simply standing next to their fish, celebrating at the tournament dinner, and accepting trophies. He became the tournament social director, creating and hosting wild costume and theme parties that became as popular as the fishing. He combined his work with his love of music and, with his bass ukulele, led calypso concerts. Fortune Five Hundred chairmen and presidents joined in with improvised instruments such as gut-bucket fiddles made with galvanized wash tubs, broom handles and fish line, old washboards strummed with spoons, and a solid percussion line with anything that could be beaten together, pounded or otherwise make noise.

Dade's photography and parties became so popular that he was soon asked to join what he referred to as the "Tournament Trail," following his clients to tournaments around the world as their official photographer and social director. The tournament business and completing the albums took six months each year but generated sufficient income that Dade was able to quit his portrait and wedding photography and pursue his love of wildlife and nature photography in the remaining time.

He was never a fisherman but he was such a presence on the tournament scene that in 2001 he was inducted into the Interna-

**Dade the
Tournament Entertainer**

tional Game Fish Association Hall of Fame. The Hall of Fame is located in Ft. Lauderdale, Florida and includes such luminaries as Ernest Hemingway, Zane Grey, Ted Williams, and Lord Baden-Powell, the founder of the Boy Scouts, among others. I attended my father's induction ceremony with my college roommate and fraternity brother, Paul Stanton, who lives in the Miami area. We were both excited to find that Curt Gowdy, the famed sports broadcaster, was my father's presenter. Paul and I had spent many Sunday afternoons together watching American Football League games with Curt Gowdy doing the play-by-play. He was a legend to us. Having him induct my father into the IGFA Hall of Fame was very special.

While Dade's tournament photography business kept him traveling, he still found time to serve as president of the Tropical Audubon Society and later the Florida Audubon Society. Despite his bohemian appearance and manic approach to life, he ran board meetings with the smooth efficiency of a gray-flannel-suited CEO in strict accordance with Robert's Rules of Order. Business was conducted with adequate discussion but when comments became redundant he called for the question, so the meetings were mercifully short. I was a junior board member of the Tropical Audubon Society. Most of the discussions were dreadfully boring to an adolescent, but I learned how to run an efficient meeting from watching my dad deal with his board. It was a useful skill in my later life.

The field trips led by Dade were legendary in Audubon circles. One of the most popular was a trip to an ibis and egret rookery located about a half mile off the remote Forty Mile Bend road in Everglades National Park. Dade would lead a group of assorted bird watchers through thigh-high swamp water, which was canopied by towering cypress trees with knobby knees breaking the surface, a silent tripping hazard, pointing out ghost orchids, and tree snails. Occasionally, he would spot and capture a water moccasin slithering through the water or curled on a cypress tree knob. There were never stragglers on Dade's hikes through the swamp.

I once remarked to my father that he didn't have the melody exactly right on a popular song he was singing, that it didn't sound like the record. He dismissed my comment by saying that he had his own style. That was true not only of his music, but of almost everything in his life. Dade didn't want to sound, look, or act like anyone else, and he accomplished his objective.

At one point, I had seemed destined to become the fourth-generation artist-photographer of the Thornton clan, but in the transition from childhood to adolescence I began to realize that Dade was a hard act to follow. More importantly, I recognized that I did not want to try. Dade was right. He was one of a kind, and I was inclined to leave it at that.

THREE

A Splinter Emerges from the Old Board

When I was in my mid-twenties and newly married, Dade gave me two photo albums as Christmas presents. The first was embossed with gold leaf lettering on the cover, "The Life and Times of Dade Whitney Thornton the Elder, or How to Grow Old Gracefully." The album contained photographs chronicling Dade's life as an outdoorsman, snake hunter, musician, and tournament photographer. The photographs were in rough chronological order and presented a man whose behavior was increasingly outrageous, at least in the eyes of his lawyer son.

As a companion volume, Dade also presented me with an album titled "The Life and Times of Dade Whitney Thornton the Younger: A Splinter Emerges from the Old Board." That album contained photographs of me from my childhood into the early teen years, engaged with my father in his various pursuits, with me either focused intently on the activity or gazing at him with obvious respect and adoration. There were some photographs taken in my later teen years that hinted at an underlying stress. In those images I was unsmiling, sullen; perhaps it was only the pose of a typical teenager, but at the time there was tension between my father and me that is evident in the photographs.

As we both grew older I felt that the constellation of friends circling around my father was weird; he tried too hard to be liked, to be the center of attention. Perhaps my resentment was that I was competing for his attention and felt lost in the crowd that always surrounded him. I began to feel that it was a one-way relationship, my father dispensing his wisdom and hangers-on lapping it up. I decided that was not me and I gradually disengaged, released from his gravitational pull, floating off to find a constellation of my own. This transition shows in the images captured in the photographs.

I recall having mixed feelings about the albums. I had recently married Jane, whom I had dated through college and law school. Jane came from a background very different from my own. She was from Babylon, Long Island. Her father, Charlie, was Executive Vice President of Fairchild Industries, a major defense contractor. He was the polar opposite of Dade. Charlie belonged to the Yacht Club, the Country Club, shopped at Brooks Brothers, and read *The New York Times* every morning. Charlie was the All American boy. He had been a life guard in the summer, played football, graduated salutatorian of his high school class, and married his high school sweetheart, Margaret, who was the valedictorian. He graduated from Brown University with a degree in electrical engineering and joined a small start-up aerospace company above the Babylon Post Office that later was acquired by Republic Aviation and ultimately became Fairchild Industries. Charlie was rock solid and a classic success story of those times. He was the role model that I had been looking to emulate.

Dade intuitively sensed that he was in a battle with Charlie for my soul. It was Jack Kerouac pitted against the *Man in the Grey Flannel Suit.*

Some photographs in the albums recalled good times. However, I felt that he had made the album of photographs about his flamboyant lifestyle to embarrass me. I interpreted his "Splinter emerging from the Old Board" reference as a heavy-handed reminder of where I had come from and that he was still the big man whom I could emulate but never replace. In retrospect, I may have made too much of it, but Dade was extremely competitive, and I felt that his most intense competition was with me.

It started with my name. My full name is Dade Whitney Thornton II. My father is Dade Whitney Thornton. Accordingly to the etiquette guru Emily Post, a man named after his father is "Jr." One named after a grandfather, uncle, or cousin, is "II." I wrote a paper for one of my college psychology courses on the psychological reason my father broke convention and named me "II." My theory was that "Jr." eventually becomes "Sr." but "II" can never become "I." I felt my father wanted a child who would emulate him but never replace him. He taught me skills, but when I became proficient in the craft or sport, the teacher became a competitor determined to remain better than the student. In response, I gradually found my own interests and outlets for my competitive juices.

While a man of Dade's talent and eccentricity naturally drew people into his circle, like mice to cheese, a casual acquaintance or friend could enjoy the feast and when sated, they could leave, take a break and when hungry for more rejoin the activities. For a family member, however, there was no break from the show. As a child and young teenager the non-stop pace and unusual interests of Dade's life were exciting, and I was a miniature mirror image, sharing his love of music, photography, reptiles, and the outdoors. I was the apple of his eye at that stage of my life.

As I matured into adolescence, however, the dramatic difference between Dade and the other male influences on my life caused me to reflect on who I wanted to be. I went in the opposite direction. Instead of taking over my father's tournament photography business, I went to law school and became a lawyer. My idea of non-conformity was to wear a coat and tie on casual Friday. I had truly become my father's shadow opposite.

Some years after law school I was working on a case with Fred Stant, a fine lawyer from Newport News, Virginia. We had worked on the case together for several years and had become good friends. One day I happened to casually mention that I was meeting my father at a fishing tournament at Hatteras, North Carolina. Fred regarded me with a puzzled look and said, "You aren't related to Dade Thornton?" It turned out that Fred was an angler who frequently fished the Hatteras tournament and knew my father well. I replied, "Yes, the one and only."

Fred's jaw dropped and he stood silent for several moments, slowly shaking his head. Then he kept repeating, "No way." "No way. There's no way that you're Dade Thornton's son." I asked him why not. He kept shaking his head and said, "You two are nothing alike." "Face it, you're a stuffed shirt and Dade hardly wears a shirt." "You must be adopted." I'm not sure that I ever convinced Fred that I was Dade Thornton's son. But I don't blame him since as adults my dad and I were two very different people.

Although I was Dade's shadow opposite, he instilled a drive in me—I became an Eagle Scout at twelve, the youngest ever in Florida, passed the bar at 23, was made partner at a Washington, D.C. law firm at 30, named president of a major West Coast ship repair company at 36. I ran through life at a full speed, perhaps chasing my father's shadow. Now I was preparing to chase my own.

And while I devoted my life to being as different from my father as I could be, as I aged I found myself wondering if I had been running from myself. Was the quiet, introverted lawyer that I had become so very different from the wild, extroverted show-man whose lifestyle I had rejected, or was there some common ground that blood and genes inexorably pulled us toward?

Perhaps the answer could be found in my youth if I could only recapture it. In my journal I had the map to guide me but did I have the physical and mental strength to follow where the journey would lead?

FOUR

Journeys of Discovery

On my library bookshelves are five black leather-bound record books with red cloth spines that chronicle annual summer camping vacations through the national parks from 1959 through 1963, when I was twelve through sixteen years of age. I enjoyed writing. Each record book starts with good penmanship and descriptive prose but gradually over the trip deteriorates into an almost illegible cursive-block letter hybrid with little more than a basic recitation of the day's events. Journal keeping became a chore but one that created an invaluable heirloom, a map to my youth.

I have moved a number of times since the journals were created but I have always known where they were kept. In musings where I've wondered if there was a fire or other disaster, and I only had minutes to save irreplaceable items, of what would be on the list, the black record books are always at the top. The journals have become one of my most precious possessions, like a fine wine increasing in value with the passage of time.

As companions to the journals I have photograph albums that my father made of each trip, further chronicling the events described on the journal pages. I have read and reread the journals often and studied the photographs, the combination of the two heightening my sensory perception to the point where I could hear the rush of a waterfall and smell the pungent wood smoke of the campfire. The journals and the photographs brought the trips back to me. It was a good feeling.

The trip that was the most meaningful to me was the seven week trip in 1962 when I was fifteen years old. I was just at the point of finding my own identity but I had not yet made the break from my father. The trip covered the Northwest National Parks starting with the Rocky Mountains in Colorado, then Grand Teton and Yellowstone in Wyoming, turning north to Glacier in

Montana, then west to Mt. Rainier in Washington State, then further west to Olympic, south to Crater Lake, further south to Lassen Volcanic, and then home to Miami with a stop at Arches in Utah and Mesa Verde in Southern Colorado. It was the most well-documented of the five summer trips.

In addition to the journal and my father's photographs, I carried a 16mm Bolex movie camera and shot hundreds of feet of film which I edited into a documentary of the trip. The film was silent but I gave an accompanying narration entitled, "Journey through the Northwest National Parks," and presented it to several Audubon and national park groups after the trek. I received no compensation, but the experience of speaking before groups of a hundred or so adults was good training for my later life as a lawyer. Thanks in no small measure to the seasoning gained in those lectures, I have never been uncomfortable with public speaking.

I've watched the film a hundred times or more and read the journal until the pages are imprinted in my memory. There were several life events on the trip for me. I hiked to the top of Flattop Mountain, 12,234 feet elevation, in Rocky Mountain National Park, so winded that I could only take two steps before stopping for a breather, but I made it to the top and back lugging my five pound camera and tripod. I also climbed the Grand Teton, 13,770 feet elevation, a technical climb. Fifty years later I could remember Wall Street, the friction pitch and the chimney on the Grand as if it were today.

Over the years, I set a goal to reprise the trip using the journal as a guide. The age gap between the youth in the journal and reality was increasing year by year, but when I looked at the photographs and film I did not feel older. I felt the same sense of wonder, pleasure, and accomplishment looking at those images as I recalled feeling at the time. The journal and photographs also rekindled a connection with my father that had been lost over the years, and which with his death in 1998 I thought had become irretrievable.

After years of having the trip as a goal, something to accomplish at some point in the indefinite future, I put a marker in the ground and set 2012, the 50-year anniversary of the trip, as the hard and fast date to make my second journey of discovery. This one would perhaps be the most rewarding and important of all.

FIVE

Getting Started

One of the special memories of the 1962 trip was a horseback ride and hike my father and I took to Sperry Glacier in Glacier National Park when we spent the night at Sperry Chalet, a hundred-year-old stone structure, one of several in the park constructed by the Great Northern Railway to attract tourists, as revenue producing rail passengers. Space is limited at the Chalet, and I assumed that reservations should best be obtained early. The week after Thanksgiving in 2011, I found the reservation website for Sperry Chalet on the Internet. To my surprise and chagrin, the entire 2012 season was already booked solid; reservations were being taken for the 2013 season.

The next day I mulled over this unhappy fact, then with a faint hope that perhaps there may have been some mistake, I called the telephone number on the website to confirm whether in fact there were no openings in 2012. A pleasant young man answered the phone, advising me that I was in luck. There had been a cancellation for a room on August 28th. I immediately booked the room. Jane, who would be my co-pilot on the trip, and I had our night at Sperry Chalet; we could now plan the trip around that fulcrum point.

While my objective was to repeat the 1962 trip as closely as possible, I was now living in Santa Clara, California, at the foot of the San Francisco Bay. Starting the reprise in Miami would mean traveling 2,500 miles across the country before the real trip began, wasting at least four or five precious days.

The first meaningful milestone of the 1962 trip was Rocky Mountain National Park. The four-day journey from Miami to my first view of the Rockies rising sharply above the flat plains provided memorable scenery, notably the Ozarks, and some points of interest, including Boot Hill in Dodge City, Kansas, but the trip was really centered on the national parks. It was a string of eleven pearls. Each pearl was a park, and it did not significantly matter which pearl was first touched. Jane and I decided that we would intersect the 1962 trip at the nearest point to where we now lived and continue the journey from there.

In 2010 and 2011, Jane and I had taken short "shakedown" cruises of national parks in California, Arizona, and Utah, to test RV camping, making sure that an epic six-week road trip was something that Jane would enjoy. She loved it. Our test runs of RV camping proved instructive in that they highlighted the necessity of advance reservations.

I reread my 1962 journal, making a day-by-day summary of our route, where we camped, and our activities. With August 28 fixed as when we would be at Sperry Chalet, I mapped an itinerary for 2012 based on my 1962 journal summary. Each day included a list of objectives corresponding to the hikes made and places visited in 1962. In setting our campsites I made some compromises with Jane. In consideration for her willingness to "rough it" at park campgrounds, we substituted several campground nights for reservations at famed lodges, including Jackson Lake Lodge in Grand Teton and Many Glacier Hotel in Glacier National Park. I tried to find the original motels where we stayed in 1962, but they all seemed to have disappeared, probably for the better as they were Class C accommodations at best in 1962; with the passage of 50 years, I was sure they were best left unfound.

With respect to the 1962 trip, I do not remember much of the planning that went into it. I recall writing to the Department of the Interior and receiving brochures on each of the national parks we would visit. I do remember poring over the brochures, reviewing the maps, looking for interesting trails. But I don't believe my father made any advance reservations for campsites. We would have to proceed differently for this trip if we were to follow the map of the 1962 journal and stay at the same campgrounds.

The parks are incredibly popular, particularly with foreign tourists who seem to enjoy camping. Campgrounds at the major national parks are typically full by noon. Late arrivals without reservations are relegated to secondary sites or overflow campgrounds. Based on this fact, at the first opportunity, which was six months in advance of our planned dates of stay, I logged into the park reservation system at www.recreation.gov and reserved a site at each campground where we camped in 1962, if it was still operating and permitted advance reservations.

The computer and Internet have revolutionized trip planning over the past 50 years. The park reservation system is definitely a modern convenience that is an improvement over the first come, first served system of the past. With the increase in the number of visitors, the reservation system rewards planning, but the parks are still sufficiently flexible to accommodate spontaneity and travel changes.

Jane and I had researched RVs for several years, attending outdoor shows and reading literature. We focused in on RVs built on a diesel Mercedes Sprinter chassis, which provided good handling and fuel economy. In 2010 we rented a Winnebago View. From that experience we learned that some national parks have vehicle length restrictions on trailhead parking lots and a few roads. We purchased a 23-foot Roadtrek Adventurous RS as our best option, providing sufficient space and storage for two people yet small enough to access most park facilities. It was an upgrade from the transportation our family used in 1962.

Before our 1962 trip, my father bought a Corvair 95 van. It had six cylinders, 80 horsepower, and a 3-speed manual transmission packed in a red and white box. With two front doors, a sliding side door, and two rear doors, the Corvair 95 provided easy access to the incredible amount of gear that could be stuffed into its rectangular confines. The air-cooled engine was mounted in the rear under a slightly raised deck behind the second row bench seat. The cargo space could be increased by removing the bench seat, which we did, replacing the bolted-in bench with a folding lawn chair for the third passenger, usually my mother.

In 1965, three years after my father purchased our Corvair 95, muckraking activist Ralph Nader penned an explosive diatribe against General Motors' new Corvair automobile line titled, "Unsafe at Any Speed." The book claimed the Corvair was unstable, with a defective design that caused the car to roll over on sharp turns. These claims were later debunked, but not before they terminally wounded the Corvair's reputation, resulting in the early demise of a sporty, relatively inexpensive auto. Recalling our modified Corvair 95, however, with a folding lawn chair for the backseat passenger, it was truly "unsafe at any speed."

"Unsafe at any speed" in 1962

Definitely an upgrade in 2012

For the 2012 trip our Roadtrek was the perfect adventure vehicle for two people. Instead of having to set up multiple tents, tarps, tables and cooking gear as we had at each campsite in 1962, we were self-contained with a sofa that converted to a queen size bed, a toilet, shower, refrigerator, convection oven, and stove, all powered by batteries, propane, and a propane generator. We also had sufficient storage space for the clothes and gear required for the journey. While the Corvair 95 and Roadtrek Adventurous were two very different vehicles, after 50 years of technological advancement the mileage on the two was the same, about 15 miles per gallon.

One of the key parts of planning the trip was determining the route. In 1962, we had a Rand McNally map of the United States for guidance. At our first fuel stop in each new state, we would get a state road map provided free of charge by the oil company. The interstate highway system was in its early stages in 1962, having been authorized in 1956 as the Eisenhower National System of Interstate and Defense Highways. We took advantage of the new system where we could, but much of our travel was on the *Blue Highways* of William Least Heat Moon's lyrical odyssey.

On maps, primary roads are marked in red and secondary roads are colored blue. Those are the two-lane blacktops that course through the small towns without traffic lights, marked at the outskirts by a weathered sign bearing the town name and population, rarely exceeding three figures. As Least Heat Moon described, there are great stories to be found along those quiet byways for voyagers with the time and an ear for listening.

As I plotted our route for the reprise, I scoured my journal for notations of towns, names, and sites that provided clues on the 1962 route's waypoints. On this trip we did not have to rely on oil company state maps for route guidance. We had a Tom-Tom Global Positioning System unit in the Roadtrek backed up by American Automobile Association state and regional maps, and a set of DeLorme detailed topographic maps.

In 1962, the United States launched Telstar I. This first telecommunications satellite provided a space-based relay for television pictures and telephone calls, and provided the first live transatlantic television feed. Thirty-two years later, in 1994, the GPS became fully operational. Ground users with a receiver and line of sight access to four GPS satellites can pinpoint their position and, with the right software, can do everything from navigating across the country or across town, to improving their golf game with accurate yardage information.

In addition to the GPS unit in the Roadtrek which gave highway route navigation, for the trip I purchased a Delorme PN-60 with SPOT communicator to provide trail maps and emergency locator assistance. The PN-60 is a handheld GPS unit that can download topographic maps and aerial photographs to provide detailed navigation for hikers. I downloaded sectional maps covering every hike we planned to take on the trip.

The SPOT locator is a one-way satellite communicator that allows sending short messages to selected email addresses with location information of the sender. There is also an emergency feature that will send an SOS message to a dispatcher who can transmit location information to rescue units. As SPOT is satellite- based, it works in remote areas where there is no cell phone coverage. It was an inexpensive alternative to a satellite phone and provided Jane some measure of comfort since some of the more strenuous hikes on the itinerary I would be making solo.

As the trip would take six weeks and we would be off the grid much of the time, in places where there was no cell phone, email or Internet access, I originally planned to retire from my job at Lockheed Martin Space Systems Company before the start. I did not want any distractions from work to interfere with my mission, which was to immerse myself in the experience of being transported back to 1962, measuring myself against benchmarks of my youth and connecting with past memories. However, my colleagues assured me that the office could run very well without me. They would leave me alone but expected progress reports along the way. With the encouragement of my colleagues I deferred retirement and instead took an extended vacation.

Work would not be an issue but both Jane and I were at the stage in life where a call in the middle of the night likely meant a flight east and a week of funeral arrangements for our last parent. My mother was 90 years old, living in a nursing home in Lakeland, Florida. As an only child, I had no one to share the responsibility for arrangements if she passed on while we were on the trip. Jane's mother, who was also 90, had dementia and was in an assisted living facility in Greenwich, Connecticut. Jane's sister, Joy, lived nearby and could handle any immediate needs, but if Margaret died Jane and I would want to attend the services even if it meant suspending the trip at some point and resuming it later. We worked out phone numbers and checkpoints where we could be contacted. We hoped that this part of our planning would prove to be unnecessary.

With our planning complete we had a detailed itinerary, reservations and a route. We made a stop at REI outfitters to purchase the few items of gear that we had not accumulated over our past two shorter camping trips, had the RV equipment serviced at a Roadtrek shop, then routine maintenance performed at a Mercedes dealership. We purchased our Roadtrek in October 2010, but with only a short weekend trip to Pinnacles National Monument and the two week shakedown cruise to Utah and Arizona, we had only accumulated slightly more than 5,000 miles, hardly sufficient to break-in the engine properly. We were still learning about the full capabilities of the Roadtrek and the idiosyncrasies of a diesel engine.

Being gone for six weeks presents a number of logistics issues, including mail, bills, Jane's treasured houseplants, our dog, Joe, a border collie/huskie mix, and as a reminder of our age, bottles of prescription medication that would not last the entire trip. None of these were issues to a fifteen year old in 1962. I had packed my clothes, gear and that was it. I was ready to go.

For the reprise trip, the logistics of arranging for what we would leave behind was almost as daunting as the planning for the journey itself. Close friends watered Jane's plants and collected our mail. Jane paid ahead for our expected bills. After some research, we found a great place to board Joe. Runamuck Farms is located in Watsonville, California, near the coast where the weather is cool. It is a three acre working farm where the dogs are off leash and uncaged. When we took Joe there for an initial visit, he immediately explored the area, mingled with the other dogs, and was ready to play. We were confident that he would be well taken care of while we were gone.

Finally, we were ready to begin. I had a new black red-spine record book to write a daily journal. Each day I planned to review the entry from my 1962 journal, travel back in time and see where it would lead.

———— DAY 1 ————

Friday • August 3, 2012

The alarm rang as usual at six a.m. The wake-up was unnecessary as I had slept fitfully during the night in anticipation of the long awaited start. My eyes were closed but my mind was racing with the list of what we needed for the trip, mentally checking off items. Counting sheep may act as a sedative; counting camping gear does not.

I quickly dressed, feeling surprisingly energized for as little sleep as I managed during the night. Anticipation long held and finally released is like a rush of caffeine or a shot of adrenaline.

The night before I had added Martha Reinthaler, the legal office manager at Lockheed Martin Space Systems Company and a good friend, to the list of recipients of SPOT messages that I planned to send each night when we reached our campsite. Our daughter,

Liz, had insisted that we had to let her know we arrived safely at each destination or she would assume the worst and initiate a missing persons action. We could use the SPOT Satellite Communicator paired with the Delorme P60 GPS unit to send her an email that we had arrived safely, together with a link that showed our location. Martha was the interface to my other colleagues at Lockheed Martin and would keep them advised of our progress.

After adding Martha's email address to the SPOT Communicator list, I tried to pair the device with the DeLorme P60 unit without success. The GPS mapping function was working but without pairing of the two devices I would not be able to send messages. Knowing Liz's overactive imagination, I could assume that she would call for a search by the Highway Patrol, Park Service, National Guard, and the Boy Scouts, if she didn't hear from us in some manner each night.

Thinking of Liz waiting for our arrival messages triggered memories of a canoe trip with my dad, his good friend Jack Partusch and his daughter Annie, who was several years younger than I, over the Easter Holidays around 1960. We had tried to canoe Fisheating Creek from the Highway 27 Bridge at Palmdale to Lake Okeechobee. The creek was wild, meandering through Florida scrub pines, prairie and swamp, dividing into a maze of blind dead-end watercourses choked with water hyacinths. The true channel was always disguised and the last we tried. The overnight trip extended into a second night and third day.

At several points where the hyacinths were thick, my dad and Jack would jump into the black water up to their shoulders and drag the canoes through the green matted morass while Annie and I paddled, keeping a lookout for alligators and snakes. We could hear the blasts of the shotguns from the duck hunters on Lake Okeechobee, but the hyacinths became impassible and we were forced to give up short of the Lake. My dad and Jack walked back to Highway 27, a considerable distance, then hitched a ride to where we had expected to emerge from the creek, while Annie and I waited at the canoes. We cooked the last of our food, hushpuppy dough mixed with swamp water, fried without grease in a cast iron skillet over a fire made with dead palmetto fronds. Nothing has ever tasted as good.

While Annie and I ate we heard an airplane overhead and we hid, assuming that it might be a search looking for us. We knew our mothers had most likely reported us missing since we were over a day late from our expected return. However, we were not lost and we did not need to be rescued. Rescue would be ignominious. Annie and I got home without being rescued, but as we expected, we had been reported missing. If we had a SPOT we could have sent an email that we were safe but delayed. But space-based communications had not yet been invented.

It was humorous to think of that story years later, but my disinclination to be rescued if I were not in desperate need was no less strong. I had to make sure Jane and I could communicate with Liz while we were on the trip and keep her finger off the panic button. I had checked the cell phone coverage maps. For most of the trip we would be in a cell phone service dead zone. It was too late to rent a satellite phone. The only solution was the SPOT satellite communicator. I had to get it working.

I called Delorme Technical Support. The Delorme tech was great and fixed the setting problem over the phone within two minutes. We would have the ability to send one-way email messages and location information by satellite from each destination on our itinerary.

With the communication problem resolved, we packed the Roadtrek and left Santa Clara at 9:50 a.m., headed for Grizzly Ranch, our second home, the first stop on our journey, where we had stored the rest of the gear we would need for the next six weeks.

The trip to Grizzly Ranch was uneventful. We had made the 265 mile drive dozens of times since August 2006 when we first visited the development four miles outside of Portola, California, only ten miles from Graeagle where we had vacationed annually since 1983 when my cousin Carl Bryan, a Superior Court Judge in Nevada City, recommended it to us for great golf and hiking. Grizzly Ranch is on the Eastern slope of the Sierras, a development of 280 lots centered around a beautiful Bob Cupp-designed golf course ranked by Golf Digest in the top 3% of all courses in California.

The drive up the mountain along Interstate 80, while beautiful as you enter the foothills, is stressful, with maneuvering around eighteen wheelers, and avoiding ambush by lurking highway patrolmen with radar guns. In winter there is the constant threat of road closure with rapidly changing weather conditions or accidents. But summer or winter, once I turned off I-80 onto Highway 89 at Truckee and headed north along the Truckee River towards the Sierra Valley, the largest alpine valley in the United States, with each mile the stress perceptibly lessened. By the Sierraville crossroads, it was gone, replaced with a Sierra serenity, part altitude induced but mostly a product of scenery and pace of life, slow and quiet. All glitz and pretense is left behind, shed with each town passed until the last flicker disappears with Truckee in the rear view mirror.

When we arrived we organized the remaining items for the trip, and I went into Portola for cash from the bank and a few items from Leonard's grocery. Portola is what Truckee may have looked like thirty or forty years ago, a bit worn, a little seedy, but solid. It was founded on railroading and timber, two dying industries. But freight trains still operate through the Feather River canyon. One of the delights of Grizzly Ranch is to hear the train whistle, muted through the pines, as a train rumbles through the Sierra Valley. Late on summer nights the coyotes will howl in chorus after the train whistles, seeming to occupy every hilltop in the area, a stereophonic symphony of the wild.

Portola was in the process of making a comeback, transitioning from trains and timber, attracting tourists, vacationers, and retirees to world-class fishing, hiking, golfing, and other outdoor activities supported by the lakes, rivers, and forests of the surrounding Sierra Nevada Mountains, but the economic downturn in 2009 hit the area hard. Nonetheless, scrappy Portola continues to be a place where you can find almost anything you want and everything you need.

Our close friends and nearest full-time neighbors, Dave Dicklich and Linda Moraga, invited us to dinner at their home in Grizzly Ranch, giving us a wonderful send-off with grilled steak and asparagus, which would become a frequent campfire staple in the weeks ahead. We made it an early night and went home to bed, excited to begin the next day's journey. It would be the second day of the trip but this first day had only been a continuation of the preparation stage. The true journey had yet to begin, what I was calling, "The déjà vu '62 Tour." Jane hates the name. She thinks it sounds like a geriatric rock band reunion but it does describe us. So for now the name sticks. The tour would start with the sunrise.

SIX

The Loneliest Road and the Expanding National Park System

Great Basin National Park
and
Arches National Park

In July 1986, *Life Magazine* described the 287 mile stretch of US Route 50 from Fallon to Ely, Nevada as the "Loneliest Road in America." It passes through bleak high desert country, over a number of mountain passes, with only two weathered mining towns, Eureka and Austin, breaking the monotony of the nearly straight asphalt ribbon and offering travelers the few necessities for the road. Travelers were cautioned to avoid the highway unless they had survival skills. But while it may have been infrequently traveled, it was far from uninteresting.

The high desert has a beauty of its own. Ever changing colors stretch across alkaline flats dotted with sage brush and salt bush that merge into high mountain ranges crossing back and forth across the Great Basin. The massive bowl, which covers most of Nevada and parts of four other states, collects the little moisture from the Pacific not blocked by the wall of the Sierras, letting no water pass to the sea. The highway winds through eight mountain passes, topped by Austin Pass at 7,864 feet. Pinyon pines, aspen, and juniper grow at the higher elevation, adding variety to the colors and textures of the desert flora.

Silver was not the first draw of settlers to the area. There are several ancient petroglyphs and pictographs along the highway, evidence of human presence centuries before miners arrived. Also, the road roughly follows the route of the short-lived Pony Express, which was eclipsed by the completion of the transcontinental telegraph line on October 24, 1861. Rendered obsolete by technology, the Pony Express ceased operations two days later. The ruins of a Pony Express way station are located at Cold Springs, sixty-five miles west of Austin, Nevada.

Other notable features of the Loneliest Road are the solar powered Loneliest Telephone, located adjacent to Sand Mountain, a 600-feet-high white dune, and the Shoetree, a quirky roadside dead tree festooned with scores of shoes tied together by their laces, mostly tennis shoes.

The State of Nevada and the merchants along Highway 50 have made the moniker of the Loneliest Road into a marketing positive. Travelers at either terminus can get a Loneliest Road card that can be stamped by a merchant at each checkpoint, Ely, Eureka, Austin, and Fallon. A completed card earns a Certificate of Survival of the Loneliest Road. Enterprising marketers also sell tee shirts emblazoned with "I Survived the Loneliest Road—Highway 50."

When we took the road in 1962, it had not yet received its ominous designation by *Life Magazine*. Highway 50 was simply the shortest route between Reno, Nevada and Arches National Monument, our next stop. I vaguely remember a vain search for a gold mine but I had no memory of the road, although my journal notes that the scenery was "beautiful."

In September 2003, I made a deal with my oldest daughter, Elizabeth. As consideration for letting her have our old Ford Explorer for her senior year at the University of Colorado, she and I drove back to Boulder, Colorado via the Loneliest Road instead of the usual trucker's route along Interstate 80 that her friends always took, faster perhaps, but considerably boring.

It turned out to be a special trip for both of us. We stopped at every point of interest and she earned her Survival Certificate and tee shirt. We visited Great Basin National Park and took the Devils Garden loop hike in Arches National Park, racing an advancing thunderstorm the last several miles. I can still hear the thunder echoing through the red stone canyons behind us as we ran breathless down the trail towards the safety of our car at the trailhead parking lot. It was a memorable experience on Highway 50 with my daughter. The Loneliest Road would be a fitting place to start the journey to recapture my youth.

The Antiquities Act of 1906 gives the President the authority to set aside "historic landmarks, historic and prehistoric structures, and other objects of historic or scientific interest" on public lands as a national monument. This broad authority may be exercised by executive order without further action by Congress. It was first used by Teddy Roosevelt to establish the Devils Tower National Monument. Later, he used the Act to create the Grand Canyon National Monument as a first step to protecting that cathedral of stone. Under the executive order process authorized by the Act, the President can, with the scratch of a pen, preserve endangered lands, eliminating the lengthy legislative process that is required to establish a national park.

The executive authority provided under the Antiquities Act has not been without controversy. There were bitter complaints from some quarters as almost two million acres of multi-use Bureau of Land Management land, potentially available for mining and oil exploration, were suddenly restricted to recreational use only in 1996, when President Clinton established Grand Staircase-Escalante National Monument, the largest ever created.

In some instances, the establishment of a national monument has been a first step to full national park status, which requires Congressional action. Arches was a national monument when we visited it in 1962 and it became a national park in 1971.

Lehman Caves in Eastern Nevada, located a few miles off the Loneliest Road, was an obscure national monument in 1962. I'm sure we were aware of its existence but we had visited Carlsbad Caverns and Mammoth Cave, both full-fledged national parks, on prior summer journeys. They were famed caverns. It was late in the day, and we passed little known Lehman Caves without stopping. Had it been a national park we no doubt would have made it a priority to visit. In 1986, President Reagan signed into law an act establishing Great Basin National Park, which incorporated the former Lehman Caves National Monument as well as 13,063 foot Wheeler Peak with its 5,000-year-old bristlecone pine trees that grow stunted and gnarled on its glacial moraines.

A brief visit to Great Basin National Park with my daughter in 2003 had whet my desire to see more of the park. Moreover, Highway 50 had become Jane's and my personal "Oregon Trail" on our trips to visit parks in Utah, Arizona and points east. Great

Basin National Park is the traditional first stop, an easy day's drive from our home at Grizzly Ranch in the Sierras.

On our introduction to RVing in 2010, Great Basin was our last stop before home. In 2011 it was our first campsite. The park that we had bypassed in 1962 would once again be the first stop of what I hoped would be a grand adventure.

Map of
Great Basin National Park

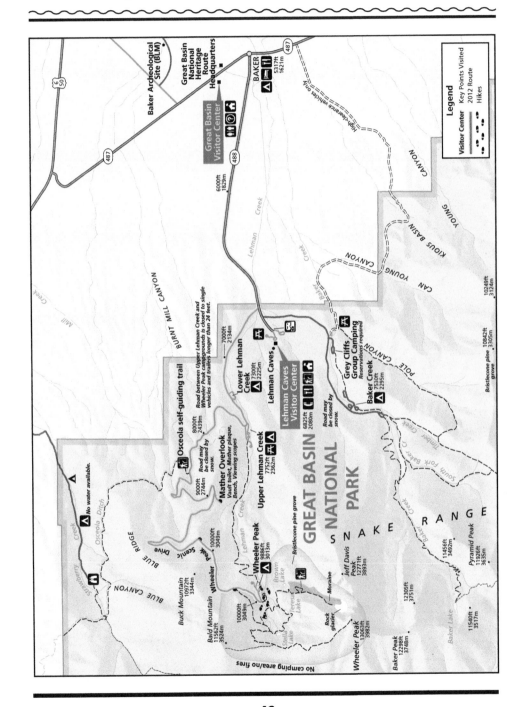

Great Basin Archeological Site (BLM)

Great Basin National Heritage Route Headquarters

BAKER

5317ft 1621m

487

487

488

Great Basin Visitor Center

6000ft 1829m

Lehman Creek

YOUNG

CANYON

KIOUS BASIN

CAN YOUNG CANYON

10249ft 3124m

Legend

Visitor Center — Key Points Visited

2012 Route

Hikes

Mill Creek

BURNT MILL CANYON

Osceola self-guiding trail

Road between Upper Lehman Creek and Wheeler Peak campgrounds is closed to single vehicles and trailers longer than 24 feet.

7000ft 2134m

Lower Lehman Creek
7300ft 2225m

Lehman Caves

Baker Creek

POLE CANYON

Grey Cliffs Group Camping
Reservations required

Baker Creek
7530ft 2295m

Bristlecone pine grove
10842ft 3305m

Lehman Caves Visitor Center
6825ft 2080m

Road may be closed by snow.

Timber Creek

South Fork Baker Cr.

Baker Creek

9000ft 2744m

Road may be closed by snow.

Mather Overlook
Vault toilet, Mather plaque, Bench, Viewing scopes

Upper Lehman Creek
7752ft 2362m

GREAT BASIN

NATIONAL

PARK

SNAKE

RANGE

No water available.

Osceola Ditch

BLUE RIDGE

BLUE CANYON

Strawberry Creek

Buck Mountain
11562ft 3344m

Wheeler Peak Scenic Drive

10000ft 3049m

Bald Mountain
10000ft 3049m

Wheeler Peak
9886ft 3013m

Bristlecone pine grove

Lehman Creek

Brown Lake

Stella Lake

Teresa Lake

Rock glacier

Moraine

Jeff Davis Peak
12771ft 3893m

12305ft 3751m

Pyramid Peak
11926ft 3635m

11456ft 3492m

Wheeler Peak
13063ft 3982m

Baker Peak
12298ft 3748m

11540ft 3517m

Baker Lake

No camping area/no fires

Map of
Arches National Park

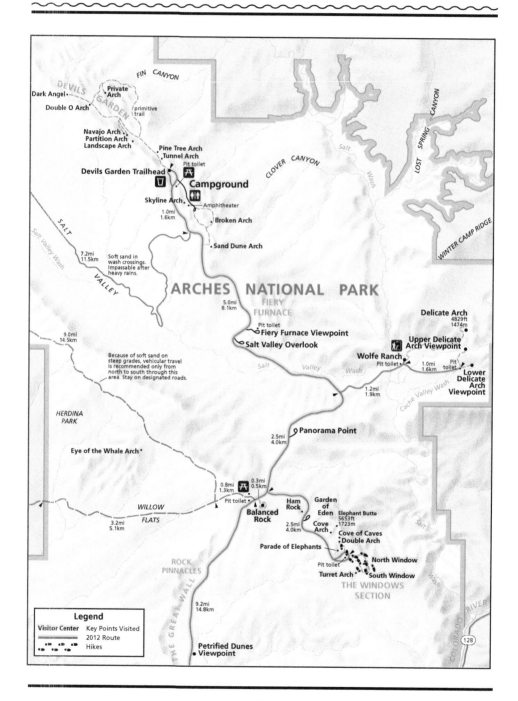

FIN CANYON

DEVILS GARDEN

Dark Angel •
Private Arch •
Double O Arch •
primitive trail

Navajo Arch •
Partition Arch •
Landscape Arch

Pine Tree Arch •
Tunnel Arch •
Pit toilet

Devils Garden Trailhead

Campground

Skyline Arch •
Amphitheater

1.0mi
1.6km

Broken Arch •

SALT

Sand Dune Arch •

7.2mi
11.5km

Soft sand in wash crossings. Impassable after heavy rains.

VALLEY

Salt Valley Wash

CLOVER CANYON

Salt
Wash

LOST SPRING CANYON

WINTER CAMP RIDGE

ARCHES NATIONAL PARK

FIERY FURNACE

5.0mi
8.1km

Pit toilet

Fiery Furnace Viewpoint

Salt Valley Overlook

Delicate Arch
4829ft
1474m

Upper Delicate Arch Viewpoint

9.0mi
14.5km

Because of soft sand on steep grades, vehicular travel is recommended only from north to south through this area. Stay on designated roads.

Wolfe Ranch
Pit toilet

1.0mi
1.6km

Pit toilet

Lower Delicate Arch Viewpoint

Salt   Valley   Wash

1.2mi
1.9km

Cache Valley Wash

HERDINA PARK

Eye of the Whale Arch •

Panorama Point

2.5mi
4.0km

0.8mi
1.3km

0.3mi
0.5km

Pit toilet

WILLOW FLATS

3.2mi
5.1km

Balanced Rock

Ham Rock •

Garden of Eden

Elephant Butte
5653ft
1723m

Cove Arch •

Cove of Caves
Double Arch

Parade of Elephants

Pit toilet

North Window

Turret Arch •

South Window

THE WINDOWS SECTION

ROCK PINNACLES

THE GREAT WALL

9.2mi
14.8km

2.5mi
4.0km

COLORADO RIVER

128

Legend

Visitor Center	Key Points Visited
⎯⎯⎯	2012 Route
•∙•∙•∙•	Hikes

Petrified Dunes Viewpoint •

Friday • August 24, 1962

We got up early drove on. After eating breakfast we hunted for a gold mine without any luck. The scenery was beautiful. After lunch we were in Utah. We drove for a long time and stopped in Provo, Utah for the night.

Saturday • August 25, 1962

We got up early and ate breakfast. We stopped at a geyser then at Arches National Monument we stopped and drove through and photographed some of the beautiful formations. . . .

——— DAY 2 ———

Saturday • August 4, 2012

We arose at daybreak, ate breakfast and packed the few remaining personal items not previously stowed in the Roadtrek, then carefully loaded the small Dometic refrigerator with the food perishables we would be consuming until our next stop for provisions. We were settled into our comfortable leather Captain's chairs, driving east on Highway 70 towards Reno while the sun was still low on the horizon, wisps of white trailing south across a slate blue sky. We were Captain America and Billy off to discover America, astride a Mercedes Sprinter instead of Harleys. The contraband stuffed in the dark places of our ride were not foil wrapped bricks of cocaine but boxes of estrogen patches and packages of Tena Men's Pads, the latter a daily reminder of my prostate surgery in 2009 which left me cancer free and with working plumbing except for an occasional faucet drip, hence the pads. Considering the other possible outcomes, I never considered the pads to be more than a minor inconvenience, less burdensome than shaving.

Hallelujah Junction, Reno, and Fallon—we were past the familiar points close to Grizzly. We were now on the part of Highway 50 known as the Loneliest Road. I reflexively checked the fuel gauge.

In the middle of the high desert, half circled by mountains the color of amethyst, is a stark white dune. Sand Mountain looks misplaced, artificial, as if a load of beach sand had been dumped to sand highways for the next century or perhaps to replenish bunkers in some nearby upscale Brobdingnagian country club. There seems no natural explanation for the unusual feature; then you feel the wind and remember this area was all underwater long ago. The receding seas left sand on the desert floor. Over the centuries the wind blew the sand across the desert to the slopes of the mountains that formed a barrier, trapping the sand, ultimately creating a two mile long, six hundred feet high silicon dune that continues to shape-shift with the zephyrs.

As we passed Sand Mountain, we could see that the visitor improvements that were under construction last summer, funded by the Stimulus, aka the American Recovery and Investment Act, had been completed. The parking area was already full with trucks, RVs, and trailers for dune buggies. We could see sprays of sand as buggies raced up the steep slope, turned sharply at the top then roared to the bottom. The buggies were small black specks moving like erratic water bugs on a tilted white pond. We hoped to get to Great Basin in time for an afternoon hike, so we did not stop.

At Cold Springs, we passed the Pony Express marker, climbed out of the high desert and over Paradise Range at New Pass Summit, and then followed the road down to the Reese River and up the western slope of the Toiyabe Range to Austin, the half-way point on the Loneliest Road. Austin has been referred to as a "living ghost town." Founded in 1861 by silver miners, it grew to 10,000 people before a series of boom and busts left a town remarkably preserved but with only 192 residents.

Austin is a window in time. Remove the contemporary vehicles from the streets and the modern fuel pumps from the gas stations and you are transported back 100 years. The buildings look old but new. The architecture is from the 1800s but they do not have the worn look of an aged mining town. Austin is a place where one could spend some enjoyable time browsing through the historic buildings, speaking with the residents on local lore, but instead we fueled the RV and were on our way, leaving questions for another trip.

The traffic on US Route 50 was light but we passed another Roadtrek Sprinter. The drive across the Basin is starkly beautiful. There was less wind than the last several times we traveled the road. On the stretch of high desert after crossing Hickison Summit, we stopped for lunch at a roadside rest area. It was the same place we had stopped on our trip to Great Basin last year. It is not particularly scenic in itself, but there are tables covered by shade awnings with a long view of the Diamond Mountains to the east, the next in a series of six mountain ranges we had to cross before reaching our destination at Great Basin National Park.

As I munched on a tortilla wrap slathered with almond butter and blueberry jam, sipping a diet Coke, I thought to myself that this landscape could not have changed from when I viewed it in 1962 as we passed on our way to Arches National Monument. I had thought then that the scenery was beautiful. I still do. I wondered if the rest of the country that we would be visiting remained as unchanged, untouched, as this lonely stretch of Nevada. Perhaps with the protection of the National Park Service it has stayed as I remember, but fifty years is a long time. The impact of throngs of visitors over the period, my imperfect memory, and the forces of nature, itself, could all have conspired to dramatically change how I would perceive the parks this time. I was looking forward to finding the answer.

At some point along this road in 1962 my interest in the scenery waned and I began to read a paperback novel, my head down trying to get comfortable in the back seat lawn chair. My dad looked at me in the rear view mirror with a disapproving scowl. When he was disappointed or angry he didn't have to say a word, he thrust his lower jaw at a canted angle. It was "the signal." I stopped reading and resumed looking at the passing scenery. In his view I could read books at home, this was a time to absorb the beauty of the outdoors. At the time, I was resentful of his unspoken rules enforced by "the signal." I was no longer a mini-version of Dade, mirroring his every like and dislike, and this was a disappointment to him. We were nearing the end of the seven week trip. It had been a great experience but I was ready to get back to my friends and start school. The tension was starting to build between us as I started to establish my own identity.

Jane and I made good time and arrived at Great Basin Visitor Center in the early afternoon. Great Basin is a park that does not accept reservations, so I had not been able to secure a campsite in advance. We asked the ranger at the visitor center desk about campsite availability in the park's four campgrounds, Baker Creek, Lower Lehman Creek, Upper Lehman Creek, and Wheeler Peak.

On our previous visits we had camped at Lower Lehman Creek, a sheltered area with 11 secluded sites, each within sound of a gurgling creek. We had hoped to stay there again but the ranger said the lower campgrounds were likely all full with our best option being the big Wheeler Peak campground with 37 sites. With that campground at an elevation of almost 10,000 feet, early arrivals generally opted for the lower sites instead of braving the chillier nights, longer cooking times, and less oxygen of Wheeler Peak, but for the first night of our journey we had no option.

While at the visitor center I asked the ranger whether we were in time to participate in one of Great Basin's famed full moon hikes. Great Basin's night sky is one of the darkest in the country, and on nights of the full moon, rangers lead hikes after sunset that traverse the park under a moonlit sky. We had read about the hikes on previous visits but were never in the park on the right night. We were out of luck again. The Sturgeon Moon hike had been held two nights earlier on August 2nd, leaving another activity on my list yet to be checked off.

We bought firewood in Baker, a tiny town outside the park, then drove the twelve mile scenic road to the Wheeler Peak campground. Our 23-feet 6-inch-long Roadtrek Adventurous just met the 24 feet limit for vehicles on the road beyond Upper Lehman Creek Campground. The restricted part of the scenic road is steep (8 per cent grade) and winding with turnouts overlooking the valley. At the campground we found a level site with a good fire pit and checked in at the kiosk.

One of the best bargains available to U.S. citizens and permanent residents, 62 years or older, is the Lifetime Senior Pass issued by the park service. It only cost $10 and covers the pass holder and vehicle occupants. I bought one when I became eligible and it is the best investment I've made. It provides free entry to national parks and federal recreational lands. It also provides a half-price discount for most campsites. For seniors visiting the parks it is a great deal. Great Basin has no entrance fee but we saved $6 off the $12 per night fee at the campground.

After setting up the campsite we hiked the Alpine Loop Trail, a 2.7 mile circle that starts at the Wheeler Peak parking area and winds through a dense subalpine forest of Engleman spruce and Douglas fir. The starting elevation is 9,800 feet, then rises another 600 feet. A small stream crossed the trail not far from the trailhead. The silver tinkling of the rushing water over the smooth worn rocks broke what was otherwise complete silence except for the muffled sound our hiking boots made with each stride and an occasional bird call or squirrel chatter.

The dense forest was broken by a few meadows that afforded good views of Wheeler Peak rising another 3,000 feet above us with small glaciers and snow packs clinging to its steep serrated edges. The gathering dark and the altitude turned us back before we reached the Alpine Lakes.

At the trailhead, we took the short self-guiding nature trail that loops around a wet meadow. The trail was flat, a good cool-down from our Alpine Lakes hike. According to our Delorme P60, we had hiked a total of 1.68 miles, not much, but this was our first day and we were at altitude. I felt good. I had been winded a bit on the steeper sections of the trail but not enough to slow my pace. I remember how difficult Flattop Mountain, 12,234 feet elevation, in Rocky Mountain National Park had been for me in 1962. That will be the test if I am ready for the Grand Teton. Everything else is preliminary.

Back at camp, I split the wood we purchased in Baker into kindling with a small hand axe, crumpled a wad of newspaper in the fire pit, then carefully stacked the kindling teepee style against the paper as I had learned as a Boy Scout and done dozens of times on the camping trips with my parents. I used a long BBQ match to light the paper at the four corners, watching the flames consume the paper, lick the thin wood kindling, then engulf the larger pieces on the outside. One match. It never failed.

I waited until the bright white, yellow-orange flames sterilized the fire pit grate, neutralizing anything harmful that had been on it. Then, for good measure, I gave the hot grill another vigorous scraping with a stiff steel grill brush. When camping there is nothing like cooking on an open wood fire. Splitting the wood, making the fire, tending it until the wood transforms to red hot charcoal and the flames have subsided to just the right level, then turning the meat, poultry or fish at the proper time, moving it to the right spot on the grill so that it is not under- or over-cooked, are all tasks that bring us closer to the spirit of our pioneer forefathers. Campfire cooking is work, which makes the meal taste the better for it.

Each Friday in the summer months, Sierra Valley Farms on County Road A-23, four miles east of Portola, California, hosts a farmer's market that is one of the best in California with organic fruits and vegetables, grass-fed lean beef, and fresh fish from an Oregon fisherman with his own boat and access to the best catch from other sources. The market draws savvy consumers from far beyond the Portola region. Before leaving on our trip, we had purchased a fresh wild Pacific salmon from the fish monger. I grilled it on the hot wood fire along with fresh asparagus. The salmon was delicious, firm yet moist. The asparagus was overcooked, shriveled and blackened but edible. I would have to be more careful when grilling vegetables. On a very hot, open wood fire there is little margin between cooked moist and crispy black.

After dinner we walked to the campfire talk where the ranger spoke on ghost towns—why they were built and why people left. The answer is gold, where it is and where it isn't. The nightly campfire talks at the national parks are always informative and enjoyable. The audience usually includes a wide range of ages, sophistication, and knowledge, but the rangers and naturalists making the presentations skillfully provide something of interest for everyone. I enjoyed the campfire presentations as a know-it-all teenager and still get enjoyment as an inquisitive senior. It is part of the camping experience that Jane also relishes.

Dark was fast approaching as we walked back to the campsite. The aspens along the trail pointed boney white fingers upwards, grasping vainly at the fading light. The sun had dipped below the mountain, casting a shadow over everything except the apex of Wheeler Peak, which was splashed with a yellow-tinged glow. With the creeping darkness, the temperature rapidly dropped. The cool temperature of the high elevation was a welcome respite from the heat on the Basin floor. We cracked open the windows of the RV for fresh air, making sure the bedding was with the warm side up, as we expected the temperature might approach freezing overnight.

The bed sack is convertible for winter and summer. For warmer nights the summer weight side is placed on top and when the weather is cooler the comforter is reversed with the winter weight on top. The system is flexible, providing comfort under a range of weather conditions.

—— **DAY 3** ——

Sunday • August 5, 2012

I awoke at 5:45 a.m., turned on the hot water heater, then quickly showered when the water warmed, and dressed. It had been a chilly night but the sleeping sacks worked well.

The campsite was quiet; no other campers were moving. Wheeler Peak was again illuminated with a bright yellowish glow, this time in the low light of early morning instead of the fading rays of dusk. The highest point catches the first and last light.

After breakfast we organized the RV and drove down the scenic road. I knew there was no dump site or water at Arches, our next stop, so we dumped the holding tank even though it was less than a third full, and topped off the potable water tank. This was my third RV trip. I was getting proficient at the dump station. But I remember the first time I dumped the black water tank in the Winnebago View we rented as an experiment to see if RVing was for us. The instructions we were provided on the View's systems at the rental agency were rapid fire, condensed into a fifteen-minute monologue by a bored employee with two more presentations before closing time. We only half heard the instructions as we were anxious to be on the road to our first night's campsite in Yosemite. It was almost three hours away and we wanted to be there before dark. Three days later, I stood in a puddle of foul smelling effluent at a dump station in Sequoia National Park, holding a hose with my bare hands trying to remember where it connected when a friendly gentlemen from the RV queued behind me approached with a pair of disposable gloves, saying, "Put these on. You look like you could use some help."

That was my introduction to the brotherhood of the dump station where it is all for one and one for all. If you have an emergency and need a wrench, duct tape, or the loan of the dump fee, your dump station brethren will willingly share. I'm not sure if the sharing is driven by a sense of community or the urge to get the line moving and get one's self off the dump station as quickly as possible. On reflection, I think it is the latter.

Great Basin is a hidden jewel of a park. Although the campgrounds were full, there was a feeling that the park was uncrowded. The parking lots were half empty, few people were on the trails.

In contrast to our previous visits to the marquee parks, Yosemite, Sequoia, Bryce, Zion, and the Grand Canyon, where each parking lot looked and sounded like an assembly of the United Nations, we didn't see a single foreign visitor at Great Basin. It's remoteness on the eastern edge of Nevada, far from any other attraction of note, makes the park either the final destination or a waypoint for the few intrepid travelers, such as Jane and I, on the Loneliest Road. The Loneliest Park on the Loneliest Road, both well worth the extra effort they entail to get there.

We fueled up at the Stateline Station, where Liz and I stayed when we took her back to the University of Colorado at Boulder. The motel hadn't changed. It seemed nondescript from the outside but the beds were comfortable and, as I recalled, the food at the café was good.

We passed into Mountain Time Zone in Utah. The news on the satellite radio was a shooting at a Sikh Temple in Wisconsin. The tragedy of the shooting was jarring in contrast to the serenity of the sagebrush valley and mountain ranges in Utah along Route 50.

By late afternoon, we were off Highway 50, once again having survived the Loneliest Road, and were back on the interstate system. Interstate 70 is one of the most scenic Interstates in the country. We were quickly in red rock country. Our view of the colorful sandstone temporarily was obscured as we passed through a heavy rain storm rent by distant lightning. Within a few miles the temperature dropped from a blazing 92 degrees to a cool 65 degrees. After the rain stopped the temperature climbed back into the 70's. We stopped at the Sand Bench rest area where Liz and I had stopped. The Native Americans were still selling their jewelry and pottery laid out on mats atop the parking area retaining wall.

South from the overlook a white sandstone bench falls off into red siltstone desert spotted with green clumps of sage brush before Cedar Mountain rises blue-purple in the distance, merging west with the dark green of the Fishlake National Forest, framed by the weathered bones of an ancient juniper long dead. Dark cumulus gathered in the west with light fingers of virga streaming eastward.

We could have watched the developing storm with its shifting effect on the colors of the desert and mountains for hours.

It was as if an artist, unsatisfied with his work, dabbed the paint brush at the palette, changing with a light brush stroke the tone of the scene, pausing momentarily, then trying again to improve on perfection.

At Green River we saw the sign for Crystal Geyser, but we didn't stop. I didn't remember the geyser from my earlier trip in 1962, but my journal records that we stopped there. Crystal Geyser is unusual in that it is not caused by geothermal activity but is a rare example of a cold water dissolved carbon dioxide geyser. The geyser is located at a drilled well that has tapped into a pocket of carbon dioxide. The gas seeks an outlet that forms the geyser until expended. Carbon dioxide then continues to seep into the well, creating pressure until the cycle repeats itself.

Past Green River we turned off I-70 towards Moab and Arches National Park. When we entered Arches we drove straight to Devil's Garden campground and checked in. The campground host had our reservation. Although the temperature was hovering around 100 degrees, the parking areas were full with scores of people out on the trails.

After we checked in and offloaded our chairs to mark that our campsite was occupied we drove into Moab, stopping first at the Park Avenue turnout, one of our stops in 1962. The smooth, high red walls and spires of Park Avenue are epic. We rushed through Arches in 1962; it was the end of our trip, school started the day after Labor Day and we were due to arrive home on August 30 with only a few days to unpack and shop for school clothes and supplies.

There was no time to explore Arches, but both my father and I sensed that in the few hours we were there we had but grazed the surface of a wondrous place. Trails through colorful rock formations beckoned but we had to leave. We did not even see the famed Delicate Arch. Regrettably, my father would never get back. I have returned twice, once with Liz and once with Jane. This now was my third visit since I first gazed down Park Avenue in 1962 feeling that this is a special place. Each visit confirmed my first impression.

In Moab we had dinner at Zax, the same restaurant where we had dinner last year, an informal place with great burgers and good service. After dinner we got ice cream and headed to the Windows area to catch the sunset. The only stop we made in Arches in 1962, other than Park Avenue, had been the Windows area and famed Double Arch. Although we were only in the monument for a couple of hours in 1962, essentially a flyby, we had seen one of the great sandstone canyons in Park Avenue and representative samples of the arches for which the area is named. It was enough to make a lifelong impression with red rust capped by cerulean one of my favorite color combinations, always invoking good feelings.

The evening was overcast and did not look promising to get much of a glow on the arches from the late light or a colorful sunset. We hiked to the Windows and Turret Arch, viewed the blue shadowed La Sal Mountains to the southeast, and took some photographs in less than ideal light.

Sunset looked like a bust so we drove the short distance to the Double Arch parking area, then hiked to the arch. Double Arch looked eerily like my father's photograph in his album of the 1962

**Double Arch
1962**

**Double Arch
2012**

trip. I should not have been surprised, as the monolithic sandstone could not have changed perceptibly from when he took the picture but it was strange; the photograph taken in 1962 had captured a scene that has remained unchanged except for the transitory entry and exit of visitors walking the path to the arch.

I was not in my father's photograph of Double Arch, but in other pictures from that trip where I am included, my visage is outwardly more youthful looking than now, but I did not feel any older as I stood in the same place as then. I felt a connection with the place, with myself, and with my father, a sense of continuity and timelessness. It was a good feeling.

Sunset at Balanced Rock — 2012

I took a couple of photographs at Double Arch and headed back to camp, disappointed in the nondescript sunset that had failed to light the Windows in a final encore to the day. It appeared that the band had left the stage without playing the fans' favorite song. But as we drove away from Windows, the dying sunset suddenly burst into a golden glow. It was as if a match had been tossed on a gasoline-doused sky.

We quickly pulled over onto a small gravel patch, bringing the RV to a stop mostly off the pavement. We were eager to get photographs before the sun disappeared below the horizon, dragging the colorful sky with it into the darkness of night. I grabbed the Nikon D90 and photographed the sunset with Balanced Rock outlined in black against the flame colored sky. As I was transfixed by the sunset, Jane said to look behind me. The setting sun had cast a spotlight on the cliffs and arches, bathing them in a brilliant reddish glow. The raging sun fire before me had leapt the dark barrier to set aflame the rocks behind me.

Sunset at Elephant Butte – 2012

The visitors who had been waiting for the sunset had left early, apparently convinced that the overcast on the horizon would thwart any show worth seeing. We were alone. The park was our personal theater. I could not decide which way to look; both fires pulled for my attention like giant red black holes. When night released the sun's grip, we went back to camp, satisfied that we had seen Arches at its finest. The final encore had been a greatest hits medley, enough to please everyone.

At the campground, we sat outside on the reclining chairs as full darkness fell around us. The night stars revealed themselves one by one until the black sky was spotted with a thousand dots of light.

Jane was concerned about cougars coming into the RV during the night. On our visit last year, a cougar was reported to have been sighted in the campsite next to us on a night when we had the rear doors open for ventilation. She stacked our chairs against the back of the RV to provide a barrier but I told her it was more of a ramp into the RV than an impediment for an intruder. She reluctantly agreed to remove them.

The night air was very warm and still. It would be a dramatic change from the previous cold night at Great Basin.

SEVEN

A Journey Back in Time

Mesa Verde National Park

It was getting late, they were cold, bone-tired from searching for stray cattle up the brush-filled canyons that crisscrossed the flat green table mountain the Spanish called Mesa Verde rising 2,000 feet above the Montezuma Valley in Southwestern Colorado. Richard Wetherill, and his brother-in-law, Charles Mason, had heard stories about ancient cities from the Utes in the area but they had never seen any Indian ruins in these canyons.

It was December 18, 1888. The wind freshened as snow began to fall. Wetherill and Mason dismounted and led their mounts along the narrow slippery trail. Visibility decreased, then lifted, as if a curtain had parted to reveal a massive stone city three stories high immediately before them. The cowboys had stumbled upon Cliff Palace, the largest of the dwellings at Mesa Verde with over 150 rooms. They explored the ruins for several hours, then went home to report their incredible discovery.

Mesa Verde was populated from 550 to 1300 AD with increasingly complex societies. The cliff dwellings most associated with Mesa Verde were built between the late 1190s to the late 1270s. Prior to that time, the Ancestral Puebloans who settled there lived first in pit houses, then in above-ground dwellings with wood and mud walls. The civilization grew and seemed prosperous when suddenly around 1300 they left, never to return, leaving behind stone and wood cities that would withstand the harsh elements for another 800 years and counting. Few clues remain as to the reason for their departure. It is another mystery of history. Speculation abounds as to the cause, including war, drought, and pestilence, but like the tale of the Lost Colony of Roanoke, we may never know for certain.

The stone cities on the cliffs discovered inadvertently by cowboys in 1888 became known nationwide and drew archeologists, anthropologists, curiosity seekers, and "pot hunters" looking for relics. Mesa Verde was established as a national park in 1906 by President Teddy Roosevelt. It is unique in that it is the only national park established to "preserve the works of man." All others preserve the works of nature.

Mesa Verde was the last park we visited in 1962, the end of a long odyssey. My journal entries became short, declarative statements devoid of descriptive language. I was ready to go home and begin my junior year in high school. However, unlike the Ancestral Puebloans, I would return.

Map of
Mesa Verde National Park

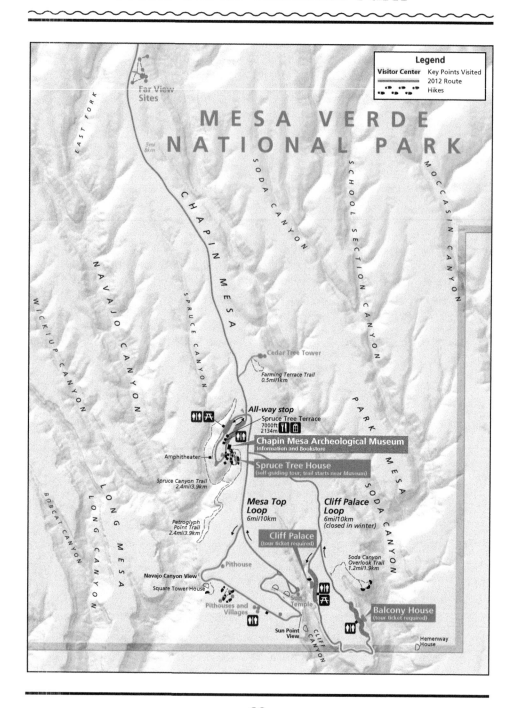

Legend

Visitor Center   Key Points Visited
2012 Route
Hikes

MESA VERDE
NATIONAL PARK

EAST FORK

Far View
Sites

5mi
8km

CHAPIN MESA

SODA CANYON

SCHOOL SECTION CANYON

MOCCASIN CANYON

NAVAJO CANYON

WICKIUP CANYON

SPRUCE CANYON

PARK MESA

SODA CANYON

BOBCAT CANYON

LONG MESA

LONG CANYON

Cedar Tree Tower

Farming Terrace Trail
0.5mi/1km

All-way stop
Spruce Tree Terrace
7000ft
2134m

Chapin Mesa Archeological Museum
Information and Bookstore

Amphitheater

Spruce Tree House
(self-guiding tour; trail starts near Museum)

Spruce Canyon Trail
2.4mi/3.9km

Mesa Top Loop
6mi/10km

Cliff Palace Loop
6mi/10km
(closed in winter)

Petroglyph
Point Trail
2.4mi/3.9km

Cliff Palace
(tour ticket required)

Soda Canyon
Overlook Trail
1.2mi/1.9km

Pithouse

Navajo Canyon View

Square Tower House

Pithouses and
Villages

Sun
Temple

Sun Point
View

CLIFF CANYON

Balcony House
(tour ticket required)

Hemenway
House

Saturday • August 25, 1962

We then drove on to Mesa Verde. There we set up camp at an overflow area then went to the Park Headquarters to hear the campfire program. On the way we saw a few deer. At the campfire the amphitheater was almost filled. The talk was on Navajo sand painting and it was magnificent. After the talk Navajo Indians performed dances for the people. Then we drove back to camp and went to bed.

Sunday • August 26, 1962

We got up early and went into Cortez for breakfast. We then drove up to the museum and got the information we needed. The first cliff house we saw was the Spruce Tree house but we didn't go down to it. We took the loops stopping at all the overlooks including Cliff Palace which we went into and Balcony House. We took the first loop too, including the pit houses and pueblos. The tour was very interesting. Then we went back to Spruce Tree House and took the self-guiding nature trail. Back at camp we packed quickly and left. At Pagosa Springs we ate supper and spent the night.

——— DAY 4 ———

Monday • August 6, 2012

We slept all night with the back doors open, lying on top of the bedding in a vain attempt to escape the heat. The temperature never went below 80 degrees.

We got up at six a.m., leisurely ate breakfast and prepared to leave Arches. The low slanting morning light highlighted the sandstone formations, casting shadows that defined each crack and knob, belying the mirage of smoothness seen in direct light. While we ate, a solitary rabbit munched on grass outside the RV and chipmunks scampered around the sandstone rocks.

I had tweaked my back on the first day of the trip so I did some stretching exercises on the table before we left. The table had a steel grate top instead of the usual smooth wood planks. It made me feel like I was stretching on a nail bed. After I got used to the sensation, however, it acted as a massage for the tightness in my back, adding another element to my stretches. The exercises helped, but I was concerned that my planned Teton climb was only 10 days away. The climb would be difficult enough without the encumbrance of a sore back.

A group of young Germans was at the campground restroom. The girls were pouting and the boys were sullen. They looked sunburned and hot even in the relative cool of the morning. Whatever was on their agenda for the day, they did not look enthusiastic but it may have been the hour. It was early and most of the campground had not yet stirred. I was again struck by the number of foreign tourists who now frequent our popular national parks as compared with 1962. The only foreign tourists I remember from the trips in the sixties were two German women at the South Rim of the Grand Canyon. They were memorable to me at the time because they were first women I had ever seen with unshaven legs, hairy as two men in shorts. I still can recall my shock, or perhaps it was envy. The wispy down on my legs at that time was no match for the awesome forest on the legs of those two otherwise very attractive women.

We drove out of Arches without stopping except for a brief pause at the visitor center to buy post cards, write a note to my mother and mail it. It was a relatively short drive of three and a half hours to Mesa Verde as compared to the marathons of the first two days. We stopped in Cortez for milk and entered the park at about 12:30 p.m. From Cortez, Mesa Verde looms straight up from the Colorado Plateau. It seems impossible that there is a road to the top of the mesa but as we drove closer we could see the switchbacks. Mesa Verde holds ancient and modern feats of engineering: the cliff dwellings that have survived virtually unchanged for centuries and the steep, serpentine road that provides access for the half million people per year who visit those dwellings.

The radio reminded me that 50 years ago that day Marilyn Monroe was found dead from an overdose. I remembered that we heard of her death when we walked into a restaurant outside Glacier National Park. In retrospect it was the end of the age of innocence, but at the time it was only the tragic death of a film icon much too young.

The Cuban missile crisis was still several months away. As I explored the national parks in 1962, the potential for thermonuclear war with the Soviet Union never entered my mind. The turbulence of the sixties with the deaths of John Kennedy, Robert Kennedy and Martin Luther King, Jr., the riots and divisiveness of the Vietnam War would come later. We so-called Baby Boomers, born after World War II, spent our childhood in the relative tranquility of the fifties, then made the transition to adulthood fired in the hot crucible of the sixties, an unprecedented period of triumph and tragedy. We had a young, exciting president who had energized the country. To a fifteen-year-old, the decade of the sixties held unlimited promise for America and those of us fortunate to live here. It was a wonderful time to be young. As the years passed, the draw of that earlier, purer period before Marilyn Monroe's death pulled stronger. This trip, in part, was a response to that tug of a past time.

We checked in at the Morefield Campground and found our campsite, number 175, a secluded spot thick with Utah Juniper and Mountain Mahogany with a view of the plateau rim. We ate lunch at the campsite and went to the Far View Visitor Center to buy tickets required for the ranger guided tour of Balcony House and Cliff Palace. On my last visit, tickets were not required; instead, the ruins were open to explore at your own schedule and pace without a ranger guide.

We decided to take the 3:30 p.m. tour of Balcony House and do the 9:30 a.m. tour of Cliff Palace the next morning before leaving the park. We drove straight to Balcony House, where a ranger explained that the tour involved climbing a 32-foot ladder, crawling for 12 feet through an 18-inch wide crevice, scrambling up a 60-foot cliff face using stone steps, then climbing two 10-foot ladders back to the rim where we started. Jane has a bad knee and opted to stay on top. I was concerned about crawling through the crevice with my strained back, but I made it through without a problem.

The tour reminded me of Disneyland—a long queue and a short activity with a fresh young person providing a scripted narrative. The ranger was informative, but when you are in a large group you lose some of the mystical feeling of being in the ruins; there is no time to sit and contemplate the mystery of the place. There was a German family with older adults and several twenty year olds. The adults obviously could not speak English. The father kept wandering outside the group disinterested in a narrtive he did not understand. The ranger asked politely at first, then sharply, that he rejoin the tour. When he ignored her direction, the son barked an order in German, startling the man who quickly returned to the fold. The scene repeated itself again and again as the tour progressed, the wandering father like a wayward unruly child.

Spruce Tree House Kiva, 1962

The same spot in 2012

In 1962 I had scrambled down rickety ladders and explored the ruins on my own. However, with the increase in the number of visitors, some limits had to be instituted to preserve the ruins for future generations. I feel fortunate to have been able to have visited Mesa Verde before visits to the cliff dwellings became so regimented and structured. But the preservation effort has been successful. The cliff dwellings are essentially unchanged over the past fifty years. Preservation of Mesa Verde is the most important objective, with access being important but secondary.

After Balcony House, we went to Spruce Tree House ruins. I walked down to the ruins on the nature trail, as I had with my father. I was glad to see you could still go into the Kiva. It was a memorable experience from my 1962 trip, and it was still special. The ceremonial room is reached by a ladder through a small opening in the roof which provides the only light, which streams through the opening like a spotlight illuminating a column of space within the Kiva, displaying dust particles suspended in the air, the dark corners of the room barely visible. I was struck by the fact that the dust floating in the air may have been the same dust I inhaled when descending into the Kiva in 1962. It certainly had not been cleaned in fifty years and there was nowhere for the dust to go. The ladder is sturdier and a safety rail had been installed on the open side of the Kiva entrance, modern concessions to OSHA regulations, but otherwise everything was the same. It was truly traveling back in time for me.

We took the Mesa Top Loop road and stopped at the pit house ruins, dating from 550 to 750 AD. These were the dwellings used by the predecessors of the cliff dwellers. Little remains except for the excavated shallow pits which the original inhabitants covered with a roof. Later, the villagers built above-ground houses with walls of wood poles and mud; the pits became ceremonial kivas.

After our full day of exploring Mesa Verde, we went to the Metate Room Restaurant at the Far View Lodge for dinner. The food was excellent. We had a table by the window with a great view of the East Rim, the sunset painting the ridge with a brush stroke of alpine glow before fading to purple then gray-black. A doe with its fawn emerged from the brush and grazed below the window. Later, a young buck joined her. After dinner, we went back to camp and to bed, too tired for the campfire program.

———— **DAY 5** ————

Tuesday • August 7, 2012

We arose early to leave Mesa Verde, dumped the tanks and advised the camp store that we were leaving a day early. Instead of making an exhausting marathon drive straight through to Rocky Mountain National Park tomorrow, we decided to get an earlier start this afternoon and spend the night at a hotel halfway to the park.

We drove straight to Cliff Palace, the largest cliff dwelling, for the 9:30 a.m. tour. While not as physically demanding as Balcony House, the hour-long tour requires descending uneven stone steps and scaling five ladders for a 100-foot climb. Jane has an aversion to ladders with her bad knee, so she took another pass, deciding to wait for me on the mesa top.

I turned on the generator and the air conditioner in the RV so Jane would be comfortable and went off to find my tour. Our group was about 30 people including, as always, a large contingent of foreign visitors. However, Mesa Verde seems favored by Germans. We didn't see any Asian visitors in either Arches or Mesa Verde.

At the starting point for the Cliff Palace tour a woman asked the ranger if she knew Nevada Barr, the author. The ranger replied that Barr no longer worked for the Park Service, adding that Barr made her job seem much more adventurous than it was. The woman seemed disappointed, saying she had read one of her books. Nevada Barr novels are murder mysteries set in national parks with the protagonist, Anna Pigeon, a park ranger. Barr's books are a riveting, enjoyable read. Happily, risk of murder in the national parks is low.

The ruins were as I remembered, but the ladders were much sturdier. My memory of 1962 was that the ladder was lashed together and wobbled when I climbed it. There is nothing like being able to go at your own pace. Touring the ruins with a guided group was a much different experience than being able to explore the area on your own. It is difficult to lose yourself in time and feel the presence of the ancients when surrounded by a cacophonous group of tourists, many conversing in foreign tongues.

I caught up with Jane in the parking area at the completion of the tour and we departed Mesa Verde. We fueled up at the

Cliff Palace, 1962

Cliff Palace, 2012

entrance to the park and photographed the mesa, looking like a green table for which it is named.

It was a seven-hour drive to Colorado Springs. Just out of Durango on US 160, a rock hit the windshield and left a quarter-size spider break. I hoped the jolt from a pothole would not spread the crack across the entire windshield. We were lucky and the break did not expand. We were able to delay replacement of the windshield until after our return home.

The drive between Pagosa Springs and Del Norte over the Great Divide is one of the most beautiful we've ever taken. The road parallels a river that runs through a mountain valley flanked by high mountains. A thunderstorm draped the mountains with a gray shroud streaked with lightning. The Divide crested at Wolf Pass, 10,500 feet in elevation. The valley is crisscrossed by ranches with cattle grazing on lush river bottom grass. The drive was truly memorable, but I had no recollection of it from 1962.

There was intermittent rain the entire drive. We finally arrived in Colorado Springs at 7:00 p.m. The final segment after crossing east of the Rockies was long and monotonous. We checked into the Fairfield Inn too exhausted to go out for dinner. Instead, we microwaved frozen entrees we purchased at the front desk, palatable but a far cry from the meals we had been enjoying up to now.

Microwave was a new invention, unknown, at least on a consumer level, in 1962. I remember TV dinners, those tasteless chicken or mystery meat meals in aluminum foil packages that you heated in an oven. They always included a glob of mashed potatoes that crusted over when cooked and had the consistency of the paste we used in grade school. The sodium content must of have been off the charts. TV dinners were quick if not tasty. On our 1962 trip, we didn't have a microwave or an oven, so there were no TV dinners. Everything was cooked on a Coleman stove or the campfire. When traveling between campgrounds we ate in restaurants. My father enjoyed good food, but his interest in cooking came later.

We organized our gear for the next day, charged the electronics and went to bed to the staccato cadence of a room air-conditioner instead of the wind rustling through the trees and other soothing night sounds of a campground.

EIGHT

Every Breath I Take

Rocky Mountain National Park

In 1962, we were four days from the flat sand beaches of Miami when the Rockies appeared before us, rising straight out of the plains, sharp edged and dark. These were not like the Appalachians, masquerading as low lying clouds on the horizon. Wearing no disguise, the Rockies emerged full form before us.

Rocky Mountain National Park was the first park on our trip. I was looking forward to a serious solo hike to test myself and establish my independence. The park has the highest average elevation of any national park, with nearly a third of it above the tree line at 11,400 feet.

On my third day in the park, I made the 8.8 mile roundtrip hike from Bear Lake to Flattop Mountain, elevation 12,324 feet, climbing 2,849 feet in the process with my 16mm Bolex movie camera, tripod and daypack. By the time I reached the summit, I was stopping every two steps to catch my breath. My 15-year-old Floridian body, though young and eager, had not been sufficiently acclimated to the high altitude.

I was laboring for breath much like I did when I had asthma attacks, which I had endured more or less continually from the time I was a baby through young adulthood. I had asthma every night when we camped, brought on by the mildew in the tent or jungle hammock where I slept. The areas where we stored the camping gear when it was not in use was hot and humid in the blazing Florida summers, a recipe for brewing mildew. My parents finally installed air conditioning, years after I left for college. I had asthma for so long it was nothing more than an annoyance. I did not let it prevent me from doing anything I wanted to do. So long as I had an inhaler and a sufficient supply of adrenaline it was not a problem. A couple of puffs and I could breathe.

The memory of the difficulty I'd had with the Flattop Mountain hike stayed with me. As I planned for the repeat trip I worried if my added years would prove to be too much even though I felt I was in good physical shape. If I could not successfully climb Flattop Mountain, which was only a steep hike, there was no way I could make the summit of the Grand Teton, a technical rock climb a thousand feet higher and one of the most important objectives of this reprise effort. The only way to find out would be to try.

Map of
Rocky Mountain National Park

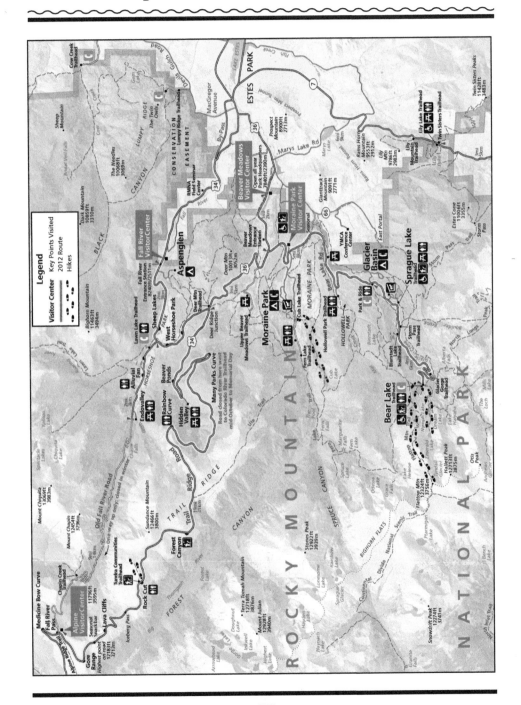

Saturday • July 14, 1962

It was 6:30 when we crossed into the Mountain Standard Time Zone. A few miles down the road we stopped for coffee. Kansas is plains stretching to the horizon, dotted with occasional farms and trees. We saw our first magpie outside of Takin. Coming up to small knolls vast panoramas open up before us. The Arkansas River on our right is distinguished by a line of trees. It is about a mile away.

We crossed into Colorado and the scenery didn't change much—rolling hills and big ranches. At Pueblo we stopped at the Koshare Indian Museum. It is a replica of a Kiva owned and operated by Explorer Scouts. In the museum were artifacts worth thousands of dollars: paintings, blankets, carvings, baskets, pottery, etc. We stayed there about an hour then rode on.

We got on a super highway and shortly we saw the thin blue line that marked the mountains. We caught US 25 outside of Colorado Springs and rode right in. In Colorado Springs we went to Manito Springs. There we saw Pike's Peak. We ate in a restaurant there and looked around for an hour and left.

Just before we got to Denver the fan belt broke and we had to take all our gear out of the car and fix it. At Denver we got groceries and ice.

The drive up to the [Rocky Mountain National] Park was very beautiful but our car had no power. It was slow moving uphill with the accelerator to the floor. We first went to the Endo Valley campground but it was full. Then we went to Glacier Basin. We went around the circle twice and then stopped a park naturalist, Stan Franklin. He told us we might be able to find a camp by talking to a ranger. We did this and wound up with a magnificent campsite out of the way with plenty of room.

Sunday • July 15, 1962

We got up late and ate breakfast then finished up the camp putting up the tarp. After we did this we went to Moraine Park Visitor Center. There they had great dioramas of the animals in the park in their natural state. They also had an exhibit on wild flowers of the park. I asked the man about my hike to Grand Lake and he said he wouldn't advise it under the circumstances. We went to Mr. Franklin's house in Moraine Park and left a message. Then we went to Glacier Park for a picnic lunch. There we saw beaver dams.

At Bear Lake we took the walk around the lake. At the start we photographed gray jays, Clark's nutcrackers, golden mantled ground squirrels and chipmunks. About half-way around the lake it started raining so we hurried on through.

I took the hike from Glacier Gorge to the campground, 3.7 miles. On the trail I saw beaver, ducks, chipmunks, and beautiful scenery. Back at camp, Mother was fixing supper when Stan Franklin, his wife and two children came by. We talked about the park until it was time to go to the program at Moraine Park.

The talk was by Dr. Dallas Sutton on mammals. After the talk we went to Mr. Franklin's house and he took us through one of the meadows hunting beaver. We heard one but didn't see any.

Monday • July 16, 1962

We got up and ate breakfast then went to Estes Park. We stopped at a Phillips 66 dealer for gas and oil. From there we ate breakfast and went to the park headquarters. Mother and I went on a tram ride up Prospect Mountain. We saw the continental divide, the plains and Flattop Mountain. When we came down the car had a problem. We took it to Arnold's but he said it would take a long time so we took it to another 66 dealer who fixed it perfectly.

We ate lunch and then went on the Trail Ridge Road. We stopped at a few places but it was too cold to do much. I got to get in snow for the first time. Dad got sick and Mr. Franklin drove us back to camp. Back at camp I went to photograph the picket pins. We ate supper and I packed for my hike and went to bed.

Tuesday • July 17, 1962

We got up at 4:00 am and ate cereal then drove down to Bear Lake. I was on the trail to Flat Top Mountain by 6:00 and it was uphill all the way. I had to stop every 50 yards to catch my breath. At the Dream Lake overlook I got a magnificent view of the lake. A little farther down the trail a chickadee stopped and chattered at me. At the Emerald Lake overlook I could see Hallett Peak and Tyndall Glacier. About 3 miles up the trail was the timberline. In the rocks I saw many pikas. I had to cross 200 yards of snow to get to the top. At the top I could see Dream, Bear, Emerald, Helenes, Bierstadt, Odessa, and Fern lakes. The Never Summer Mountains were at my back and a cold wind blew around me. A blue haze prevented my viewing the plains. It started to rain so I headed back. It took 5 hours up and 3 hours down. I caught a ride back to camp.

After I got back to camp we went into Estes Park for a doctor for my mother and looked at gift shops. She had an upset stomach. I caught 4 trout at a commercial trout hatchery. Then we came back to camp. There we photographed the picket pins for a while then ate supper. After supper we went on a beaver hike and saw quite a few.

Wednesday • July 18, 1962

I got up late and Mother and Dad had already come back from photographing beaver at Sprague's Lake. Our breakfast was pancakes and they were very good. After washing dishes we took some pictures of the camp and photographed golden mantled ground squirrels and the broad tailed hummingbird. The hummingbirds were very common and consistently came to the feeder we had hung from the tarp.

Mom and Dad took a nap and I worked on photographing some more animals. A chickadee was up in a pine tree, eating and fell out. This made him very mad and he really scolded. After they got up we packed the camera gear and went to Bear Lake. This time we got a booklet and read the signs to the self-guided nature trail. Along the trail a golden mantled ground squirrel came and stood up on a rock against the background of the mountains. Half way around the lake it started raining so we hurried back to the car.

From Bear Lake we drove directly into town for supper. We looked around then decided on the Continental Restaurant. It was a bad mistake. First the waiter dropped our dinner and then quit. After this farce we went into a donut shop and then went to the

Blue Spruce. There they had some beautiful carvings. Some were by an Indian named Dee for $1.50.

Thursday • July 19, 1962

We got up fairly early and ate breakfast. After washing dishes we started up Trail Ridge road. Our first stop was outside the Beaver Meadows entrance. There we shot pictures and pictorials. At Many Parks Curve we stopped and shot some more pictorials. Half way between Rainbow Curve and Iceberg Lake we stopped and shot snow scenes of Mom and I having a snow ball fight.

At Forest Canyon overlook we saw a couple of marmots. We also shot some scenics. At Rock Cut we got out and saw a marmot and shot pictures of Never Summer Mountains. A storm came up and we got pictures of that. At an overlook this side of Fall River it snowed. This was a real thrill but it melted quickly.

At Fall River we ate a few hotdogs and had some hot chocolate. We drove on down to Milner Pass but the weather was awful. It hailed at the pass and we didn't climb Specimen Mountain. We drove on back to Fall River and there we photographed the mountain blue bird. At Rock Cut we waited for and got photographs of pika. But the marmots didn't show up. We took the hike up to the Toll Memorial Mountain Index over the tundra trail. Up at the memorial was a bronze dish pointing out the mountains. We walked on back and drove down to camp.

At Moraine Park we stopped at the visitor center and went on the trail. It was very interesting and well-constructed. Just before we got to camp we tried to photograph a beautiful sunset. At camp we fixed supper and worked on the cameras then went to sleep.

Friday • July 20, 1962

We all got up early and ate breakfast then Dad and I went off. At Horseshoe Park we saw a weasel. At the Endo Valley campground we drove around. The camp didn't look as good as Glacier Basin.

At the Trail Ridge Road we headed straight up to Rock Cut. There we saw marmots all over the place. We set up our gear and photographed a couple. I saw a pika and got some footage of him.

We stayed there for a while then went back to photograph the dwarf spruce and dead trees. While we were photographing the dead trees I saw a deer. We stalked him over snow and down the mountainside but never got a picture of him.

At Rainbow Curve we stopped and took some pictures of the chipmunks and Clark's nutcrackers. Back at camp we ate lunch then went to Bear Lake where we took the trail to Nymph Lake a half mile away. On the trail we saw a Steller's jay. At the lake we fed chipmunks.

On the way back we went into Estes Park for supper. I went on a trampoline. We ate trout. Back at camp we took down the tarp and went to bed.

Saturday • July 21, 1962

We got up early then took the camp down. After that we head straight for Rock Cut. Dad photographed the marmots while Mother and I went on the Tundra Trail.

At Fall River we had some hot dogs and hot chocolate and then went to Milner Pass. There we saw the bighorn sheep and Dad and I took off up Sheep Rock after them. We saw them twice more but didn't get pictures. At the Timber Creek Campground we had a drink then went to Grand Lake. A few miles outside the park we saw a sign that said, "Yellowstone Park, shortest, most scenic route," so we took it.

In the Arapaho National Forest we stopped and ate lunch and I fished. We also went into a mine. At Willow Creek Pass we crossed the Continental Divide. In Wyoming the roads were pretty bad at first. We stopped and got gas and a drink just across the State Line. We saw a lot of magpies and other birds.

At Rawlins we got gas and ate at a Mexican restaurant and had some real good food. We hunted for a motel but all the prices were high. We finally stayed at a motel called Dreamland and went to sleep.

—— DAY 6 ——

Wednesday • August 8, 2012

I was awakened by a hotel noise, a shower, door opening, or the cranky start of the fan, a sound that was incongruous with the quiet solitude of park campsites where we had been sleeping for the past week. The red-lighted numbers on the bedside clock showed that it was still early but I was now awake, ready for the day. With the extra hour of found time, I took advantage of the fact that we had Internet access for the first time since we left Grizzly Ranch to search through the myriad of junk emails for the few that were of interest.

One of the major differences between the 1962 trip and 2012 is the fact that we now live in the electronic age. Whenever possible, we use every available outlet to refresh our precious battery-powered devices. Our key equipment had recharged overnight. We should be set until the next water hole. I swapped in my spare camera batteries to top off their charge before we left.

At breakfast, we met a young couple with three young children, who were headed home to Kansas City after a 6500 mile trip through western national parks, including Yellowstone, Glacier, and Mount Rainier. They planned to make the trip again when the children were a little older. Glacier was their favorite park. With his eyes widening, the oldest child described to me that they had seen grizzly bears! As I asked the children more about their trip I wondered what memories would remain with them the rest of their lives. Would they carry a life-long urge, as I have, to return to the scenes of their youth?

After breakfast, we packed and drove to Estes Park just outside the entrance to Rocky Mountain National Park, where we replenished our grocery supplies at the Safeway. We stowed the food in the refrigerator and cabinets, filled the cooler with ice and soft drinks, then drove into the park, stopping at the Moraine Park Visitor Center. The wildlife dioramas that had so impressed me as a youth were still there. I'm not sure if the animals were the same ones, but if so they were prepared by a great taxidermist to have remained so lifelike after fifty years. My father always said that when he died he wanted to be stuffed and put on display. I thought it was his usual attempt at being outrageous, but perhaps not. He always sought attention and reveled in the spotlight. I think he would have enjoyed being gawked at in a museum—Dade Thornton, photographer, naturalist, eccentric, the last of his kind.

Outside the visitor center was a picnic area that looked very much like the scene in my film where we had lunch. After looking around, I was certain it was the same place. Jane and I found a picnic table in the shade and had our standard fare, tortillas with a generous spread of almond butter covered with blueberry jam for me and peanut butter with blackberry jelly for her. I have a mild peanut allergy that triggers a migraine headache if I have more than a dab of peanut butter. Almonds are not a problem and I stocked up on fresh almond butter before we left on the trip. A tortilla, almond butter, blueberry jam wrap became my daily mid-day energy boost, much as a can of Vienna sausage and sardines on Saltine crackers with a block of cheddar cheese was our standard fare in 1962. I had always found Vienna sausages tasty until I happened to read the ingredients on the label; after that I stayed with sardines, crackers and cheese.

I saw several Wyoming ground squirrels at the picnic area. They are also called picket pins because when alarmed they stand erect like the small wood posts used to hitch horses. In 1962, my father and I had patiently staked out burrow holes after lunch to get good photographs of these wary creatures. We tried to draw them out of their burrows with our version of what we thought were squirrel calls, clumsy clicks and whistles that were ignored by our prey. My father had a good ear for bird calls. He could mimic a barred owl and draw a response from an interested mate. He could also imitate the cry of baby alligators, bringing the mother gator to investigate. Picket pins were a different story. Our seductive calls did not work. Nonetheless, when we stopped the noise, the squirrels eventually came out and my father got some good photographs while I captured them on film.

After lunch, Jane and I checked in at the Moraine Park Campground where we had a reservation. I previously had camped at Glacier Basin campground but it was closed for the 2012 season for updating and repairs. While it was disappointing not to be able to camp at the same campground, our campsite at Moraine Park, number C247, was great. It had shade and was close to the trail to Cub Lake that we intended to take the next day.

One of our favorite places in Rocky Mountain National Park is Bear Lake. Whenever we visited our daughter Elizabeth at the University of Colorado in Boulder, which is only 45 minutes from the park, we would drive to Bear Lake and take the short trail that loops around the lake. It always brought back memories of the trip with my parents, the tough hike up Flattop Mountain that starts there, and fueled the yearning that burned within me to revisit all of the places of that memorable trip in 1962.

In addition to the closure of Glacier Basin Campground, we discovered major repairs in progress on the Bear Lake Road. Due to the construction work, the road past the Moraine Park Visitor Center was closed to private vehicles from 9:00 a.m. to 4:00 p.m. Although the shuttle bus service ran every twenty minutes from the visitor center, we decided to wait until after 4:00 pm to drive to Bear Lake for a hike.

When the road opened to private vehicles, we drove to Bear Lake, parked in the near empty lot, and took the half mile hike to Nymph Lake and then continued on another .6 miles to Dream Lake. The trail winds through the subalpine ecosystem dominated by Engelmann spruce and subalpine fir. At times it emerges from the woods to track alongside a rushing stream cascading from Tyndall Glacier down Tyndall Gorge that connects Emerald, Dream and Nymph lakes. The icy water tumbles over stones ground smooth by glacier action and the polishing effect of the fast moving stream. The sound it made was loud and musical, masking our labored breathing as we ascended the trail.

There were views of Hallett Peak, elevation 12,713 feet, a huge cliff-faced granite block angled sharply to its summit straddling the Continental Divide at the head of the Gorge, with Flattop Mountain, elevation 12,234 feet, lying just to the north, looking less formidable but stirring memories of a tough hike long ago. I was anxious to test my conditioning and stamina against the bench mark I set on that hike when I was young. Along the trail, we saw a chipmunk gorging itself and a chickaree hauling off a mushroom the size of itself.

We took the Bear Lake loop and I looked for the rock where I photographed a golden mantled ground squirrel 50 years ago. With Hallett Peak in the background, I think I found the same rock at the edge of the lake among several that looked similar. Two thirds around the trail, we spotted two female elk swimming across the lake. Once across, they stopped in the shallows and drank deeply from the still water, seeming to enjoy the cool soaking on the warm day, oblivious to the visitors crowding in openings along the trail to get a glimpse of them. We got photographs of the elk in the water before they had their fill and exited into the woods. According to our GPS, the total hike to Nymph and Dream lakes and the Bear Lake loop was 3.2 miles, an easy workout that started at 9,475 feet and climbed 425 feet in elevation.

Back at camp, we bought firewood from a vendor at the campground entrance who also sold ice cream. He was there every night at five p.m. and stayed until he sold out his inventory, which did not take long. A line of campers queued up before he arrived to ensure they got their favorite flavor.

I grilled bratwurst on the campfire and sautéed asparagus in a cast iron skillet using Newman's Own Lite Italian salad dressing. Either the food was great or we were famished from a long day and our hike. Anything would have tasted extraordinary.

After dinner we went to a campfire program on squirrels, chipmunks and marmots. It was a terrific talk and very informative. One fact that made an impression was how deadly salt can be to small animals. The ranger emphasized the importance of not feeding the chipmunks and ground squirrels that are abundant in the campground and to make sure that chips and any other food not be left out. These animals are so small and their body weight is so light, the salt from potato chips or other processed foods can cause salt poisoning and death.

After the talk, we walked back to our campsite in full darkness using our headlights. Light from lanterns and campfires in various stages from blazing bonfires to dying embers broke the blackness outside our light beams. Muted sounds of campers settling in for the night came from the shadows of tents and RVs. After cleaning the dishes we went to bed tired. Sleep came quickly.

---   **DAY 7**   ---

Thursday • August 9, 2012

Jane had a headache and I let her sleep late while I had my usual breakfast of orange juice, Starbucks Via instant coffee to satisfy my caffeine craving, and shredded wheat topped with honey and blueberries. A diet Coke and Tylenol worked its magic with Jane, rallying her sufficiently that we were able to drive to the Cub Lake trailhead by 9:00 am. The trailhead parking lot was already full, so we parked in the overflow parking area.

The trail to Cub Lake crosses Big Thompson River and then skirts Moraine Park meadow. Belying its impressive name, the river is hardly more than a shallow stream, easily fordable but spanned by a sturdy foot bridge of whole logs. I can imagine that in the early summer when the winter snow melts and the river rages the bridge is a necessity. But this year the snow pack was unusually light and the summer runoff more a dripping faucet than a torrent.

The trail start was firm, packed solid by hikers without the dust created by horses. The 2.5 mile hike was a gradual uphill grade with the last short section a fairly steep climb. The elevation gain was about 500 feet. It was cool when we started but the temperature gradually increased. We shared the trail with numerous chipmunks, golden mantled ground squirrels and red squirrels. We also saw a rabbit and a marmot in the meadow.

The lake had a shroud of lily pads that added green color patches to the dark blue water. Tall pines and boulders lined the lake shore, providing shade and seats. We ate lunch and rested before heading back down the trail. On the way, we were passed by a trail runner wearing high tech footwear that looked like bare feet complete with ten toes. The trail was strewn with sharp edged rocks and crisscrossed with thick roots. The thin rubber shoes offered no support or protection against these hazards. The runner's gait was a toe dance down the path, alternating short hops and long strides. Yet she deftly picked her way between the rocks and roots. She looked like a concert pianist playing Rachmaninoff with her feet.

The rest of the afternoon we rested at the campsite. We were first in line for firewood and ice cream from the camp vendor. I got lazy and also bought a bundle of ready-made kindling, avoiding having to split my own. The firewood was well seasoned, catching fire once again with a single match and a crumpled section of USA Today. I grilled chicken over the campfire before going to the ranger program.

The program was on the Trail Ridge Road, completed in 1932, which traverses the park, opening up the high wilderness to automobiles and making it accessible to visitors. The road, which is 12,183 feet at its maximum elevation, is the highest paved road in the United States. It replaced the Fall River Road, which opened in 1921, a single lane steep grade byway that proved inadequate for motor traffic but for the adventurous it is still a one-way option from Lawn Lake to Fall River Pass. We thought briefly about making a loop going out the Fall River Road and returning by the Trail Ridge Road, but RV's are discouraged on the steep grade of the old road.

The next day I planned to hike to the summit of Flattop Mountain, hopefully a successful prelude and confidence builder for my Grand Teton climb. I was apprehensive as I remembered how difficult it was the last time I made the hike, but I felt ready.

——— DAY 8 ———

Friday • August 10, 2012

I set the alarm for 5:30 am but slept through it, awaking with a start at 5:50, the sky just beginning to lighten at the rim of the mountains in that still period of dawn just before sunrise. The campground was quiet as I filled my Camelback bladder with water, made an almond butter/blueberry jam wrap, and assembled the rest of my gear.

I wanted to duplicate my first Flattop Mountain hike as near as possible. I strapped my graphite Induro tripod to my Camelback pack, conceding that it was lighter than the aluminum one I had lugged around the last time. Instead of the five pound Bolex 16 mm movie camera I carried a Nikon D90 camera using a Cotton Carrier vest that attached it to my chest with the weight off my neck. I also carried a Sony video camera.

For the Grand Teton climb, Exum Guides require that all climbers wear one of several recommended brand boots. Prior to leaving on the trip I had ordered a pair of La Sportiva approach shoes from REI. La Sportiva tends to run narrow while I have a wide foot with high instep. I had to send back my usual ten-and-a-half shoe for an eleven-and-a-half to get a comfortable width. Flattop Mountain would be a break-in trial for my brand new puke green Sportiva boots. The rest of my wardrobe might be inconspicuous but my boots can be seen from a mile away. I grabbed my trekking poles and was ready for the hike.

We were on the road to Bear Lake at 7:00 a.m. There were few other cars and we avoided any construction delays. Jane dropped me off at the trailhead and I was on the trail to Flattop Mountain at 7:45. The morning was cool and still. The trail was a steady climb upward from Bear Lake through a thick forest that gradually thinned out to the tree line, where rocks and boulders extended across the landscape without any barrier for either view or wind.

I kept a steady pace without stopping, except for brief conversations with other hikers. There were many more hikers on the trail than I remembered in 1962. I passed a number of groups. Only one hiker, a young man who looked to be in his early twenties, passed me. I felt a bit of perverse pride each time I strode past a group, silently noting to myself whether they looked younger than I. The younger they looked, the greater the energy boost I received from leaving them in my dust. When I hiked with Jane, I could slow down and smell the flowers. On this hike I was in a competition with myself and everyone else on the trail. This was a test of stamina, wind, and endurance, with a fifty-year-old bench mark against which to measure myself. If I could pass this first test with high marks, I should be in good shape for the remaining physical challenges of the trip and, most importantly, the Grand Teton climb.

Near the summit, a guided party on horseback came up behind me. I knew there was a livery near Bear Lake with trail rides to Flattop Mountain, but the trail up the mountain had been devoid of the usual signs of horse travel. The dust did not rise up to my knees with each step, pulverized by the heavy shod hoofs of horses weighted with riders, nor were there piles of hardened and fresh manure scattered along the path. I remember hiking the North Rim of the Grand Canyon almost asphyxiated by the clouds of thick dust stirred with each step, the constant equine traffic pounding the trail foundation to a powder. I much prefer the hikers-only trails.

Shortly after the horses passed, I reached the summit of Flattop Mountain, elevation 12,324 feet. I could not find a summit marker but I was standing on the highest point, looking down in all directions except to the south, where an ascending ridge line intersected with Hallett Peak, some 400 feet higher than Flatttop Mountain. I thought briefly about trying for the summit of Hallett Peak. It looked so close, but reality took hold, and I decided that my original goal of returning to Flattop Mountain was a sufficient accomplishment for this day.

I checked my watch for the time, calculating that I had made the summit in two hours, fifteen minutes, quite an improvement from the five struggling hours it took me to reach the top in 1962, a one way distance of 4.4 miles with an elevation change of 2,849 feet. In 1962, the crest had been snow covered. Today there were only bare rocks and boulders on the summit. There were not even isolated patches of snow lingering in the shadows of the boulders.

I did a 360 degree survey of the view: to the west was the Never Summer Range; to the north was the Trail Ridge; to the south Hallett Peak was the dominant landmark; and to the west down Tyndall Gorge in succession were Emerald, Dream and Nymph Lakes, sparkling light blue in the high sun. I noticed that when I stopped hiking I could feel the cool wind, particularly on my bare arms. I had a sweater in my pack, but I sat down in the lee of some rocks where the sun was warm, took off my Camelback and camera, then lay back and thought about the last time I was here.

Flattop Mountain - 2012

On that hike, a half century ago, when I reached the summit I set up the movie camera on the tripod, starting shooting film on automatic, then made a wide arc to get in front of the camera, photographing myself slogging through the snow towards the lens. It had taken so long to get to the summit, I was far behind schedule and had to start back immediately. Moreover, with snow everywhere there was no place to sit and rest. It was much different this time. I had the time to enjoy the experience and good resting spots were everywhere.

I called Jane on the mobile radio, and to my surprise she answered. She was in Estes Park at the Safeway parking lot about eleven miles away as the crow flies. I told her I was at the summit. She was surprised and relieved to hear from me. When I bragged about how quickly I had made it to the summit she warned me to take it slower on the way down. She's my voice of reason letting me know that my mind may think I'm fifteen again but the body is showing some wear. The brief rest felt great and the cool temperature was refreshing.

After a snack and a 30 minute rest I started down. A mile from the summit a yellow-bellied marmot was busily engaged eating something on a rock beside the trail. Its head was down and I was waiting for a better photograph when the marmot moved directly to me touching my lime-green boot with its nose. It seemed as if it were sniffing it. It then moved up into the boulders.

A curious marmot - 2012

Another quarter mile down the trail the pikas were very active. I waited and got some good photographs of one.

The hike down the trail was very hard because of numerous rocks and roots. Tripping was a constant hazard. I made it back to Bear Lake in two hours and fifteen minutes, the same time as my ascent, even with my leisurely photographing the marmot and pika. The bus to Moraine Park left shortly after I arrived at Bear Lake with the shuttle to the campground waiting at the visitor center when we got there.

The shuttle service was quicker than the hitchhiking that I had done the last time. Hitchhiking as a fifteen-year-old seems so risky now but looking back there were not a lot of options. There was no shuttle service. Cell phones had not been invented. The timetable for my hike had been an optimistic guess, wildly inaccurate, that would have left my parents waiting at the Bear Lake trailhead for hours. The best solution was for me to make it back from Bear Lake to Glacier Basin Campground by the best means possible – hitchhike if I could catch a ride or hike the three miles if necessary. The decision was up to me. I did not know it at the time but the latitude that my parents gave me to be independent, self-sufficient, and test my abilities was perhaps their greatest gift to me. It made me the person I am today.

Jane had shopped for groceries in Estes Park while I was on the hike. I had been the exclusive driver on the trip. This were her first time behind the wheel of the RV since she had dropped me off for a solo hike on the Chimney Rock trail in Capitol Reef National Park the previous year. While the Roadtrek handles well, its length can be deceiving in tight spaces. Jane had a fender bender in the parking lot of the Safeway, cutting the corner too close to a truck, denting the right rear fender of the RV and ripping the molding, but fortunately doing no visible damage to the truck.

The molding flapped in the wind stream at a right angle to the fender, when the RV was in motion. I retrieved a roll of duct tape from the storage well in the rear of the RV and secured the wayward molding with a latticework of cross strips, functional, but giving our heretofore pristine Roadtrek the look of a battered fighter when viewed from the side. We would both give trucks a wide berth in crowded parking lots from now on.

At camp a light drizzle dampened the ground and wet the picnic table. I had the foresight to have wrapped the firewood in a plastic garbage bag, placing it under the table before leaving on the hike, and it remained dry. I started a fire in the rain and we were able to reheat the leftover chicken, bratwurst and macaroni. I was famished and exhausted. Leftovers never tasted so good. I lay down to the sound of the rain drumming a metallic rhythm on the roof of the RV. Liquid fingers danced on a steel drumhead fast drawing me into a deep, hypnotic sleep.

—————— **DAY 9** ——————

Saturday • August 11, 2012

I rose at 6:00 a.m., thinking ahead to the Grand Teton. My confidence, which had surged yesterday when I bettered my performance from 1962 on the Flattop Mountain hike, ebbed as I reminded myself it had only been a hike. Grand Teton was a thousand feet higher and was a technical climb requiring not just stamina and wind but physical upper body strength as well. I had passed the first test, but that did not mean I was ready for the final exam. Everyone I know thinks I'm crazy for attempting the Grand Teton climb at my age—Jane, my daughters, Virginia and Elizabeth, friends. But I don't accept that at sixty-five I am old. You become old if you stop setting goals for yourself. You stay young by continuing to test yourself, physically and mentally.

We started up Trail Ridge Road at 8:00 am as a cold front came through with the temperature dropping precipitously. The dark cumulonimbus clouds along the leading edge front looked ominous. A light rain fell as we climbed the road.

We stopped at Many Parks Curve and I took some photographs. The spot looked very familiar from my father's photographs and my film. The view from the overlook looks south towards the flat meadows of Moraine Park, then beyond to Long's Peak, at 14,259 feet the highest point in the park.

We continued on to Forest Canyon Overlook where a cold gusting wind sent my hat flying as I stepped out of the RV. I chased it down, stowing it safely in the RV. It was not a day for hats or any other untethered object. I walked out to the overlook while Jane stayed in the RV. My father and I had stalked marmots in the field below the overlook and I could hear them whistle, but it was too cold to wait for one to appear for a photograph. To the west was the Never Summer Range. It was now the Summer Range. As on the summit of Flattop, there was no snow on the mountains. I had heard rangers talking with visitors that this past winter was one of the lightest snowfalls on record. It was a very dry summer with a high fire danger.

**Forest Canyon Overlook
1962**

**Forest Canyon Overlook
2012**

A few miles past Forest Canyon is a natural gap called Rock Cut where Trail Ridge Road was routed without the necessity to blast through the granite cliff. I walked back along the road to get a photograph, noticing along the way the rock "V" in the embankment I had filmed in 1962. I thought then and still do that it was more impressive than the famed Rock Cut. The primary difference is that the "V" provides a thoroughfare for marmots instead of motorcars. As I walked back to the turnout I saw several marmots poking out from the rocks below with their mouths stuffed with dry grass. At the campfire presentation I had learned that marmots are very fastidious, changing their nest material almost daily. The marmots I saw were in the middle of changing sheets.

A frigid hike on the Tundra Communities Trail - 2012

Back at Rock Cut I hiked the half mile Tundra Communities Trail to the Toll Memorial, a bronze plaque at the top of a stone outcrop honoring Roger Wolcott Toll, Superintendent of Rocky Mountain National Park from 1921 to 1929. The trail is the highest trailhead in the park, starting at 12,110 feet, climbing to 12,310 feet at the Memorial. The trail is paved to encourage hikers to stay on the path and off the fragile tundra environment where careless footsteps can destroy plants, leading to the thin layer of topsoil being blown away by the high winds, with the recovery process taking hundreds of years.

The short walk to the memorial was bitter cold with wind whipping across the tundra. A massive blue-black storm cloud moved over the area, seeming to rise from the ground and descend from the sky at the same time, spitting small bits of hail and light flurries of snow. I thought of the verse of the Judy Collins song *Someday Soon*, "So blow, You Old Blue Norther." This was what I had imagined a "Blue Norther" must look like the hundreds of time I heard that song. Beautiful, powerful, ominous. I was surprised to see that Jane had ventured out on the trail but I caught her halfway back to trailhead, shortly after she had turned back, giving in to the chill. She was bracing herself against the wind, head down, holding her jacket hood tight. We both were glad when we reached the warm, safe confines of the RV.

Trail Ridge Road continued in a serpentine weave along the ridge separated from a steep drop off by a ribbon-thin guardrail that seemed more of a marker than a protective barrier to block an inattentive driver or runaway vehicle from the abyss. It was hard to concentrate on driving, as the Siren-like scenery drew my attention at every turn.

At Fall River Pass, we stopped at the Alpine Visitor Center and its snack shop for hot chocolate, just as I had in 1962. With the chilled temperature and a light rain falling, it was delicious in taste and memory. The original snack bar has been expanded to include a large gift shop. Most of the wares were the usual tourist items, but there was a side alcove with Native American jewelry and crafts that were quality. We looked but there was nothing that we wanted to buy.

Jane and I are not collectors like my father. He collected owls, snakes, wood carvings (particularly birds), Kachina dolls, hats, smoking pipes, beetles, antique tools, ethnic musical instruments, crafts in general, practically anything that he found interesting. On our trips in my youth we would scour gift shops at each stop, looking for unique items for his collections. Some we would pack into the few remaining crannies of the Corvair van, others we would ship home, hoping they would arrive undamaged, or in some instances arrive at all. Our last glimpse of the item was in the hands of a weathered old proprietor of a gas station curio shop at an unnamed crossroads, who assured my father he would pack the treasure well and mail it to our address in Miami. To the best of my memory everything we purchased did arrive in Miami as had been promised, unbroken.

Our Miami home looked like a museum with all of the "stuff" my father collected. To my mother, the collectibles were simply items that gathered dust. At first I was an active participant in his search for collectables, looking through shops with him for carvings and crafts. It may have been an extension of the stage every young boy goes through where there is a natural tendency to accumulate things. As a child, I had been an avid collector of stamps and coins.

I still have my childhood stamp collection, bound in a well-worn Coronet Deluxe World Stamp Album, 1955 edition, organized by countries, some of whom have disappeared into history. Others still exist but under new names. Stamp collecting was a wonderful introduction to world geography, transporting me to distant and exotic locations like Tristan da Cunha, a remote island in the South Pacific with a population of only 275 people but issuing stamps that were major jewels in the collections of many youngsters, myself included. I still have a mint condition beige stamp from Tristan da Cunha featuring a rose colored Tristan crawfish with a profile of a young Queen Elizabeth in the right corner. I remember looking at a globe to find where Tristan da Cunha was located and marveling at the journey the stamp had taken to get to me.

Later, as my father's collections grew and I approached adulthood, his obsession began to seem a bit strange to me. As I tilted toward conformity I jettisoned the pastimes of my father that, to me, were outliers to conventional society. Obsessive collecting was removed from my list of favorite activities.

A few years before he died Dad gave a lecture on "The Art of Collecting" to a Brevard, North Carolina, civic group. The lecture was videotaped, and he gave me a copy. At the time, as I viewed the tape, I was slightly embarrassed. He exaggerated the extent of his collections when the truth was impressive enough. His passion for excess was on full display.

My father had managed to cart an incredible sampling of his collections from his home to the Jim Bob Tinsley Museum, where he regaled a rapt audience with vivid tales of how the items had come into his possession. He flaunted his eccentricities in the curios he shared with his audience and his description of the hundreds of additional treasures he had displayed in his house and the several barns on his property in Rosman, North Carolina.

While, like most of what he did, his collecting was excessive, he claimed that the collectibles enabled him to recall the great experiences that he had on the trips where he obtained the individual items. He was right about that. The few items I have from his collection bring back vivid memories, connecting me with past times, people gone, and places far distant. Having a few items to remember is good.

Jane and I left the gift shop at Fall River Pass, driving past Milner Pass at the Continental Divide, expecting to stop there on our return to Moraine Park campground later in the afternoon. We looked at Timber Creek campground as a possible lunch site, but it was in the open and not as nice as our Moraine Park campsite. We decided to continue on in hope of finding some place more interesting for a rest stop.

The road down to Grand Lake was very scenic. Grand Lake was much like Estes Park, with streets lined with shops, some quaint, others tacky. The sidewalks were jammed with tourists and bumper-to-bumper traffic. We drove through town to the historic Grand Lake Lodge, parking close to an antique tour bus. The lodge was old but comfortable, a huge wood and log structure on a hill overlooking the lake. We explored the lodge grounds then drove back to the park towards Estes Park.

At Harbison Meadows we had lunch, looking west across the meadows towards the meandering Colorado River. If the Colorado were a person stretching one arm and hand full length pointing north, the river at this point would be near the mid-joint of a crooked forefinger, the headwaters nigh. I was always surprised when the Colorado River appeared unannounced outside the Grand Canyon. When I took Liz back to Boulder in 2003 we had kayaked on the Colorado in Moab, Utah after hiking in Arches National Park the previous day. It seemed we followed the river into the State of Colorado almost to Denver, on a highway jammed with vehicles and the white water paralleling the road equally crowded with rafts and kayaks. For some reason, I had this thought that the Colorado started and ended within the walls of the Grand Canyon. I know that was not true, but the river is so closely associated with the Canyon that it was disorienting to find it in another location.

Interestingly, prior to 1921, although the Territory of Colorado was named on the fact that the headwaters of the great river were in its mountains, the Colorado first emerged at the confluence of the Green and Grand Rivers, which converge in Utah near the Colorado state border. The entire stretch of river within its borders was named the "Grand." In 1921, a Colorado Congressman sought to have the Grand River renamed so that the entire length of the mighty river from its headwaters in the high mountains of his state to the Gulf of Mexico would be known as the Colorado River. There was some opposition by supporters of the Green River who argued that under standard geographical convention, the Green, which was a longer tributary, should have been designated as the Colorado. The supporters of the Grand countered that it contributed more water flow to the Colorado than the longer but smaller Green River. On July 25, 1921, a resolution was passed by the United States Senate and House of Representatives changing the name of the Grand River to the Colorado River, giving the State of Colorado the honor of cradling its namesake on the first leg of its 1450 mile journey to the sea.

After lunch and my musing about the Colorado River, we continued back toward camp on Trail Ridge Road. The Milner Pass parking lot was full so we did not stop as we had intended. Shortly past Milner Pass there was an elk jam. Cars were pulled over on both sides of the road, still half on the pavement, bumper to bumper for fifty yards in both directions. A bull elk was grazing in a meadow approximately 100 yards east of the road. People were lining the roadside trying to get a good view of the magnificent animal. I jostled for a space, then noticed a middle-aged woman extremely close to the elk, separated by a small fir tree, trying to photograph it. The elk pawed the ground, obviously distracted. The elk would move and the woman moved in synchronicity with it, trying to keep the tree between her and the beast while at the same time peeking around it to get a picture. It was an act of sheer stupidity. The elk stood twice her height. It reminded me of the bear jams I witnessed as a youth in the Smoky Mountain National Park where city folks would foolishly feed the black bears at the pullouts, then run for the safety of their cars when the bears came after the food source looking for more handouts. The "Do Not Feed the Bears" signs were ignored as much as the speed limit postings. Some people do not understand that the parks are not Disneyland; wildlife is wild and for our sake and theirs must remain so.

At Deer Ridge Junction we took the turn to Horseshoe Park and stopped at Sheep Lakes. A very informative ranger talked about big horn sheep that come down to the lake to eat the mineral rich mud. It does not sound very appetizing, but apparently the sheep crave the minerals and are drawn to the lake mud. There were no sheep at the lake at this time. Jane and I scanned the rocks above the lake with our binoculars for signs of sheep, but they must have been elsewhere.

We went into Estes Park for groceries at the Safeway then returned to camp. On the drive I saw a picket pin standing watch, straight as a rod.

After dinner, we walked down to the meadow and went inside the elk enclosure to watch the sunset, but there were only a few clouds and the sky darkened without showing much color.

We walked around the meadow, crossed the Big Thompson River, which was only a rivulet at this point, a mere 18 inches deep. As I looked at the harmless shallows it seemed inconceivable that it contained a latent potential for immense destruction. However, on July 31, 1976, the year of the Colorado Centennial, a late afternoon thunderstorm stalled over the Big Thompson Canyon, only a few miles east from where we stood, dumping twelve inches of rain on the rocky slopes in four hours, causing a flash flood that roared down the canyon carrying huge boulders, cars, trees, destroying everything in its path. One hundred forty-three campers and visitors were killed, five of whom were never found.

I looked again at the rivulet and tried to imagine the death and destruction that it had caused, but the scene was too peaceful to conjure up dark images. It was much like my trips to Civil War battlefields. Except for geography, the carefully landscaped fields of today's historical parks have little in common with the blood and gore soaked fields of the actual battles. The silent monuments of men in military pose and the ever present cannon are the only indications of the bloodshed that took place on those pastoral fields.

We went back to the campsite for the night. The campground was quiet except for the sound of a few children working off the last of their unexpended energy.

—— **DAY 10** ——

Sunday • August 12, 2012

Today was a getaway day, but as a treat I cooked bacon and scrambled eggs on the campfire in the cast iron skillet. Supposedly bears can smell bacon frying up to five miles away. With 12 ounces of bacon sizzling on the campfire, I was surprised we didn't get a visit from one of the park's 25 black bears. A golden mantled ground squirrel darted around looking for a morsel but the ranger's warning about the harm salt can do the delicate systems of these critters was fresh in my mind so we were careful not be leave any crumbs. The campfire smoke swirled in all directions, stinging my eyes while I cooked, but a few minutes of discomfort was a small price to pay for a delicious breakfast.

When we cleaned the dishes we found the RV sinks were clogged. I bailed the kitchen sink and found that the vanity sink also was not draining. On the way out of the campground we dumped the tanks and it solved the problem. We had to pay closer attention to the gray water tank level. I thought we had more capacity, but the combination of my morning showers and the nightly dishwashing produces more gray water discharge than I had anticipated. Although we've had the RV almost two years this was only the second trip we had taken in it other than a weekend to Pinnacles National Monument shortly after our impulse purchase. We were still learning the intricacies of the Roadtrek.

The weather on Trail Ridge Road was much milder than the day before. There were a great number of bicyclists pedaling up and down grade, but even in yesterday's frigid temperature there had been a few hardy souls pumping on bikes, heads down against the blustery wind. I don't remember any cyclists on the road in 1962. Road cycling is a recent phenomenon. With the steep grade and high altitude, it takes incredible fitness to cycle Trail Ridge Road.

We drove the Trail Ridge Road enjoying the views but did not stop at any overlooks. Outside of Grand Lake, we took US 40 and then Colorado Highway 125. The sign reading "Shortest Most Scenic Route to Yellowstone" that took us on the shortcut in 1962 is no longer there. However, the road is still very scenic.

There was a huge area of thousands of acres of dead trees in the Arapaho National Forest, probably killed by the mountain pine beetle epidemic that is afflicting Colorado. The devastation that the tiny insect is causing to the western forests is tragic. After the trees die, forest fires become a real threat because the tinder dry trees are an explosive fuel waiting for the natural spark of a lightning strike or the hot ash of a careless camper. To minimize the potential damage, the Forest Service tries to harvest the dead trees. A harvesting operation was ongoing as we passed through the afflicted area.

The route through the Arapaho National Forest in Colorado rises along a river course to the Continental Divide at Willow Creek Pass, elevation 9621 feet. Once through the national forest, the route passes several small towns including Rand and Walden in Colorado, then Saratoga nestled along the North Platte River in Wyoming. Walden is a quaint town of less than 700 people with old brick buildings, situated in North Park, a high basin where the headwaters of the North Platte rise surrounded by mountain ranges. Walden was established in 1889 and looks it. There were several dilapidated log cabins, looking vacant, visible from the road.

In both Colorado and Wyoming large ranches abut the road with cattle grazing on the sparse sage grass. Jane and I commented that we would rather have beef fed on the lush grass in the valley outside Pagosa Springs than the coarse sage grass of Northern Colorado and Southern Wyoming. I had noted in 1962 that when we entered Wyoming the roads became poor. The quality of the roads has much improved over the past 50 years. The Wyoming roads are now just fine. We made good time on the scenic byway with no bone-jarring potholes, cracks or buckled asphalt.

In Saratoga, Wyoming, we stopped and had lunch, consisting of my usual tortilla sandwich of almond butter but this time topped with the rest of the bacon left over from breakfast. It was a delicious indulgence.

We arrived in Rawlins, Wyoming, around 2:30 p.m., delighted that the Hampton Inn had a room ready for us. We had a triple load of laundry and once again every power outlet in the room was quickly filled with our electronic necessities, including Jane's Nook, my iPad, various batteries for cameras and phones. I broke a vow, checked my office email and was relieved to find that the work world had continued fine without me. At our last hotel stop in Colorado Springs, I had posted a comment on my Facebook Wall about starting this trip and also posted a photo of the fantastic sunset at Balanced Rock in Arches National Park. I was not sure it had uploaded but I was heartened to see I had several "likes" and a few comments from friends on the post and photograph. At least for the day we were back on the "grid," but I must admit that there is something liberating about being away from phones, emails and computers. I looked forward to unplugging and plunging once again into the black void of communication silence where no news is good news.

On a recommendation from a young woman at the hotel front desk, we ended up at Buck's Sports Bar and Grill for dinner. Jane asked if they served wine, and the desk clerk said that she was too young to be served so she didn't know. It turned out they did. Buck's was fun. The décor was rustic with a combination of sports photographs and outdoor trophies. The food was good and we left "fat and happy" as the desk clerk had promised. Our next stop was Grand Teton National Park. I went to bed reliving my climb of fifty years ago, asleep right after we roped in on Wall Street, before the real climb began. A dreamless sleep gave me no premonition of how my attempt at a second climb would turn out.

NINE

A Long Hard Day

Grand Teton National Park

People often ask, "Which national park is your favorite?" It is a difficult question. The national parks are so complex. Each is unique, spectacular in its own right. But a short list would certainly include Grand Teton. It has everything a visitor could want: accessible wildlife, memorable hikes, stunning scenery, and world class mountain climbing on the granite peaks of the Teton Range.

Almost all of my father's photographic work has been lost. The thousands of Ektochrome slides and scores of 16 x 20 museum mounted photographs that he displayed in a traveling exhibit on the national parks disappeared at some time between his permanent move from Miami to his retreat in Rosman, North Carolina, and his death in 1998. Fortunately, I have in my possession three of the original 16 x 20 photographs. My favorite is a panoramic view of the Teton Range from the Snake River Overlook, the dark river a winding "S" below the jagged Grand Teton. The sky is also dark, highlighted with bright, billowy cumulous clouds. The contrast is sharpened by my father's innovative use of infra-red film and filters.

I've always loved the photograph. I longed to return to the site where it was taken.

Another photograph that has a special meaning to me was taken on my climb of the Grand Teton in 1962. It is the only photograph I have of that climb. I carried a small camera with me but never took it out of my pocket as all of my attention was focused on the intensity of the climb. After we had summited and were at the rappel point on the way down, I asked one of climbers in my party to take my camera and photograph me rappelling down

Snake River – Grand Teton, 1962

the mountain. The photograph of me in jeans wearing a hooded sweatshirt and thin nylon windbreaker, dangling in the sling on the rappel rope, sliding down out of the fog in a free rappel, the vertical face of the mountain parallel to the rope, has haunted me, a Siren call to return.

Map of
Grand Teton National Park

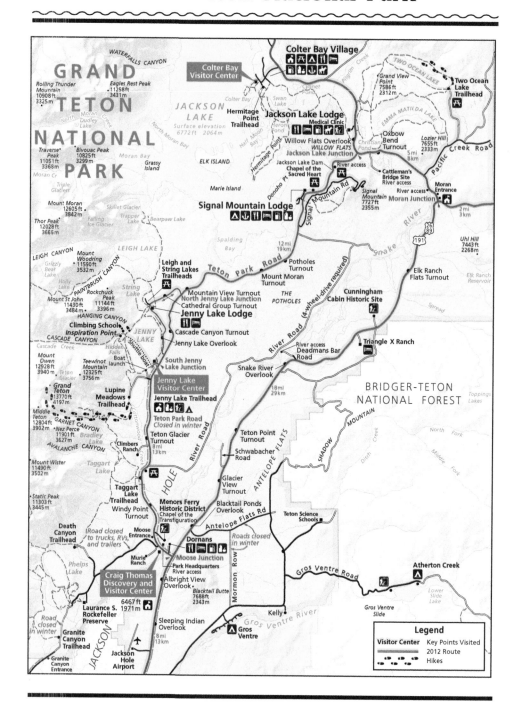

Sunday • July 22, 1962

We got up, dressed and quickly headed out of Rawlins. A lot of dead rabbits were on the road. We stopped and photographed a ptarmigan on US 287 and saw an antelope. A few miles down the road we saw more and Dad photographed them. We saw more and more antelope and magpies.

At Lamont we ate breakfast then went on. We saw more antelope. Between Rawlins and Lander we saw about 150 head of antelope. We also saw two mule deer. Outside of Lander we found a dead antelope and hunted for beetles. I got the jaw bone. We also found a prairie rattlesnake and photographed it. The road was great for wildlife.

At Grand Teton National Park we stopped at the Jackson Hole Wildlife Refuge and saw the exhibits and bison. They told us that all the campgrounds were full. At the Jackson Lake campground we stopped and it was full. At the Coulter Bay campground we got a fire permit to camp at Two Ocean Lake. We set up a short camp and ate supper. We met a couple from New York and talked for a while then went to bed.

Monday • July 23, 1962

Dad and I got up early and hiked part way around the lake but we didn't see anything. Back at camp we had breakfast then took down the camp and left.

At Jenny Lake campground we found a party that was just leaving so we got their campsite and set up camp. Dad and I walked down to register and look at the museum. There they had exhibits on climbing. It looked like fun. At the gift shop we looked around and saw some nice plaster work. From there we walked over to the Exum School of Mountaineering and I registered for the climbing school. Back at camp we ate lunch.

After securing the camp we left for Jackson. At the Menon Ferry we stopped and looked at the pioneer ferry and exhibits on life in Jackson Hole. Then we went on into Jackson. On the road we passed the elk refuge and the trumpeter swan pond.

At Jackson we got gas and changed our clothes at a Phillips 66 dealer. I got my cable release and my Bolex and took them to Camera Corral. They spent about an hour on it while we watched a hanging in the street of old Dover the Killer. Back at the camera shop we picked up our equipment then went to eat supper.

Tuesday • July 24, 1962

We got up fairly early and ate breakfast. I got my knapsack, packed lunch and then went down to the School. From there we went to the boat docks and took a launch over by Hidden Falls. There we walked up about a half mile, stopped under some shade trees, tied ropes and heard about pitons and carabineers. After about an hour we went up the trail and filled our canteens.

At the base of a rocky slope we roped in and started our climb. First the leader went up and belayed the next man and so on down the line. The first part was easy but the pitch gradually got steeper and slicker. At the top we waited for the rest of the party then hiked up to a stream where we ate a quiet lunch in the shade. After resting we went back and learned rappelling (body and sling). First we rappelled down the slope we had climbed then we went higher and did a 20 foot free rappel. After finishing our work we hiked back to the boat dock and got a ride to the school then I went to camp and rested for a few minutes.

After that we went to the Coulter Bay Store and got food for my Grand Teton excursion. After getting this done we went back to camp and ate supper then looked at the program and went to bed.

Wednesday • July 25, 1962

When I got up, Mother and Dad were already gone for the day. I fixed breakfast and packed then I walked on over to the school and got everything situated. At 10:00 a.m. we all piled into cars and headed for the start of the Glacier Trail. At the trail we got into our places and started off. The pace was fairly fast and our first stop for water came two miles out. At a stream just below the Black Dyke on Middle Teton we stopped for lunch. The sky looked threatening so we didn't rest very long. The rest of the trail up to the Saddle is on the crest of a moraine. We stopped a couple of times to rest and finally we came to the steep cliff just below the hut. Here there was a rope. We climbed up and I made it easily. At the hut we looked over to the Idaho side and the view was magnificent. The Alaska Basin, Death Canyon and Pierre's Hole spread out in a wide panorama before us. After our soups were cooked we ate them and drank tea then went straight to bed.

Thursday • July 26, 1962

At 2:30 a.m. the guides got us up and we had a snack for breakfast. The sky was dark and the sun had not risen. The mile hike up the ridge to the Dyke was torture. No one said a word and the wind was whipping around the west and froze our ears. At the Dyke we continued east along the ridge to the Needle. There we stopped to decide which route we were going to take. The Owen Route was the easiest and safest, but the Exum was more fun. The danger was being caught in a storm. We decided on the Exum Route and slowly worked our way along Wall Street. Almost to the end of the Street we roped in and started climbing. The first belay was around a huge boulder in the middle of the path with a dropoff straight down. After several pitches which were hard and strenuous we came to the vertical friction pitch. There were no handholds and we used a lie back technique. We used a couple of more belays, then we walked and boulder scrambled to the top.

At the top were a plaque and a register. The Mountain was still socked in and visibility was only 50 feet. We stayed at the top for about an hour and then started down. The trip down to the Rappel Point was cold. Getting ready for the rappel the wind was in our face. Finally my turn came and I went down the 150 foot free rappel. At the bottom we rested until everyone was down, then we climbed down to the base camp. There we ate lunch. While we were eating it hailed and snowed.

We cut our lunch short and started down. On the moraine we divided into two parties – the express and the slow group. I got in the express and we made it down the 9 miles in 3 hours. At the school we got our certificates of ascent and I went back to camp and went to sleep. The Dilleys came over for supper and I woke up.

After supper we went over to their house. We saw his slides and then went back to camp and slept.

Friday • July 27, 1962

We got up and ate breakfast then Dad and I hiked up to the Moose Pond. We didn't see anything there. We came back to camp and fixed things up and had lunch. Mr. Dilley came over and we took a ride with him first to Swan Lake where we saw the trumpeter swans then to Hedrick Pond where we saw two more. We rode the Antelope Flats Road a while and saw quite a few hawks. We went up the Gros Ventre Slide Road. We drove around to the Moose Ponds but didn't see anything then he took us back to camp.

At camp Dick James was there and we decided to eat at the Chuck Wagon so we headed to the restaurant. After eating we got Bill Dilley and came back for beaver. We waited about an hour then went back to camp and had a campfire.

Saturday • July 28, 1962

We got up early and went down for beaver and I fished. I caught a sucker fish but no beaver were around. We headed out for the Moose Ponds but didn't see anything there. At camp we fixed things up and ate breakfast. Dad walked to the Moose Ponds. I stayed at camp and tried to photograph the western tanagers. After Dad came back we stayed at camp for a while then went on the Jenny Lake nature trail. We got some good pictorials of the lake and went back to camp and ate lunch. We then photographed the camp. After that we went up to Signal Mountain but it was raining so we couldn't see much. We drove around the Moose Ponds again then went to photograph the beaver but didn't see anything.

We stopped by to shoot marmots and did very well. We stopped and looked at a pond and a calf moose was there. We didn't have the camera and didn't get a picture. On the way back we stopped by Mr. Dilley's to say goodbye, then went back to camp and went to bed.

——— **DAY 11** ———

Monday • August 13, 2012

We ate breakfast at the Hampton Inn and left Rawlins about 8:00 am. The town looked like Portola, California on a Saturday night. Rush hour traffic consisted of our RV. We saw a group of pronghorn antelope kids grazing in a field between the Hampton Inn and US Route 287, practically in the middle of town. They were without adult supervision. Shortly outside of town Jane had to use the restroom. We were low on water in the RV so I asked her to hold it until the next gas station. Unfortunately, the next point of any civilization turned out to be Lamont, essentially a ghost town, almost thirty miles down 287.

At Lamont, the only commercial building was a falling down structure called the Antelope Café which had an "open" sign. It looked like a place out of a bad western, but by this time we were desperate. I kept the motor running for a quick getaway if necessary and Jane bravely went in. She came out five minutes later, looking relieved, but she said the inside looked much like the outside, dilapidated and filled with a blue haze of cigarette smoke trumped by the pungent smell of deep fried kitchen grease. The rough looking occupants, however, were friendly.

The road to Lander passed through sage brush prairie. There were several dead antelope, but we did not see any live ones. I scanned the empty plain as I drove, looking for movement, but there was none. The scores of pronghorns that had roamed this lonely stretch of highway in 1962 had disappeared.

Shortly before entering Lander, we saw a sign for "Old books and fresh eggs," an interesting, even enticing, combination, but we didn't pursue it. At Lander we stopped for groceries at one of the most beautiful Safeway stores I've ever been in. The architecture of the building reminded me of a large ranch house. We also stopped at the Palace Pharmacy to get an icepack. Jane was having trouble with her foot, and we thought that ice would help. She took off her shoe and rode with her leg full extended, resting on the dash with the ice pack atop her foot like a massive hood ornament. It looked uncomfortable, but she said it helped.

Outside of Lander, we entered the Wind River Indian Reservation. At Fort Washakie we passed the gravesite of Sacajawea, the young Shoshone woman who served as a guide for the Lewis and Clark expedition. The terrain became more rolling with small rises and ravines. I finally spotted a herd of antelope a couple of hundred yards off to the side of the road. When I stopped to get a closer look they spooked, dashing across a ridge and out of sight before I could raise my field glasses.

Somewhere around Burns, I saw a sign that read "Slow Cattle in Road." A few miles later there was a herd of about twenty cattle grazing on the road shoulder, passing from one side to the other. The sign had been correct in either reading; it was good that I slowed down and the cattle in the road were indeed slow.

The town of Dubois is very quaint, situated in the river valley between the Absaroka and the Wind River Mountain Ranges. It caters to outdoor activities and has a rich cowboy history. US 287 follows the Wind River through this area and is very scenic. It looks like a great place for trout fishing.

We crossed the Continental Divide at Togwotee Pass, elevation 9658 feet. To the north was a jagged range of peaks that looked like a miniature Teton Range. There was road construction in the area and a sign that said "Expect delays and great scenery." We got both.

When we first glimpsed the Teton Range, it was a faint blue purple mirage. Fires in Idaho were causing substantial overcast, washing out the natural colors of the mountains. As we entered the park, the view of the peaks improved, but the overcast was as if we were looking at them through a thin layer of silk gauze. It was a much different view of the Tetons than the crystal sharp images in my father's black and white photographs taken with a Hasselblad 120 film format and Graflex 4x5, each capturing the smallest details of the mountains. The Teton Range that I saw before me now looked muted, sharp edges dulled by the corrosive haze, its ferocity dampened by the gossamer shroud of smoke.

We drove directly to Coulter Bay and found there was road construction between Jackson Lake and Coulter Bay with limited one-way traffic. There would be delays going to and from camp. We checked in at the RV camp and Jane decided she would rather be in the regular campground than at a full hook-up RV site. We would have more amenities at an RV site, but it had less privacy. We found an open site in the campground and told the RV site attendant that we were moving to the campground. She said she would credit our fee if the site was rebooked, but she didn't think it would be a problem.

After putting out our chairs on site 229 and paying for the three nights we intended to stay there, we started on the Grand Loop. We stopped first at South Jenny Lake to check in with Exum Guides. They said to be there at 7:45 am on Wednesday for climbing school. We were tired, so instead of continuing on into Jackson, we went back to Coulter Bay. We stopped at the grocery, which was well stocked, and picked up pork tenderloins for dinner. I grilled them with our usual asparagus on the campfire. They were delicious. By the time we finished eating and cleaning up, it was time for bed.

─── DAY 12 ───

Tuesday • August 14, 2012

We were on the road to Two Ocean Lake at 8:30 a.m. On the drive there I saw a bobcat cross the road several hundred yards in front of us, but when we got to the point that led into the woods there was no sign of it. We also saw two large hawks roosting in the aspens next to the road. They flew off before I could get the camera out.

Two Ocean Lake is now a picnic area and trailhead. The smoke from the fires was so thick that you could not see Mt. Moran from the lake. The site looked much the same as in 1962, except for the lack of a view of Mt. Moran. I could see a faint muddy trail following the shoreline. A fly fisherman was casting for trout from the bank. The improvised shore trail used by the fisherman is the one that my dad and I took when we hiked part way around the lake in 1962.

The morning fog rising from the lake on that day had been thick, obscuring Mt. Moran, much like the screen of smoke on this trip. My dad and I walked around the shore of the lake in silence. We rarely talked on our hikes. Both of us intently listened for wood sounds that would foretell the presence of wildlife or birds. He always had his hands on his camera, ready for a quick shot. On that day we walked the lakeshore alone. There were no moose, bear, or any other critters of note. I remember that our shoes got muddy. I wore boots when hiking but my dad always wore moccasins or slip-on sneakers. For all the time we spent together in the woods, I never saw him wear boots. I think he grew up used to slogging through the swamps of Florida where canvas shoes that drain and dry were preferable to leather boots.

There is a now a loop trail around the lake that runs several hundred yards inland. It is more of a worn single track footpath than a trail. Jane and I took the path for about a half mile around the north side of the lake but did not see anything. The dearth of wildlife may have been the result of the cacophony of noise we made on the trail. At the trail start there was a warning sign in bold red lettering, "Bear Attack: Are You Prepared to Avoid One?" with a further admonition to make noise, which Jane did with her large "bear bell" jangling loudly at each step. The bears were duly warned of our arrival as was every other creature in the woods; hence we passed in solitude, if not in silence.

The fact that our society's enthrallment with warning labels to reinforce the obvious has penetrated into the wilds of our national parks is perhaps a sign of our society's litigiousness. In addition to warning of the danger, at the bottom of the bear warning sign was a disclaimer advising hikers that "there is no guarantee of your safety in bear country." I was not aware that I am "guaranteed" safety anywhere, that there is someone or an organization that I can look to for relief for breach of a guarantee. I have an old-fashioned notion that I am responsible for my own actions, be they reasoned or foolish, and there are no guaranteed outcomes in life.

From Two Ocean Lake we took Rockefeller Parkway to the Snake River Overlook. We tried to recreate the photograph of me at the overlook in 1962. However, the haze from the fires made the view of the Tetons much different from the dramatic sharp image of the range my father took in 1962. Also, the bend of the Snake River had changed slightly and the trees have grown substantially taller over the past fifty years. The log where I had stood was gone, and there was now a stone wall encircling the perimeter of the overlook. While the view is still spectacular, it does not compare with the view in 1962.

We also stopped at the Teton Point turnout and then the Blacktail Ponds Overlook where we had lunch before following the path to the ponds and back. Blacktail Ponds are marked as beaver habitat, situated in a lush meadow fed with small streams flowing into the Snake River. Rabbit brush lined the meadow with yellow blooms forming a colorful foreground to the blurred pastel shadow of the Teton Range barely visible through the filter of lingering smoke from the Idaho fires.

Snake River Overlook, 1962

Snake River Overlook in 2012

At the tiny village of Dornans I looked in the Moosely Mountaineering Store for a few clothes I still needed for my Teton climb.
The Exum Guide instructions are adamant that no cotton clothing is permitted on the climb. Even in cool temperatures, climbers work up a sweat that cotton absorbs. Wet cotton clothing can
result in hypothermia, dangerous in any situation but life-threat-
ening at thirteen thousand feet on a technical climb. Moosely had
synthetic Kuhl shorts and a Mountain Hard Wear shirt that I purchased to complete my kit. All the other items I needed from the
Exum Guides list I had obtained at REI before we left Santa Clara.

While I was browsing the Moosely store, I got into a discussion of the Grand Teton climb with a young saleswoman who
was a serious climber. She and her friends had climbed the Grand
Teton several times along with other peaks in the Teton Range.
She said that her best advice for me would be to take Emergent C
to combat the effects of altitude sickness. I made a mental note to
put Emergent C on my list of items to buy along with food for the
two days on the mountain.

At Moose Junction, appropriately, there was a moose jam. A
bull moose was stuffing himself on willow leaves on the banks
of the Snake River, oblivious to the pack of spectators he had attracted. While we watched the moose feeding, a bald eagle flew
overhead, soaring, wings outstretched with its distinctive white
head moving slowing side to side, scanning the shallows of the
Snake for a meal. The fishing must have been poor today. I never
saw it make a dive. I watched it fly down river until it was a small
dot, then disappeared.

The moose ate non-stop, practically stripping the willow tree
of all leaves and branches before moving to the next tree. The
massive animal had a look of utter contentment, head moving
slowly side to side, up and down, as it chewed its way through
the willow patch along the Snake, much like a gardener trimming
a tall bushy hedge with sharp clippers but leaving no cuttings.

We left our ravenous moose before he denuded the entire east
bank of the Snake River to visit the Menors Ferry Historic Dis-
trict, where I walked the short path to the restored ferry and the
old Menors Store while Jane waited out of the sun in the cool-
ness of the RV. As I was watching the ferry get ready to make a
crossing, two women floated by on the river in a rubber raft. At
the point the fast moving Snake River turned from swift current

into a patch of white water, the women lost control of their raft, madly slapping at the water with their paddles. The raft spun in circles as it sped through the wavelets. It looked like Mr. Toad's Wild Ride on water. The women grasped their paddles with both hands at the blade, vainly trying to push the water as the raft continued to spin crazily until it hit a shallow bar. The two women staggered out of the raft and hauled it to shore. I do not think it was anywhere near the designated takeout point but they looked relieved to be anywhere on dry ground. The women did not look like they would venture on this ride again.

At Windy Point turnout, I got a good view of the Lower Saddle and the Grand Teton. It looked imposing. I hoped to be sleeping on the Saddle two nights hence.

We drove toward North Jenny Lake Junction and took the one-way scenic drive. We stopped at Jenny Lake overlook for a view of Mt. Moran and the lake. The smoke lifted slightly, and while the colors were still washed out, the features of the mountains were finally clear. As we walked along the lakeside path at the overlook, the Grand Teton and Cascade Canyon emerged from the haze on the far side of the lake, framed by the sun behind them. The lake was a deep sapphire blue tinged with emerald green.

I recalled walking this trail in 1962, the lake in shadow, and then when the sun emerged, the sapphire-green color flashed as if a light switch had been toggled. When clouds again obscured the sun, the colors vanished. I vividly remembered the colors. As I looked at Jenny Lake, I was heartened to see they had not faded.

We overhead one of the other walkers say that they had seen a grizzly bear on the Cascade Canyon trail. Jane looked over at me with a scowl and said, "We're wearing bells and carrying bear spray when we hike; I don't care if we sound like a train."

From Jenny Lake, we drove back to Coulter Bay to buy groceries for dinner. It seemed like a good night for something hearty, so I picked up a package of Johnsville bratwurst that I grilled on the campfire, along with the leftover pork loin. Instead of our usual grilled asparagus, I sautéed a bundle in the cast iron skillet with salad dressing. It was surprisingly good.

After dinner, we walked to Jackson Lake on a path from the campground. From the rocky shore we watched the sun set behind the Teton Range then hurried backed to camp in the gathering darkness. I packed for climbing school and went to bed restless with apprehension about the coming day.

———— **DAY 13** ————

Wednesday • August 15, 2012

We rose at 5:30 a.m. to be able to get to climbing school on time. I was concerned about a possible delay caused by the construction work between Coulter Bay and Jackson Lodge, but we made it on time.

In 1962, Exum required only one day of climbing school as a prerequisite for making the Grand Teton climb. In addition to adding an extensive list of mandatory equipment, Exum now requires climbers to attend a two-day school before attempting the Grand Teton climb. An exception is made if a private guide is engaged for one-on-one instruction and the climb; then the class requirement can be shortened to one day. Because of time constraints, I opted for a private guide for the school and climb.

My guide was Peter Ramos. It was Peter's first year with Exum Guides; but he has been climbing since he was nine years old. He was now twenty-nine and worked four days as a nurse in a clinic in West Yellowstone and three days as a guide for Exum. His mother was a surgeon in Reno, Nevada, so he was familiar with the Lake Davis area where Grizzly Ranch is located. Peter was to be my guide for climbing school and for the ascent of the Grand Teton. I was reassured to have a trained nurse as my guide. I felt in good health, but I was 65, had two cancer surgeries, chronic migraines, a history of asthma and was about to tackle the most physical challenge of my life—for a second time. If something unexpected happened, it was good to know that Peter had some medical skills.

After getting a helmet and harness, Peter and I walked over to the Jenny Lake boat dock to catch the shuttle across the lake. At the dock, the crew had a map of the United States with magnetic state pieces they placed on the map each day when a state was represented by a rider on the shuttle. There was also a white board where the crew wrote the names of countries represented by foreign visitors each day. California was already on the map when I boarded the shuttle. The crew said that California was always one of the first states on the map. I was not surprised, as we're one of the most populous states and relatively close to Grand Teton.

Once across the lake we took a short hike up the trail past Hidden Falls to the cliffs where climbing school is held. Hidden Falls was exactly as I remembered it. It is a beautiful spot. Climbing school, however, was a completely different experience. The curriculum in 1962 was kindergarten and 2012 was graduate school.

There is a split log fence bordering the trail that separates the climbing area. Peter gave me the requisite warning that when I crossed the fence I would be engaging in a hazardous activity and could be seriously injured or killed. Lawyers have entered into the process over the past fifty years. I don't remember receiving any such warning in 1962, but perhaps it is simply the fact that I was an eager fifteen-year-old then, invincible, and warnings of any kind would have failed to register. Fifty years later, I was a lawyer with over 40 years of law practice experience, acutely attuned to warnings, liability, and risk allocation. Despite my legal training, I hopped the fence into the danger zone without hesitation.

We walked a short distance into the boulder area where we went over the basic knots we would be using, including a bowline and figure eight. These knots have not changed and I already knew them well. Years of scouting and my recent training at Planet Granite put me in good stead. We then went over the technical equipment. Carabineers are now locking devices. Fifty years ago they were simply clips that did not have a screw lock. Pitons have been replaced with fancy nuts and cams that can be sized to the width and depth of the crack and removed instead of hammered in and left. In fact, Peter did not carry a hammer.

Personal equipment has changed as well. Helmets are now mandatory. No one wore a helmet in 1962, not in climbing school or on the ascent of the Grand. Footwear is much different. Fifty years ago I participated in climbing school wearing the same Keds sneakers with worn rubber soles I wore in high school gym class. Today, Exum requires climbers to wear special approach shoes with sticky rubber soles specific for rock climbing. But new equipment was only the beginning of the changes in climbing school.

The biggest surprise was the first ascent of the rock cliff. In 1962, we made a scramble up a slick granite slope that was an easy climb with prominent foot and hand holds. This time Peter chose a difficult mantle start that required a leg extension and pull up over a

Exum Climbing School, 1962

Exum Climbing School 2012 version

smooth outcrop without any handholds. My first attempts were unsuccessful and left me breathing heavily, exhausted from the effort. Peter clamored down from his belay position and demonstrated how to accomplish the difficult move. I followed his example, extending my right leg to a small toe hold in what had seemed to me to be a smooth, slick surface, then making an explosive push off with my left leg. I continued my upward momentum with an arm pushup on the mantle accompanied by thrust with my right leg as the increased angle provided leverage. It was a difficult move.

I finally was able to complete the maneuver but bruised my left palm in the process. The rest of the afternoon was equally rigorous. I kept thinking that I should have trained harder at Planet Granite. My bouldering work had been limited to novice routes, the easiest on the climbing wall. It had strengthened some underused muscles but had not pushed my limits as Peter was urging. I had trained alone and had become complacent with the small progress I made on the easy routes. I took satisfaction from the fact that I was the oldest person in the gym by at least 20 years and could reach the top of the 12-foot wall on my own, unassisted. As I stared up at a rock face of real granite, I realized that my bouldering training was helpful but had made me overconfident of my limited skills. Peter disabused me of my false expectations.

My impression of climbing school in 1962 was that it was to give novices a fun taste of the climbing experience. We were not pressed with anything difficult, and I remember that on the actual climb of the Grand in 1962 I had been shocked by how much more difficult it was than climbing school. The current climbing school recreates each of the technical moves that a climber will experience on the actual climb of the Grand Teton. Today's Exum School is both a test of capabilities as well as preparation for the climb. I struggled to absorb and process the training tips for tomorrow's climb, while concentrating on the physical and mental challenges I had to pass in order to demonstrate I could successfully make the climb without endangering myself or others.

After the demanding ascent of the vertical face of the cliff, the rappel lesson was a breeze. I just leaned back and walked backwards off the ledge. The rappel was about 100 feet from top to bottom. It was much longer than the climbing school rappel in 1962. After the rappel, we did a relatively easy climb called the Bat Cave, then, instead of another rappel, we did a walk off. I did not complain. The difficult mantle mount at the start of the day had sapped my energy, leaving me with only adrenaline to power through the climbs. Two ascents of the cliff were enough for me.

Before starting on the trip, Jane and I had serious discussions about the wisdom of my attempting the Grand Teton climb. She felt that I took unnecessary risks, liked to live on the edge, reveled in an adrenaline rush. I had flown planes, rode motorcycles, drove too fast, hiked alone in the woods—in general had a penchant for pushing my limits. To her, the climb was another risk that, at my age, was too much. However, Jane eventually acknowledged the importance of the climb to me, giving her blessing to the adventure.

Although I was tired, I had successfully completed each technical move, giving me confidence that I could repeat my goal of summiting Grand Teton. The wild card was that the mountain was some 7,000 feet higher than the climbing school cliff, with much less oxygen. Moreover, I would be even more tired after the 8 mile hike from Lupine Meadows to the Lower Saddle, where we would spend the night before starting the climb. My initial surge of confidence began to ebb with slight flickers of doubt. I began to wonder if Jane had been right in her concern that the climb was too much for me.

I asked Peter what he thought about which route we should take for the ascent. He knew I wanted to repeat the Exum Ridge, but he gave me a wry smile, paused for a moment then said quietly, "the Owen-Spaulding route would be best for you." Apparently, I had passed the class but with a less than stellar grade. I was disappointed, but the primary objective was to get back to the summit of the Grand Teton, and if it was by the Owen-Spaulding route, so be it.

Unfortunately, on our last pitch Peter injured his knee. As we walked back to the dock from the climbing school area to catch the shuttle boat across Jenny Lake, his knee began to swell. He questioned whether he would be able to make the climb the next day but thought that another guide should be available for me.
Jane was waiting for me at Exum Guides Headquarters. We learned that there was no other guide available for the next day. Tomorrow was my only opportunity to try to repeat the Grand Teton climb. If I could not go tomorrow, the climb would have to be scratched from the trip itinerary. Our seven week trip was tightly scheduled with reservations at coveted campgrounds in the national parks on our itinerary. Any delay would topple the first of a series of closely stacked dominos.

The Grand Teton climb had been the highlight for me of the 1962 trip, a life milestone. The thought that I might not be able to try to repeat it tore at my gut. No matter how wonderful the rest of the trip might be, and the start had been spectacular, not having the opportunity to attempt another summit of the Grand Teton would leave an emptiness that would preclude accomplishing my goal of reaching inside myself to find the fifteen-year-old youth from 1962 I believe is still there. It looked as if my fifty year goal of repeating the Teton climb was in jeopardy but another climber, Greg Duncan, offered to share his guide if Peter was unable to go. Greg was a 54-year-old IBM software engineer from Durham, North Carolina. He had been a serious climber in his twenties and thirties and his interest had recently renewed. Greg's objective had been to make the climb by the Exum Ridge route but he generously offered that any route would be fine with him. He said that, like me, his primary objective was to summit, the route being secondary. Greg's guide was Anneka Door, a 25-year-old experienced Exum guide from Nebraska, whose family raised sled dogs. She had led her father on a climb up Mt. Rainier, but he had no interest in climbing the Grand Teton. I was relieved that if Peter's injury was severe I had a back-up guide. But I felt terrible that I would be a burden on the group and cause Greg to have to make the climb by the "walk up" route.

Armed with the backup plan, Jane and I went to Dornans to buy food for the climb. They were well stocked with small one-person freeze-dried packages. After vacillating between beans and rice, I chose a Southwestern chili. The label looked appealing, and I gave no thought to the possible downside of digesting a spicy dish at 11,000 feet. We ate dinner at a pasta restaurant at Dornans, taking our plates to the outside tables where we had a view of the Teton Range, bluish purple as the sun set behind the mountains. I had spaghetti and meatballs and part of Jane's pasta to carbo load for the climb. The food was plain, but I was ravenous and it tasted great.

Climbing school had really exhausted me. Jane went in to get ice at Birnams, and I saw a man hobbling slowly towards the door. He was middle-aged and looked fit but his head was down and he winced with each halting step. I said, "You look like I feel." He turned to me and said, "Don't try to climb the Grand and come down the same day. It will kick your butt." I nodded with a smile but thought to myself, I may feel tired now but just think: I've got to hike up four thousand feet to the Lower Saddle tomorrow, then climb another three thousand feet to the summit and come back down seven thousand feet in the same day, and I already feel this bad. My mind may have written a check my body can't cash!

We went back to camp at Coulter Bay, and I packed for the climb and then went to bed. I was quickly asleep and slept soundly through the night.

——— **DAY 14** ———

Thursday • August 16, 2012

We were able to sleep a little later since we did not have to be at Exum headquarters until 9:45 am. We made breakfast then drove to South Jenny Lake. At Exum Guides, Peter was there and said he wouldn't be able to make the climb but Anneka would guide us.

Greg drove Anneka and me to the trailhead where we started up on the Lupine Meadows trail at about 10:30 a.m. I had taken the bladder out of my camelback and placed it in my backpack, which weighed about 20 pounds with my water, food, cooking utensils, clothes, and raingear. The trail was much as I remembered. It was a steady steep climb. I quickly found a comfortable stride using my trekking poles to provide support. Off to the left, I could see Bradley and Taggart Lakes. The smoke was not as bad as on the previous days.

Anneka kept a steady pace. We stopped first at the 1.3 mile point for a short water break and then again at three miles. I was breathing heavily but regained my wind quickly at the stops. After a series of switchbacks, we hit the Moraine where the trail became rocky and steeper. I felt a slight pressure behind my right eye, the precursor of a migraine. Left untreated it would slowly morph into a hot poker thrust through my eyeball, making the orb throb with excruciating pain. In preparation for just such an event I had packed a sumatriptan tablet in my shorts pocket where I could easily reach it. I retrieved the tablet and swallowed it with a sip from my camelback without slowing my gait.

There were several boulder areas where I had to hold my trekking poles in one hand, maintaining my balance with the other while scrambling through crevices and over huge granite blocks. Anneka continued to set a blistering pace, but Greg and I stayed close behind her, neither of us succumbing to the urge to take a short breather. At one point, where glacial water was rushing down from the mountain, we stopped and I refilled my camelback bladder. The water was icy blue pure. Anneka said she drank it straight from the stream without treating it. I was glad I had brought the camelback. I was able to sip water as we hiked up the trail and kept hydrated between rest stops. The sky was cloudless.

It was hot, a good day for shorts and a tee shirt. My head felt fine. My preemptive strike on the migraine had worked.

We reached the Headwall at about 3:00 p.m. The Headwall is a 100-foot high vertical rock face at the base of the Lower Saddle. A fixed rope has been placed there for climbers to ascend the rock although there are adequate foot and toe holds without it. I made it up the vertical wall using the fixed rope without a problem.

We arrived at the Lower Saddle at 3:30 p.m. The aluminum Quonset hut where I stayed in 1962 had been blown down the glacier some years previously, a victim of the hurricane force winds that sometimes scour the exposed saddle, which sits like a catcher's mitt awaiting invisible fast balls hurled across the open space to the west. A new plastic and aluminum hut about the same size had been erected to replace it. The view from the Saddle is unimpeded west and east to the far reach of one's vision. To the north, the Grand looms like a dark tower looking more imposing as the shadows lengthen.

Grand Teton from the Lower Saddle – 2012

The Middle Teton rises sharply to the south, the Saddle wedged snugly between the twin mountains. The first part of the climb had been successfully navigated. I made it to the base camp at 11,500 feet, an arduous 8-mile hike with a vertical climb of 4700 feet. The technical climb to Grand Teton summit and the long downhill return to the Lupine Meadow trailhead would be tomorrow's challenge.

I ate an early dinner of dehydrated Southwestern beans and chili, with a cup of bullion, and drank an Emergent C to replace the electrolytes I lost on the hike to the Lower Saddle. I left the chili in the bag with the boiling water for fifteen minutes more than recommended for the altitude but it was not fully hydrated when I ate it. The beans were semi-hard, more like boiled peanuts than beans. The chili was very spicy. My stomach immediately let me know I had made a mistake. I looked around at my fellow climbers and noticed that everyone else was eating some bland rice concoction. As my stomach began to churn and rumble, I thought of the waste kit we were provided by Exum when we were told to pack out everything. I began to worry that if nature called on the climb how was I supposed to use the waste kit, roped in on a ledge with a 2000 foot drop?

My stomach continued to roil with indignity against the spicy gruel I was spooning down my gullet. I feared the consequences that my unruly stomach foreshadowed, but I needed the calories for energy. Eating the chili and risking fumbling with the waste pack was a lesser evil than not having sufficient energy to execute the demanding physical moves required to summit and return. I ate the entire two-serving package of unappetizing chili, ruing with every mouthful that I had not chosen rice, an inexplicable decision given that rice is one of my favorite foods.

It was barely dark, but I was feeling very tired, the cumulative result of today's arduous hike and yesterday's demanding climbing school exercise. There were twelve of us in the hut, packed like sardines in a can, two rows deep, six on the top bunk, six on the bottom. The guides slept in the open, outside the hut. I chose a sleeping bag on the bottom next to the wall so that I could get out without disturbing anyone if I had to make a dash for the outside during the night. I had earplugs, but they didn't work very well. I went to bed at 9:00 p.m. but woke with a start when I was hit in the head by a pair of Oakleys dislodged from the bunk above me. No damage was done to me or the sunglasses. I fell back to sleep, but at 11:00 p.m. one of the climbers started snoring. The sound resonated through the small hut like a bass drum. I never got back to sleep.

—— **DAY 15** ——

Friday • August 17, 2012

I was already awake when the guides came in at 4:00 a.m. to start boiling water for breakfast. The climbers lined up for hot water then sat on the floor, leaning against the hut wall while we ate in silence, each deep in our own thoughts. I scarfed down a bowl of watery oatmeal and ate half of a leftover bratwurst washed down with a cup of Starbucks Via instant coffee. My stomach had settled down, and there had been no emergencies during the night. I reunited my bunkmate with his wayward Oakleys.

The guides provided us small packs for the ascent that we stuffed with rain gear, extra layers of clothing, a full 32 oz. Nalgene water bottle and energy snacks. I was wearing long underwear, synthetic pants, wool shirt, fleece, wool hat, helmet, gloves, headlight, and harness. Everything that had been on the Exum equipment list I was either wearing or was in my pack. There was not an ounce of water absorbent cotton on me or in my pack. I placed my Nikon Coolpix S8000 camera in the pocket of my fleece, where I could easily retrieve it. I hoped to have more than one photograph to commemorate this climb.

At 4:30 a.m., we started our climb to the summit, clamoring up the rocky slope towards the Black Dyke. It was still pitch black. Instead of going through the Eye of the Needle, we took the Crack of Doom route. It was like climbing in a dark cave. I could only see to the perimeter of my headlight. I was extremely winded, but again when we got a brief rest stop I quickly caught my breath. Anneka pushed us hard. Greg was behind me and I tried to hear if he was breathing heavily but could only hear my own labored breaths. However, I was keeping pace with Anneka. I might sound like a V-8 working on six cylinders, but I was close enough to draft off her.

Once through the Crack of Doom it was decision time as to which route to take to the summit. My view of the east was blocked by the mountain, but light was beginning to tint the western sky. The air was still. I told Anneka that I was willing to push myself hard. I just didn't want to do anything stupid. Greg said he was willing to go either route; that his goal was to summit, but I knew he really wanted to climb the Ridge. Anneka said that the Owens Spaulding Route would be shorter and easier and the Exum Ridge would be "a long hard day" but wouldn't be the wrong decision. I said, "Let's do the Ridge." Anneka was excited about climbing the Exum Ridge route. She said it would the first time in three years for her. Her previous trips scheduled for the Ridge had aborted due to weather or the capabilities of the climbers. I felt a rush of adrenaline.This was the climb that I remembered so vividly.

We were on Wall Street at 5:30 a.m. It was as I remembered: a long sloping ledge with a 1000-foot drop off that begins about ten feet wide, gradually narrowing to an exposed boulder outcrop that requires a big step around to continue the ascent.

"Wall Street" – Grand Teton - 2012

This is the point where Glen Exum made his famed blind leap to the unknown other side, discovering the Exum Ridge route. I had been petrified at this move when faced with this barrier in 1962. It looked impossible, but with the firm encouragement of my guides, Jake Brietenbach and Peter Lev, I pushed myself around the corner, relying on my belay man to save me from catastrophe if I fell. I still remember the feeling when I made it to the other side. It was an unbelievable combination of relief, shock, pride, and accomplishment, fired into one moment in time. It was then I realized why people climb. Although that had been my last true technical climb until today the memory was fresh, and I have wanted to recapture that feeling one more time.

This time the outcropping at the end of Wall Street seemed an easier obstacle to overcome. Perhaps it was that I knew what to expect and had made the difficult move in my mind a thousand times over the past fifty years. More likely it was that climbing school had better prepared me for this ascent. There was nothing on the Ridge Route that was more difficult than what Peter had put me through in climbing school. I was physically exhausted after climbing school, the 8-mile hike up to the Lower Saddle, virtually no sleep the night before, and the arduous hike up to the Crack of Doom. But there were enough rest periods at the belay points to gather myself for the next pitch and make my muscles move in the proper direction. The Chimney and Friction Pitch, which were so vividly scary 50 years ago, seemed routine. It could have been the training at Planet Granite, climbing school, or the equipment. La Sportiva sticky rubber ascent boots are better suited for rock climbing than Boy Scout hiking boots.

Anneka led the ascent with Greg second. As the third in line, I had no responsibility for belay. At each belay point I tried to watch Anneka and Greg make the ascent, looking at the route they took, the handholds and footholds they used, so that I could follow the same way. Some of the belay points were narrow ledges, hardly wide enough to stand sideways. I hugged the slick granite wall at those stops anxiously waiting for Greg to yell, "On belay," so that I could respond "Climbing" and start upward, comfortable that if I fell at that point Greg would arrest my fall within a few feet. A scrape or two might result but it would not be a major free fall. While waiting to climb, I periodically checked my heart rate; it never exceeded 124 beats per minute.

Several times during those minutes alone at the end of the climb-ing rope, standing on an exposed ledge with a thousand foot drop-off, cold but feeling sweat clammy against my skin, I felt a wave of exhaustion envelop me. My mouth was dry. The altitude and exer-tion were causing dehydration. I drank from my water bottle at the stops but tried to ration it as the water had to last until I returned to the Lower Saddle. I could see Greg struggle with the next pitch, and I questioned if I could make it, but turning back was not an option. There was no place to go but up. I took strength from the fact that I had done this previously, and although I was much older, I had been able to do everything else on this journey I had done as a fifteen-year-old. I was the same person and was determined to prove it.

We climbed the last pitch, scrambled over a narrow boulder ridge and were on the summit at 9:00 a.m. It was an exhilarating experience. Greg and I stood together on the summit rock, then we each had an individual moment of triumph. I raised my arms

Summit – Grand Teton, 2012

above my head with my face in a wide grin. I had done it, or at least had accomplished half my objective. I was at the top, however, I still had to make the descent. But first I wanted to enjoy the summit, something that I had missed the last time.

This time instead of a cold, thick, white impenetrable cloud barrier, I could see for miles in any direction. From the summit you get a real feel for how much higher Grand Teton is than Middle Teton and Mt. Moran. You are looking down on the world. There is nothing taller on the 360-degree view. Carved in the rocks on the summit are the names of William Owen and Frank Spaulding, the climbers who made the first ascent in 1898.

In 1962, other than the monument and the names in the rock, there was nothing to give a sense that I was on the summit. Back then, the elation of accomplishment was diminished by the lack of spatial orientation to provide the sensory confirmation that we were indeed on top of the mountain. That was not the case today. My eyes provided visual confirmation that there was no higher place within my scan. Over the years I had always felt that I had missed something having climbed the Grand Teton in total cloud cover, never experiencing the sense of exposure and height. It was true I had missed a stunning part of the experience of the Teton climb in 1962, but today I gained what I had missed then. My experience was total and complete.

I took out a paper weight replica of the geodetic monument that Liz had given me as a Christmas present and photographed it next to the real one. It was interesting that the real monument does not have an elevation inscribed. There seems to be some confusion about the true elevation. In 1962 I was told that the Grand Teton was 13,766 feet. Leigh Ortenburger's classic 1956 Climber's Guide to the Teton Range identifies the Grand at that height. The monument replica, however, shows the elevation as 13,770 feet, the elevation shown on current maps. Somehow over the last 50 years the mountain has shrunk. I can identify with that. At my annual physical checkups I now have to cheat to reach the six foot bar. Certain of nature's laws are immutable and age cannot defy gravity.

We ate a snack and then headed down the Owen Spaulding Route for the descent. There were several exposures on the way down. We bypassed the first rappel point. At the second rappel point, Greg went first with my camera. I went second. I tied in

**Free rappel off the
Grand Teton
1962**

**Fifty years later at
the same spot**

with a bowline and then snapped in the rappel attachment and backed off the cliff. On the top part, I bounced down the granite rock then I was hanging free on the rope. The rappel was a little less than I remember. I believe it was about 100 feet rather than the 150 foot in my 1962 journal, but it was long enough. At the end of the rappel I thought I might run out of rope, but it terminated just short of the ground. As the rope end slid through my hands, I safely landed on my feet.

After the rappel, we continued down the mountain to the hut. We got to the Lower Saddle at about 12:30 pm, had a quick lunch and rested. I could feel blisters burning on the balls on my feet. La Sportiva's are a narrow boot. The first pair I ordered was a half size larger but a bit tight in the arch. I exchanged them for a pair a size and a half larger than I regularly wear. They were fine on the ascent but on the steep descent my socks, wet with sweat, slid forward slightly with each step rubbing my soles raw. Fortunately, Greg gave me some of his moleskin. I finished off the last of my water and thought about the cold glacier water that sprang from the rocks trailside several miles below the Headwall. The thought made me thirsty again.

I was running on empty, my energy reserves expended, and the trail down from the Lower Saddle to Lupine Meadows was steep and rocky. The ascent of the Grand had been successful, but as tired as I felt, I knew that the hike out would be almost as dangerous. I could easily break an ankle or blow out a knee with a misstep. I had a brief thought about how much it would cost to get a helicopter lift off the Lower Saddle, but I quickly dismissed that option. In 1962, I had made it up and down the Grand Teton. If I got a ride from the Lower Saddle, this ascent would have been qualified by an asterisk. I had made it this far, and I intended to complete the climb by returning to the starting point at Lupine Meadows on my own two feet.

We started down from the Lower Saddle at 1:00 p.m. after filling our water bottles from the hose below the hut. The water had to be treated. I gave Greg some iodine tablets since his water purification system took four hours to work and the iodine tablets were effective in only a half hour. We descended the Headwall in short order, but the rest of the trail down the mountain was torturous. In 1962, I had been part of the "express" group, rocketing down the trail from the Moraine in less than three hours. This time I hiked slowly, trying to make sure that I did not sprain a knee or ankle. My pack weighed about 20 pounds and acted as a pendulum. When I twisted on a rock, the pack continued to swing in the same direction, placing more pressure on my knees. I was more concerned with completing the course without injury than in breaking a fifty-year-old speed record. My senior buns had already kicked my teenage butt in a time trial on Flattop Mountain. That was enough to satisfy my aged ego.

It was a hot day. To keep hydrated I kept drinking water. I had consumed a full 32-ounce bottle of water on the ascent, downed the remainder of my Camelback bladder at lunch, and then finished off another 32-ounce bottle on the first part of the down hike. It was a huge relief when we got to the glacial creek where we could refill our water bottles. At the creek, an up climber saw my Washington & Lee cap and asked my relationship to W&L. I told him that I had graduated from W&L and obtained my law degree there. He said his dad went there and now lived outside Lexington.

W&L is a small school but has an incredibly loyal alumni base. It was founded in 1749 in Lexington, Virginia, as Liberty Hall Academy. George Washington gave the small school a gift of stock that is still contributing to the University's endowment, and his generosity resulted in a name change to Washington College. After the Civil War, Robert E. Lee could have had his pick of insurance companies or railroads to head but chose instead to spend his last years building up a small school in the Shenandoah Valley devastated by the war. He spent the last five years of his life as president of Washington College, establishing a law school during his tenure; then after his death the College was renamed Washington & Lee University.

It is a special place for me. I received a great education, made life-long friends, matured into adulthood, and on a blind date, met my future wife Jane from Mary Baldwin College, a neighboring women's college in Staunton, Virginia, a short 30 miles from Lexington. I recently returned to W&L for my 45th college reunion. It is now co-ed, coats and ties are no longer required dress but Lexington and the campus are much the same. It is a place that draws you back like a fond memory, special and timeless, new and fresh but unchanged and comfortable as a well-worn boot.

Greg and I doggedly kept hiking down the trail with Anneka always in front, pushing us hard. When we left the jumbled boulders of the Moraine the trail improved and we picked up the pace. At the last planned rest stop we told Anneka to keep going. Shortly thereafter, I made a quick excursion into the woods to urinate - finally. It was the first time since before dark this morning that I had passed water, a sign of dehydration.

We finally emerged at the trailhead and piled into Greg's car at about 6:30 pm, fourteen hours after we had started our ascent. Both Greg and I were wearied but extremely satisfied. Anneka had spoken the truth. It had been a "long hard day" but worth every brutal step. We exchanged addresses and promised to stay in touch. Anneka did a wonderful job of guiding us up and back, pushing us to the limit of our capabilities but not beyond. I was elated that we were able to climb the Exum Ridge Route. I forever will be grateful to Anneka for the confidence she showed in me to give us the option for that route. I would always have regretted it if I had been the reason that Greg had not been able to take the route he had planned.

The successful end of a "long, hard day" with Greg and Anneka

Jane was waiting for me at Exum headquarters. Anneka gave me my certificate of ascent, then Jane drove us back to the Jackson Lake Lodge, where I took a long shower that felt wonderful as I leaned forward against the wall letting the hot spray cascade over my shoulders, down the back of my legs, soothing my tight, aching muscles. Afterwards I lay on the soft bed admiring my bloody shins and the darkening bruises on my knees. Granite is an unforgiving surface. I told Jane I wanted something easy to eat, and she got me some takeout quesadillas from the lodge diner. I could hardly finish them before I was asleep.

I kept Jane awake during the night with labored breathing but I slept the deep sleep of one fatigued, yet fulfilled. One of the last things I did before crashing was to check my pedometer; 47,212 steps for the day, almost double my previous best.

———— DAY 16 ————

Saturday •August 18, 2012

I slept well but woke up with every muscle stiff, sore, silently protesting the abuse I had subjected them to during the rigors of the past three days. Summiting the Grand Teton and the return was the hardest physical and mental challenge I had ever faced. My body was now calling for payment.

Another hot shower felt great. It energized me sufficiently to venture down to the coffee bar in the lower lobby. Jane and I got our daily caffeine ration in large cups, took quick sips and went outside for the view of the mountain range. The haze was back with a vengeance. The clear sky I enjoyed yesterday from the Teton summit had been a fortuitous window in the wall of haze. I felt blessed to have been able to enjoy it, completing a vital missing part of my previous climb experience.

I noticed a young man with a sophisticated camera on a graphite tripod looking dejectedly at the washed out Teton Range. I said, "It's too bad about the smoke from the fires. Hopefully, you were able to get some good photographs yesterday." He responded in a French accent, "I've been here for a week, it's been like this every day. Yesterday I went to Yellowstone where there was smoke. Tomorrow I leave for home. I can see the beauty but I will not be able to share it with my photographs." I wished him luck and said that I hoped he could visit again when conditions were better. In life sometimes timing is everything, yet it is beyond our control. We have to appreciate the here and now. As Stephen Stills sang, "If you can't be with the one you love, love the one you're with, love the one you're with."

As we were photographing the mountains a ground squirrel appeared, munching away on some grass. The animals are constantly eating or searching for food. It is all they do in the waking hours.

We had breakfast in the RV then hooked into the Internet through the lodge Wi-Fi. Jane suggested we stay another night at the lodge instead of moving to the campground at Gros Ventre. I did not object. The thought of one more long hot shower after a night on a large comfortable bed sounded great to me. We spent all morning sending emails and photographs of my climb to friends. We got takeout lunches from the Pioneer Grill in the lodge, then we went in search of Swan Lake and trumpeter swans.

The park map indicated there was a "Swan Lake" accessible by a trailhead at Coulter Bay campground. We drove to Coulter Bay but did not see any trail for Swan Lake. I went into the visitor center and asked a ranger about trumpeter swans and Swan Lake. He laughed and said "Swan Lake" is any water where the swans are at the time. He said he had seen some swans that morning in the wetlands of the Elk Reserve just outside of Jackson. He also said that there might be some swans at the Oxbow Bend of the Snake River. I told him about the Déjà vu '62 Tour and my climb of Grand Teton. He congratulated me and wrote out on a small scrap of paper a quote from John Muir on why men climb. "Climb the Mountains and get their good tidings. Nature's peace will flow into you as sunshine flows into trees. The winds will blow their own freshness into you, and the storms their energy, while cares will drop off like autumn leaves." It was very appropriate.

From Coulter Bay, we drove towards Jackson on the East Road. As we passed the Oxbow Bend in the distance we saw two large white birds in the water that looked like trumpeter swans. We circled back, turning down a gravel road that followed the bend to a turnout with a path to the water. I set up my 300 mm telephoto lens, and photographed the birds, which were still little more than white spots in the distance. When I digitally enlarged the image, the "trumpeter swans" turned out to be white pelicans. Disappointed, we continued our search.

We stopped in Jackson at the Jackson Hole Greater Yellowstone Visitor Center drawn by a dramatic sculpture of a confrontation between a grizzly and an elk in front of the Center. In addition to indoor exhibits, the Center has a boardwalk extending into the wetlands where we walked, but no swans were evident. We continued into Jackson to get some cash at Wells Fargo and groceries at Albertsons. Jackson has become much more gentrified from the western town where there was a hanging every day. The arch of elk antlers is still there, but the rest of the town has become much more upscale.

We navigated through the narrow, traffic-filled streets of Jackson, finished our shopping, and then happily headed back to the quiet of the park. Jane was driving while I kept looking for the elusive swans. Just outside Jackson in the National Elk Reserve wetlands, exactly where the ranger had described, there were two trumpeter swans. They were far away, and I had to use my super zoom, but they were definitely trumpeter swans. The distance was too great to hear their distinctive bugling, a three note trumpet call from which they get their name.

Satisfied that we had located "Swan Lake" and had seen swans, we went to Dornans to check out the Chuck Wagon. Jane was reluctant at first to eat there. She wanted something light. But I wanted to keep as close as possible to the events in my 1962 journal. If I was going to recapture my youth, I felt I had to do the same things, and go to the same places as I had then. Moreover, my memory from 50 years ago was that it had been a very good meal. The Chuck Wagon at Dornans has a sign that it has been there since 1948, so I was confident that it was the same place where I had eaten in 1962. The menu for the night was mashed potatoes, white beans, beef stew, and short ribs. The food was cooked in large cast iron pots hung over open wood fires. The stew had the largest carrots I have ever seen. We filled our plates and hungrily ate it all. The Chuck Wagon was just what we both needed. It was hardy, basic, filling and tasty—good Western-style grub.

We drove back to Jackson Lake Lodge thoroughly satisfied. At the Lake Overlook, we stopped for the twilight view of the Teton Range, watching elk grazing in the meadow. Back at the hotel we ordered dessert. I had cherry pie a la mode and Jane had a milkshake. After the huge dinner we had consumed at the Chuck

Wagon, I was surprised we wanted anything more, but the sweet taste was somehow soothing. The calories were not a concern. I had lost 15 pounds in three days, now weighing in at 155 pounds, the same as my weight in college. When I look in the mirror, if I ignore the gray hair and the few experience lines, I think I look much the same as the youth I'm searching for, but perhaps I'm being delusional. Although I'm the same weight, the pounds may have shifted around a bit.

———— DAY 17 ————

Sunday • August 19, 2012

I got up at 6:30 a.m., and went outside to try to photograph the alpine glow of the sunrise against the Teton Range. The smoky haze was worse than the last few days and the glow never materialized. I purchased coffee in the lobby, then went back up to the room to catch up on my journal. I had been too tired after climbing school to write. Also, I had been off on the climb, so I was several days behind. Outside the room was a balcony with comfortable chairs and tables overlooking the lobby. I settled into a large chair, transcribing the experiences of the last days into my journal, the events fresh, my pen racing over the pages scarcely able to keep up with my thoughts. My handwriting, always a challenge to decipher, was an illegible montage of half-formed first letters followed by wavy lines of varied length, depicting words. Even my skill at interpreting my unique cryptography will be sorely tested by the mystifying matrix of swirls and lines of my journal entries. I will have to transcribe this mess quickly upon the completion of the journey or hope to discover my own Rosetta stone to unlock its mysteries.

At 8:30 a.m., I took a break to call my 90 year-old mother at her nursing home in Lakeland, Florida. I had been sending her postcards from each of the national parks we had visited, reminding her of our trip in 1962. I was surprised when she told me that she had not received any of my postcards. I found out later that she was confused or was just being obstinate. She had received the cards. The staff at Lakeland Hills Center where she lived told me that they enjoyed following our trip and reading the cards to my mother. I was glad that someone enjoyed the cards even if it was not the intended recipient.

We checked out the buffet breakfast, but it looked like they were taking names for table reservations, which was much too formal for us in the morning. We again ate breakfast in the RV, then went back to the lodge where I continued to write in my journal and send emails to friends. At 11:00 a.m., it was time for checkout. The extra day at the lodge had been great for me. I was still stiff and sore, particularly my knees, but I felt better rested.

From the lodge, we drove to Signal Mountain campground, checking into campsite 56. Following my 1962 journal entries, we drove to South Jenny Lake to try to catch the Lake Shuttle to the Hidden Falls trailhead. We circled the parking lot three times without finding a parking spot. Frustrated, we finally gave up, deciding to have lunch at an overlook then take the Signal Mountain Drive.

Pulling off at Mountain View turnout, we made lunch. With the lingering haze, I lamented that we were missing the stunning views of the Teton Range that were captured in my father's photographs, but again I was thankful that I had great weather on the day of my climb.

After lunch, we drove to the top of Signal Mountain. When I was last here it had been raining and we could not see anything. This time, although it was hazy, there was a good view east towards the Wind River Range with the Snake River clearly visible as it winds through the valley. We also had a good view of the Oxbow Bend.

On the way down the mountain we stopped at the Jackson Lake turnout and got a great view of the lake and the Tetons. We then drove back to South Jenny Lake and finally found a coveted parking space. We caught the shuttle across the lake and hiked the half mile to Hidden Falls. There were a lot of people on the trail, including many Japanese tourists. At the Falls Viewpoint, a gentleman about my age noticed my W&L cap and commented that I must be a fellow Virginian. I explained that I was now a Californian but had gone to W&L. His two sons, 30 and 20 years old, had just completed an ascent of Middle Teton. The oldest had left for home that morning with his wife, but the youngest was with him, looking very tired. I said I had just completed an ascent of the Grand Teton. His eyes widened as he looked at me, shaking his head and quietly murmured "Wow." We had a nice chat. Afterwards, I showed Jane where climbing school was held. I pointed out the difference between where the school was conducted in 1962 and the difficult wall that Peter had me climb.

The last boat left at 6:00 p.m., so we headed back to the dock. It was a short but beautiful hike. My knees, however, were still creaking from the Teton climb and the downhill hike to Lupine Meadow. Each step was a reminder that payback was not yet completed.

We decided to have dinner at the Peak Restaurant at the Signal Mountain Lodge. Jane and I both had delicious Idaho trout. We returned to our campsite, wrote in our journals, and went to bed. I had accomplished everything I had wanted to do at Grand Teton National Park. Having successfully made a second ascent of the Grand Teton by the Exum Ridge route, everything else on this journey is a bonus. I recaptured my youth on the Grand Teton; the rest of the trip would be a tandem ride.

TEN

Too Popular for Its Own Good

Yellowstone National Park

At the point where the Firehole and Gibbon Rivers converge swiftly with the Madison River a mountain rises sharply above the river bottom, with the flat grassy plain a perfect camping site, protected from the wind, with plentiful fuel for a fire, and bountiful fish for supper. On the night of September 30, 1870, a small survey group led by Montana Survey General Henry Dana Washburn converged around a campfire at this spot, marveling over the spectacular beauty of the region. One of the party suggested that this area was too important for private ownership, that it should be held as a national park for all the people.

This tale may be apocryphal, but one of the members of the party, Nathaniel Pitt Langford, described this account in his journal, then lectured extensively on the wonders of the Yellowstone area and the idea of a national park. On March 1, 1872, President Ulysses S. Grant signed into law an act establishing Yellowstone as the world's first national park.

As writer and historian Wallace Stegner observed, national parks are "America's best idea." Stegner wrote that "we need wilderness preserved because it was the challenge against which our character as a people was formed. The reminder and the reassurance that it is still there is good for our spiritual health even if we never once in ten years set foot in it." In my case even a fifty-year interval does not dim the remembrance.

In the winter of 1807-1808, John Coulter explored the Yellowstone territory and came back with fantastical tales of boiling hot springs, shooting waters and yellow stone canyons. He was perhaps the first white visitor. In 1872, the year the national park system was established, there were 300 recorded visitors. In 1962, the year of my first visit, there were 1,925,000 visitors and a cumulative total of 29,383,330 from the park's inception. The popularity of the park has continued to explode, particularly with foreign visitors. By 2012, the annual number of visitors reached 3,447,729, with the total number of sojourners increasing more than fivefold to 160,143,923.

Most of these visitors view the park from the road, the crowded parking lots, or short self-guided trails less than a half mile long. The crush of visitors jam into restricted sensitive spaces and stress the delicate environment. Some of Yellowstone's most treasured and unique features are in danger of being destroyed by their very popularity. The fact that these features are so accessible to visitors has endangered their continued existence.

To address the boom in park attendance after World War II, a massive billion-dollar construction project called Mission 66 was initiated and completed over a ten-year period from 1956 to 1966. This project introduced the visitor center concept to the parks and completed construction of new roads and trails that dispersed the crowds and lessened the stress on the sensitive parks. Our trip in 1962 was during the middle of the Mission 66 building project. I found many changes on my return to Yellowstone.

Map of
Yellowstone National Park

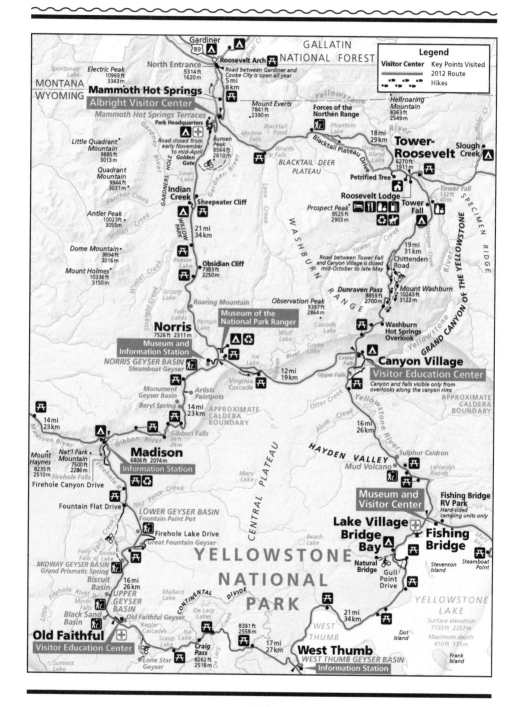

Sunday • July 29, 1962

We found out that ten climbers were lost on Grand Teton. One was dead and two were in critical condition. [They were members of the Appalachian Mountain Club that I had passed on my way down off the Grand on July 26th].

We drove around to the Snake River Overlook and shot some scenics. At Hedrick Pond we photographed the swans. At Oxbow Bend we shot some more scenics and at Coulter Bay we saw the museum.

We drove on to Yellowstone in a light rain. At West Thumb we stopped and saw our first geysers and thermal area. Yellowstone Lake was also visible. We drove on by Old Faithful and up to Madison Junction. There we saw a really nice campsite and set up camp. Dad and I walked down to the museum while Mother cooked supper. There was an exhibit of historical significance there. At the same campsite where the idea for the national parks was born is a replica of this historic event.

After setting up the rest of the camp and eating supper, we went to the campfire program. It was on wildlife. We came back, built a fire and went to bed.

Monday • July 30, 1962

We got up early and headed out towards Mammoth. At Norris Junction we stopped and walked to Steamboat Geyser and then looked around the museum. There were many animal dioramas and geological exhibits. We stopped at all the exhibits along the road, including Obsidian Cliff and Gibbon Falls where we photographed the violet green swallow.

At Mammoth we ate lunch and I got sick. Dad went the museum. When he came back we left and started for the Canyon. We stopped at several overlooks on the way and saw a black bear. At Lower Falls we got some books and went down to the overlook of the falls. It was a very beautiful view. A trail went to the bottom of the falls but we didn't take it.

At Mt. Washburn we drove up to the parking area but couldn't get to the top because the buses had stopped for the day. At the Canyon we looked around the campground, then went to the visitor center and looked around.

At the Grand Canyon of the Yellowstone we stopped at a couple of overlooks and saw the Canyon. It was nothing like the Grand Canyon but it was beautiful. We ate supper at the cafeteria then drove up the Old Norris Road to camp. After having a campfire and toasting marshmallows we went to bed.

Tuesday • July 31, 1962

We went to Mt. Washburn. At the parking lot we got a bus and drove to the observation building at the summit. We looked around there a little then went over the hill looking for bighorn sheep. The first thing we saw was a Richardson grouse. We got right next to it and got photographs. While we were doing this he sheep came down and we stalked them for about an hour. We finally got some good pictures where they separated into two bands.

We waited at the observation tower again for the bus to come back. It finally did and we got down. We drove by the Canyon again and stopped at the Craighead Boys to find out about grizzly bears.

At a campground two miles north of the Fishing Bridge we ate lunch and rested. Two boys across the river were really catching trout. At the Fishing Bridge we stopped at the visitor center and looked at the exhibits. We found out we could find moose at Pelican Bridge. Before this we had a terrific hail storm with two inches covering the ground.

At Pelican Bridge we hiked about a quarter mile into the marsh and photographed a moose feeding on the willows. At the car we drove back along the Norris Road. At camp we cooked supper and toasted marshmallows by the campfire. We then went to bed.

Wednesday • August 1, 1962

We ate a quick breakfast then drove towards Mammoth. At Mammoth we found the old road to Gardiner and took it. It was a dirt road winding through the hills. We saw a herd of antelope. A little ways down the road we saw a lone antelope lying down. We got our cameras ready and went closer, then closer, and finally closer. We got within about 75 feet of him.

At Gardiner we turned around and came back to Mammoth. There we got a haircut and we went to the museum. After that we started back to camp. We ate lunch and secured camp before going to Old Faithful.

At Old Faithful we stopped at the Fountain Paint Pots and saw and photographed a coyote. We arrived at the Geyser Basin and looked at the visitor center. There we saw the setup and exhibits and Dad got one of the naturalists to take him out to Rabbit Creek for the grizzlies. Dad left on the grizzly hike while Mother and I watched Old Faithful erupt. Then I walked around the village and had a coke. When Dad came back it was time for another eruption so we saw that one then we went to the visitor center again. In the center there are a few dioramas that are really good.

We drove back to camp and up to Moose Meadow looking for elk. I got a fire started and Mother fixed supper. While we were eating a man from Everglades National Park, Dick Nelson, came by with his wife and daughter-in-law. They stayed a while and talked and we went to bed.

Thursday • August 2, 1962

Dad got me up early and we went looking for beaver. We walked about a mile in a wet marsh three miles from camp. We didn't see any signs of beaver or everything else. We came back to camp and got breakfast started. Mother woke up and finished cooking. We took down the camp and packed.

Then we drove to Tower Geyser Basin. We arrived just as Grotto Geyser was erupting. We photographed the geyser and saw Morning Glory Pool. At the visitor center Mr. Nelson was there and he took us around to find somewhere to eat. We went to the cafeteria then saw the eruption of Old Faithful. All the restaurants were full. He took us to his house and Mrs. Nelson cooked breakfast. We left Mother there and went back for the cameras. At his house we all got together and went to see geysers.

The Castle Geyser was erupting so we watched that then we went to Biscuit Basin and saw Sapphire Pool erupt. Then we went to Rabbit Creek and tried to find a grizzly bear. We didn't

see one so we said goodbye to the Nelson's and drove out towards
the quake area. There we saw the cottages in the Lake, the Cabin
Creek Fault and the Slide. We walked to the Memorial Rock on
the top of the Slide. We drove on through Madison Canyon and
stopped for supper. At Wolf Creek we stopped at the A&H motel
for the night.

———— DAY 18 ————

Monday • August 20, 2012

At 5:30 a.m. I woke to the sound of a soft rain gently drumming
on the plastic vent. I got up and closed the ceiling vent and
went back to bed. The rain was intermittent. In light of the rain
we slept in until 8:00 am and got a late start. Between the haze
from the smoke and the low clouds from the rain there was not
much of a view of the mountains, so we decided to head straight
to Yellowstone.

Upon entering Yellowstone, we immediately saw signs of the
Great Fire of 1988. Stark dead timber fingers pointed skyward, and
detritus was everywhere on the ground. But the new growth forest
had also taken a strong hold. The regenerated trees were side by
side with their dead ancestors. We passed a bison jam around Lewis Lake, but there was no turnoff to stop so we kept driving. Off to
the right was Yellowstone Lake, stretching to the horizon, an impressive body of water. As we approached the Old Faithful area, we
decided to drive directly to Madison campground for lunch then
return to the geyser later in the day.

At Madison, I checked in with the campground host and was
assigned campsite D-131. Yellowstone is another park where you
can make advance reservations for a campsite. At Arches, we reserved a specific site based on experience from previous visits. I
used Internet research for recommendations on selecting a campsite at Rocky Mountains National Park. The information proved
valuable. We loved the site at Moraine Campground. We were
spending four nights at Madison, a long stay by our standards. I
hoped that we would be fortunate on the draw with a good site.
We were. D-131 reminded me of our campsite in 1962. It was a
wooded site, shady, with a good fire pit and privacy. Perfect.

After setting up our site I walked a short distance to where I could see National Park Mountain and the confluence of the Gibbon, Firehole and Madison Rivers. I looked for the tents that recreated the campsite where the idea for Yellowstone National Park was born, but they were no longer there. The meadow was empty. I closed my eyes and could see the scene in my mind, the white wall-type tents, slightly tilted, the canvas slapping with the wind. When I opened my eyes, the tents were still there. Then the image vanished.

We had lunch at our campsite, stowed the firewood under the table in case it rained, then drove the short distance to the National Park Service Information Center just south of the campground off the loop road. I asked a ranger about the reenactment campsite. She told me that historians had concluded that the formation of the park idea at the campsite was a myth, so the tents were taken down. There is a line from the movie, *The Man Who Shot Liberty Valance,* "When the myth is better than the fact, print the myth," or something to that effect. They should have kept the campsite; it made a good story.

As an impressionable teenager I had looked at the white canvas tents nestled in between the three fast flowing rivers framed by the background of the 7500-foot mountain looming behind them and envisioned myself at the campfire, joining in the discussion, agreeing that this magnificent place must be preserved for everyone to enjoy. It was living history, an opportunity to transport yourself into a time and space where something important occurred, to experience it in the flesh instead of reading about it on the flat dimension of a printed page. Historical accuracy is for historians; myths are more fun.

We drove back towards Old Faithful. Shortly after turning onto the road from the campground, we encountered an elk jam. Curious as the other visitors we stopped to look, adding our Roadtrek to the growing line of vehicles parked half on the roadside but still straddling the road. A few yards off in the woods an elk family - buck, doe and fawn - were grazing, moving slowly, unconcerned by the army of onlookers, some pointing cameras with large telephoto lens, myself included, trying for a clear shot through the upright bars of trees. A park ranger arrived and asked everyone to keep their vehicles off the pavement. We were one of the many culprits, so we returned to the RV without getting the perfect photograph. With the abrupt exodus of many of the viewers, the elk moved deeper into the woods, and the jam dissipated.

Shortly before we got to the Old Faithful area, it started raining in earnest, large droplets pounding the windshield, restricting our vision. Then it hailed, small ball bearings of ice accumulating on the roadway. I slowed down, leaning forward for a better view through water and ice. The hail stopped, but the rain continued in a steady downpour. It rained hard for most of the time we were at Old Faithful.

We arrived at about 4:55 p.m. and the next eruption was scheduled for 5:38. We had time to kill, so we walked over to the Snow Lodge for a cup of steaming hot chocolate. It may be that we always ordered a cup in inclement weather, but the hot chocolate in the lodges in the national parks seems to be especially good. The cup at Snow Lodge was no exception. We savored the warm sweet liquid, then ventured back into the rain to check out the visitor center.

On the way I saw a trail sign that said Morning Glory Pool was two miles away. Morning Glory Pool was one of the highlights of my previous trip to Yellowstone. With brilliant blue green waters that mimicked the colors of its namesake flower, it had been almost as popular as Old Faithful. I have beautiful film footage from 1962 of the pool. However, I did not remember packing my Bolex movie camera any distance to Morning Glory Pool. I would recall lugging the five pound camera plus tripod two miles and back.

At the visitor center, I asked a ranger where the parking lot was for Morning Glory Pool. He said that Morning Glory Pool's fame had been its demise. People vandalized the hot spring by throwing objects into it, clogging the water flow, dulling the vibrant colors of the pool. To protect the famed geothermal feature the road was rerouted. Morning Glory Pool previously had its own parking area, but now visitors have to hike at least 1.5 miles to enjoy it. I told him about the Déjà vu '62 Tour. He said it would be interesting to see how the color of the pool now compares with my memory from 1962.

It was still raining hard so we waited inside the visitor center for Old Faithful. Despite the weather, the geyser area was crowded with people cloaked in raingear or holding umbrellas. Wisps of steam rose from Old Faithful; we were teased with false starts as the geyser sputtered then retreated. Old Faithful was fashionably late by five minutes, but put on an impressive display, gushing skyward in a continuous fountain for several minutes. We got a good view from inside the visitor center while keeping dry. Those outside looked drenched even with rain gear.

After Old Faithful's eruption we walked over to the Old Faithful Lodge to look at its famed lobby. It was an impressive wood structure with balconies on each floor overlooking the lobby that centered on a massive stone fireplace. The peeled log supports provided a warm mood to the area, accented by the dim yellow lighting in the great room. The lodge was jammed with visitors with hardly room to move. The crowd caused a claustrophobic atmosphere.

We concluded that since it had rained so hard at Old Faithful, it likely had rained at the Madison campground. Although I had placed our firewood under the picnic table covered with a plastic cloth, it probably was wet and would be difficult to light. Rather than try cooking on a smoky campfire in a possible drizzle, we decided to stay in the Old Faithful area to eat. We took a look at the lodge dining room but there was a queue of at least 30 people waiting in front of the Maitre'd. Instead, we walked across the parking area to the near empty Snow Lodge Grill. I had a salmon burger and Jane a cheeseburger. The food was tasty for fast food.

We then drove to Madison campground. On the way back we saw a bison on the other side of the Firehole River. I walked through the river bottom brush to photograph it, moving slowly so not to disturb it. The bison was intent on munching great clumps of lush grass on the riverbank, ignoring me and the two other people who had ventured out for a closer look at the beast. As we watched, an occasional fish would jump. It seemed strange to see bison in a forest area rather than on the plains.

As the sun was setting, we saw two more bison grazing in the meadow just past the Lower Geyser Basin. It was a peaceful scene; a perfect transition into the quiet stillness of the night.

—— DAY 19 ——

Tuesday • August 21, 2012

I woke at 5:30 a.m. The inside of the RV was very cold, but we had reversed the Havasack to the warm side up and had been comfortable during the night. I dozed off again and suddenly it was 6:00 a.m. I turned on the RV heater for the first time on our trip. In short order the blower fan went on with warm air flowing from the floor vent. The heater worked great. The chill was quickly out of the RV. After I showered and we ate breakfast, we started on the Grand Loop tour.

Earlier in the morning, I met a camper at the campground rest room from Silver Springs, Florida. He was several years older than me. Shaking, he said he had never been so cold. He was driving a truck with a pop-out tent in the truck bed. I explained that I had an RV and that we were on the Déjà vu '62 Tour. He got excited and said that was what he was doing. He had been here when he was eight years old and he was now 68. He asked his wife to come with him but she didn't want to go, so he grabbed his dog (a small beagle) and off he went. He doesn't make reservations; he just goes where he feels like it. He has cousins in Utah he hasn't seen in 60 years, so he wants to go there and also see the Grand Canyon. I asked if he was going to the North or South Rim and he asked which was better. I told him to go to the North Rim since it was less crowded. He said that's where he'd head.

I thought about my tightly scripted itinerary and mused that his tumbleweed approach of going where the wind blew him had some advantages. But I was on a quest; he was simply out on a lark. I felt I had found my youth on the summit of Grand Teton, but to make sure, I had to continue to retrace my steps, testing myself against memories along the way. Other parks, while inviting, I must reserve for another trip.

As we drove through Gibbons Meadow towards Gibbons Falls there were bison grazing next to the road. A number of people had ventured well within the 25-yard perimeter that visitors are supposed to observe with large wildlife. One of the intruders was a slight Japanese woman with her eye fixed behind her camera, paying no attention to how close she was to a wild animal ten times her size. Fortunately, the great beasts were fixated on breakfast, ignoring the intrusion.

We walked to the overlook at Gibbons Falls, looking back upriver towards the squat cascade which appeared like an outstretched hand with white water rushing over and between the curled rock fingers. The last time here my dad and I had photographed cliff swallows, but there were none present this time.

Our next objective was Artists Paintpots. We tried to stop, driving around the parking area twice, but there was not a single open space. Yellowstone was packed with visitors. Finding a parking spot at the popular areas is much like a game of musical chairs: a steady stream of traffic moves along the park main road then detours into the parking areas of the attractions where a fortunate few may find an open spot. The others continue the game, hopeful they will get lucky at the next area.

We got lucky at Roaring Mountain, one of the less popular areas, stopping for a view of the steam oozing from multiple vents in the side of the hill. It is interesting that the thermal activity is not confined to the Yellowstone plateau but has seeped up through the side of a mountain. The escaping steam from the bare rocks is a reminder that the center of Yellowstone is a volcanic caldera that may one day erupt, dwarfing the explosions of Mount St. Helens, Mount Lassen, Mount Mazama, and other previous eruptions, a sobering thought as one passes the myriad signs of active geology.

The park map showed that Obsidian Cliffs is a few miles farther down the road from Roaring Mountain, just past the picnic area at Beaver Lake. Obsidian Cliffs was one of the places I remember from my 1962 film. As we passed Beaver Lake, we looked closely for a sign for Obsidian Cliffs but did not see one. I was surprised and disappointed. The cliffs were not a major attraction, but I had noted them in my 1962 journal, so they were on my itinerary. They were still on the park map. We must have missed the sign.

As we approached Mammoth, I thought I recognized the side loop road where we had photographed the van in 1962. It looked the same, still a gravel road. At the top of the Mammoth grade we stopped at the Golden Gate. Across the Gardner River we saw what looked like a badger but was probably a marmot.

We were fortunate to find a parking space near the Lower Terraces at Mammoth Hot Springs. We walked the boardwalk, climbing up to Minerva Terrace, a beautiful white travertine sculpture that I remember well from 1962. Although it looked much the same, the trail guide said that the cascades of travertine beside the boardwalk were formed in the 1990s. There was a thin sheet of ochre-colored water flowing in a narrow serpentine band along the boardwalk, adding minerals in a slow continuum of growth to the terrace. Farther along the boardwalk we reached the Main Terrace, where we had a view of New Blue Spring. Water was flowing down a series of flat white plates, stark against the gray hillside framed with the long green needles of the surrounding pines. It was a serene setting.

In the Mammoth Hot Springs parking lot another Roadtrekker approached me to ask if I had any tips on the vehicle. I shared the tip I had received last year in Capital Reef from a fellow Roadtrekker about frequently checking battery water levels. It had been a good tip for me. The Mercedes Sprinter battery caps are metric, and it wasn't until we got to Moab that I found an auto parts store with a metric socket wrench that fit the caps. It is a tight squeeze between the hood and the batteries. When I was finally able to remove the caps to check my battery fluid level, the cells were almost dry. The two thirsty batteries consumed a gallon of distilled water. Since that close call, I have been checking my battery fluid level regularly.

The new Roadtrekker thanked me for the advice, then asked if I had refilled the diesel exhaust fluid. He said he had put in a half gallon and asked if I thought that was enough. I had no idea what he was talking about but I nodded and said that sounded about right. I wished him a good trip then went back to the RV, pulled the owner's manual from the glove compartment and searched for "diesel exhaust fluid." I found that I should have been checking it frequently. Alarmed that the manual indicated that if the fluid level was sufficiently low the engine would be locked, we drove into Gardiner to check the oil level and buy diesel exhaust fluid. We were down a quart of oil and after adding two gallons of diesel exhaust fluid I still could not see fluid at the fill line. According to the owner's manual, the capacity is three gallons. I bought another gallon for safety, deciding to hold it as a reserve.

We drove back into the park through the impressive 50-foot-high stone Roosevelt Arch built in 1903 as the gateway to the park for visitors from the Gardiner rail depot, then continued on the Grand Loop towards Tower Falls. Between the park entrance and Mammoth Hot Springs there was a group of big horn sheep on the rocks a few yards off the road. We pulled over, and I got some great photographs along with some video. The scene was reminiscent of the big horn sheep my dad and I had followed on Mount Washburn with the lambs frolicking among themselves like juveniles of any species, seeming to play a game of tag.

Further along the road to Roosevelt, two solitary bison were resting in the grass. There seemed to be more bison than I remember from 1962 but they are usually alone, no more than two together. I thought that bison were a herd animal that traveled in a group, but I had yet to see more than two bison in the same place in Yellowstone. I'll have to ask a ranger what happened to the herd.

At Tower Falls we walked to the overlook that gave a good view of the 132-foot cascade formed by the rushing Yellowstone River. Its name was descriptive. The falls looked like a tall tower of white water springing from a forest of cone-shaped dormant fumaroles rising from bare hillsides tinged yellow. Water, fire, and earth color, the three elements that are the essence of Yellowstone were evident here. Although Tower Falls was beautiful, I knew from my previous trip it was only an appetizer: the main course was further upriver at the Grand Canyon of the Yellowstone.

Shortly after we got back on the Grand Loop Road there was a bear jam, but we did not see anything. However, at the Dunraven Pass trailhead for Mount Washburn we saw a large brown-colored bear lumber up the hill some two hundred yards in the distance. I was surprised to learn later that black bears come in various shades of brown as well as the standard black. It was too far away to tell whether it was a grizzly or a cinnamon-colored black. Perhaps its ancestor was the black bear I had seen here in 1962.

We passed Canyon Village and then stopped at the Lower Falls overlook, walking to the edge for the view of the Grand Canyon of the Yellowstone to the north and the Lower Falls to the south. Looking down at the yellow rock canyon carved by Yellowstone River, still a thundering, roiling ribbon of white water below, I was flooded with memories.

**Lower Falls of
the Yellowstone,
1962**

**Lower Falls,
2012**

I have film of this very view from 50 years ago, the colors as vibrant, the surging river and 308-foot-high falls still awesome with their power, the sound deafening though I stood more than a half mile away. I was standing in virtually the same spot as my dad and I when we photographed the falls on that trip. There are more trees now and the original ones are larger, but the river, the rocks, and the falls are essentially unchanged. Again, I felt a connection to my past, to my youth, to my father. This was a place where we had a shared experience of wonderment. It had been his first view of the Grand Canyon of the Yellowstone and the Lower Falls as it had been mine. I recall that we both were awestruck by its beauty, excited to capture it with our photography.

As I reflect on the 1962 trip, there were a number of shared moments with my father where I felt very close to him. It may have been the high-water mark in our relationship. Several years after that trip, sometime early in my senior year in high school, we were in his darkroom printing photographs; there was only the dim red light in the room. I do not remember how the matter arose, but I told him I did not want to be a professional photographer; I wanted to go to college and study history. I could not see his face. He kept working on a print, lightening and darkening the image by feathering the light from the projector with his hands, then placing the exposed photographic paper in the tray of developer solution. He never said a word. It had been an unspoken expectation since I was a child that I would follow in my grandmother's and father's footsteps to become a professional photographer.

But I did not want to be my father; I wanted to be my own person with my own identity. My decision to attend Washington & Lee University in Lexington, Virginia, was part of this breakaway. I went to W&L without having set foot on the campus and without knowing a single person at the school, but it had an excellent academic reputation and importantly was 1,000 miles from Miami and home. I needed space outside the vortex of my father's personality to become myself. W&L and Lexington were the perfect incubator for my transition to adulthood.

After I told my father I did not want to follow his path our relationship became strained. We never fought openly, but there was a distance between us; the closeness I had once felt had been ruptured irrevocably. I always felt the fault lay with him. He was overbearing. When we were together, he never let me be an individual, everything was on his terms. After he died, and as I have aged, I have become more understanding, less judgmental. I remember the good qualities, and there were many, and the estrangement that marked our relationship has been marginalized, if not forgotten. I have come to realize that this trip is as much about trying to reconnect with my father as it is a search for my youth. There are several special locations still ahead on this trip that I look forward to visiting again to see if he is there, waiting to share the time and space with me, perhaps to recapture the closeness of father and son once bonded by a mutual love of the wilderness, its serenity, beauty and creatures.

We continued through Yellowstone on the North Rim Drive to the intersection with the Loop Road then turned left onto the South Rim Drive stopping at Uncle Tom's Point to hike the trail to the Upper Falls view. The 109-foot Upper Falls are smaller than the more famous Lower Falls but are dramatic in their own right. From the Upper Falls View we could see people across the river congregated at the Brink of the Upper Falls, a lookout almost within the spray of the falls. It looked like a great place to experience the power of the falls. I am sure that the sound was deafening at that point beneath the falls; it was incredibly loud where we were standing.

With the roar of the falls still ringing in our ears, we drove back to the Canyon Visitor Center. While there I asked a ranger if there was a road sign for Obsidian Cliffs. She said there was not a sign, but she drew a map of where to turn off to see the cliffs. Apparently, the sign that had marked the site in 1962 had been removed for some reason. When I described the bear we had seen at Dunraven, she advised that grizzlies and black bears can be any color; the distinguishing feature is the hump behind the neck on grizzlies. Based on that description, the cinnamon colored bear at Dunraven was most likely a black bear.

It was late in the day and the timing was perfect to check off another event on my trip list. The Canyon Cafeteria mentioned in my 1962 journal was still operating. We picked up our trays, moved through the line, selecting entrees and desserts, then sat down at a table by the window. It was an unfortunate choice as the building was in the process of renovation. Our view was soon blocked by a crew of workman constructing a large structure with pneumatic nail guns that sounded like a battery of field artillery

Lonely Bull - 2012

firing continuously. The noise was deafening, shaking the table. We moved to the far end of the dining room, away from the vibration, where the noise, while loud, was tolerable. Despite the ambiance, the food was surprisingly good. After a full day in the fresh air both Jane and I were famished. Although I enjoy campfire cooking, a cafeteria where you can select your meal and immediately savor it has its advantages when you are tired and hungry. Afterwards, we drove the Norris-Canyon Road, a twelve mile shortcut that bisects the Grand Loop Road, back to camp.

On the way we encountered a bison strolling down the middle of the road, holding up a lengthening line of vehicles behind him. He finally ran off the road to avoid an overly aggressive El Monte RV driver approaching from the opposite direction. We saw another solitary bison in Gibbon Meadows framed against a reddish-orange sunset. The music from Herb Alpert and the Tijuana Brass' *Lonely Bull* echoed through my mind, appropriate as that classic, haunting hit had been released as a single in August 1962, about the time I was in Yellowstone. I recently played the song for the first time in years. It remains as fresh as when I first heard it, another legacy from '62 that has retained its youth.

As I watched the bison in the meadow, it occurred to me that they are more numerous than in 1962 and more accustomed to humans. They seem unconcerned with the gawkers as they chew their cud or graze leisurely by the roadside.

——— DAY 20 ———

Wednesday • August 22, 2012

The RV was not as cold as the previous night, but I still ran the heater to cut the chill. At the restroom I again ran into the gentleman from Florida and asked him what he did yesterday. He replied, "Everything. I took the three mile hike to the Geezers and saw where they were swimming in the river where it was warm." It took me a few seconds to realize that his "Geezers" were "Geysers" to me. He was a good ole boy from the South.

My main goal for today is to make the hike to the Lookout on Mt. Washburn (10,243 ft.). In 1962, buses ran from a parking lot to the summit but some years ago the bus service was stopped and the road was demolished. Now the only way to the Mt. Washburn summit is to hike a trail. I surmise that with the crush of visitors to Yellowstone, the small parking area and lookout facilities were overwhelmed, with the bighorn sheep habitat at the summit also stressed beyond its capabilities.

To reduce the impact of visitors on the environment, the National Park Service, as in the case of Morning Glory Pool, has made it more difficult, but not impossible, to tour these fragile sites. The park service could not move the mountain but it has moved the people. It is a marked difference in park philosophy; a departure from the theme of building infrastructure to bring the people to nature. If someone wants the same experience I had in 1962, they can't be a passenger transported directly to a prime view area. They have to expend some sweat, get out of their vehicles and hike. It has reduced the number of people at the sensitive areas, making it more enjoyable for those who make the effort.

We were on the road to Mt. Washburn at 8:30 a.m. The morning tourists obviously were headed to specific destinations. Bison grazed along the road, but no one stopped or even slowed for a closer view. Jane drove the RV to get comfortable behind the wheel as I had done virtually all of the driving on the trip and she would be solo for most of the day. Unlike yesterday, when it was overflowing, the Dunraven parking lot was almost empty. I wanted to start the hike from the Chittenden Road parking lot where we loaded onto buses in 1962, so we passed by Dunraven. About four winding miles later, we turned onto the gravel Crittenden Road. Jane drove the twisting bumpy road to the parking lot and let me off. I arranged with her to meet me later in the day at the Dunraven parking lot. This would be a one-way hike up Mt. Washburn and down the other side.

The trail to the lookout from the Crittenden parking lot is a steady 2.5 miles uphill with a total 1,400-foot elevation gain. Compared with my recent hikes up Flattop Mountain and to the Lower Saddle on the Grand Teton, it felt like I was walking downhill. At Jane's insistence, I was carrying bear spray and wearing a bear bell attached to the shoulder strap of my camelback pack. With each stride it jingled, adding a musical rhythm to the crunch of my boots on the gravel that was once the roadbed.

The morning air was brisk, clear, without a hint of smoke from the lingering fires. There were a few other hikers on the first section of the trail, but at my pace I passed them. I was soon alone. It was great to be away from the crowds at the turnouts and the major tourist sites. I always enjoy solitary hiking. It gives me time for thought while absorbing the beauty around me. It may stem from the fact that I am an only child, accustomed to time alone. I'm not a loner, but I prefer solitude to crowds.

At the mile and a half point a marmot darted across the trail. I fumbled for the camera but the marmot was skittish, disappearing into a jumble of rocks on the other side of the trail. I thought, "Good for you Mr. Marmot. You still have a healthy wariness of humans, not like the open zoo along the park roads." Fifty years ago it seemed that you had to work a bit harder to see wildlife and get decent photographs. There was a sense of reward and accomplishment in getting a good shot. Today, the bison practically pose for you.

I made it to the lookout in a little more than an hour. Surprisingly, there were a number of hikers already there, mostly foreign visitors. The signatures in the visitor log identified that they were from Portugal, France, and Italy. It seems that the Japanese visitors, who are in large numbers at the turnouts and at the major sites, are with tours and do not venture off the roads on extended hikes.

The lookout has a mountain index that identifies the geographic features visible from the summit. Grand Teton is 75 miles away but was obscured in a light purple haze. After I munched

**Searching for
Big Horn Sheep
on Mt. Washburn**

**Mt. Washburn
in 2012**

on a blueberry crisp Cliff bar, I went in search of big horn sheep. The topography around the summit looked familiar. To the north was a narrow rocky path leading over the crest of a hill. I followed the path towards the crest. In the dust were sheep hoof prints and fresh droppings, a good sign. I hiked about half a mile on the path then stopped, scanned the rock outcropping for movement, listening for any sound, but there were no sheep today.

However, in the quiet and solitude of the Mt. Washburn ridge, I felt a closeness to my father. I realized that it was in situations like we shared 50 years ago, patiently waiting for big horn sheep to photograph, that I felt closest to him.

He was in his element in the outdoors. He was an expert in the wilds and used great patience to capture the perfect photograph. In social interactions, he sucked the oxygen out of the room. As his son I found him difficult to be around.

I remembered one Parent's Weekend at W&L, my dad was the center of attention at my fraternity's cocktail party. While the other fathers were dressed conservatively, he was wearing a flowered sports coat, paisley ascot, and loafers with no socks. He was telling his usual tall tales when one of my fraternity brothers commented on my dad's mustache and goatee. With a straight face, my dad turned and said, "The secret to a great goatee is horse manure. You have to rub your whiskers with manure each night. I'll let you have some of my stock if you want." My fraternity brother looked squeamish. He didn't know if my dad was serious or not but he declined the offer. After the party, my fraternity brothers thought my dad was cool. I just wanted him to go home. But he was different away from people.

In the wild he blended in, quiet and observant. In the civilized world, he delighted in being a garish plaid shirt with outlandish striped pants. Socially, he was an extrovert's extrovert, my polar opposite.

The clouds looked threatening, so I cut short my sheep watch and started down the trail to Dunraven Pass. Part way down, I stopped for lunch at the base of a rock cliff with a view of the trail snaking through the forest below. I found that my plan to wrap my tortilla, almond butter, and blueberry jam sandwich in aluminum wrap had been a failure. The wrap leaked. My mobile radio and notepad were now sticky with jam juice. As I sat eating, a parade of hikers passed, going both up and down the trail. Although visitors can no longer ride a bus to the summit, Mt.

Washburn is still a popular destination. One hiker was a nun in full habit wearing sturdy looking hiking boots, carrying trekking poles. I gave her a wave as she smiled back, continuing uphill at a good pace.

I made it down to the Dunraven Pass parking lot an hour and a half early from the rendezvous time I had arranged with Jane. I tried to call her on both my cell phone and on the mobile radio but was unable to reach her. With time to kill, I found a spot in the shade up the hill with a seat on a stump where I could lean against a tree. It was fairly comfortable with only a few short branch stubs poking in my back. I was half dozing when I noticed a group of people in the parking lot excitedly pointing up the hill. I went down to ask what they saw and was told someone had seen a black bear.

A few moments later, a black bear appeared up on the slope in the trees close to the same place where I had seen the cinnamon bear the previous evening. This bear, however, was pure black. The bear came downhill partially hidden in the trees. People walked along the road trying to get a better view of it. The bear finally emerged about 150 yards up the hill and entered an open meadow. As soon as the bear hit the meadow, it started running and didn't slow down until it was in the cover of the trees again. This was a small bear, but it still had body fat that rippled in waves as it ran. They are remarkably fast animals.

Jane arrived exactly at the prearranged time of 2:30 p.m. We drove to the Norris-Canyon Road, then turned north on the Loop Road to the Obsidian Cliffs. The pull out was where the ranger had described. The exhibit explained that the Obsidian Cliffs had been plundered over the years by souvenir hunters. I then understood why the stop was no longer marked with signs. It is there if you want to find it, but the park service is not going to make it easy. That is an unfortunate recurring theme in Yellowstone: as its popularity increases, the stress on the natural wonders that are its draw likewise increases, placing the park service in the difficult position of balancing protection of the fragile environment with making the park accessible to visitors. Fortunately, in Yellowstone there is much to see from the road and the short self-guided trails that access the geyser areas. For the more adventurous willing to hike a few miles from the roadside trailheads, an even richer experience awaits.

Having checked off another milestone on my itinerary by locating the elusive Obsidian Cliffs, we turned around, driving south on the Loop Road to the Norris Geyser Basin where we walked the boardwalk to the Back Basin that contains Emerald Spring and Steamboat Geyser. Emerald Spring is a brilliant green, the combination of the rich blue of the water and the yellow of the suspended sulphur in the pool. We were fortunate to find Steamboat in the midst of a minor eruption, spewing water and hissing steam. Steamboat, the tallest active geyser in the world, can go days, months, or even years between major eruptions, which can reach more than 300 feet high.

The sky was threatening. It started to rain lightly, so we cut short the walk around the rest of the basin and went back to the RV. We continued south on the Loop Road, stopping at Artists Paint-pots where we took the one-third-mile trail to the pots. The board-walk trail climbed to a view of the colorful basin with flesh-toned bubbling pots, gurgling hot pools with plumes of white steam, interspersed with verdant green grass patches, domed by a cerulean sky. The rain had stopped with the sun shining briefly between large banks of clouds moving swiftly overhead. "Double double toil and trouble; fire burn and cauldron bubble"—the quote from Macbeth was brought to mind as the paintpots made gurgling noises like boiling asphalt. It was a witch's brew in an otherwise pastoral set-ting, an incongruity of nature—fire and brimstone amid fields of greenery. I was glad there was an empty space in the parking lot, for the short hike around the paintpots was a walk worth taking, a good end to a great day.

On the way back to camp, we stopped at an unnamed pool Jane had discovered after dropping me off for my hike to Mt. Washburn. It was an azure color and had a steam vent at the back of the pool, a small but beautiful feature in a park filled with wonders unveiled at each turn in the road. At camp, I quickly made a fire, carefully tending it until the flames subsided then I slow cooked chicken and asparagus over the glowing embers. It was delicious. After dinner we sat by the fire, feeling its warmth, writing in our journals by flashlight; then overcome by a wave of exhaustion, we went to bed, looking forward to the next day.

——— DAY 21 ———

Thursday • August 23, 2012

We rose early and after the usual preparations left for the Upper Geyser Basin to take the hike to Morning Glory Pool. There are two options to get to Morning Glory Pool from the Old Faithful Visitor Center, a paved bike path that roughly parallels the Firehole River or a boardwalk that meanders through the thermal area, connecting geysers and pools as dots along a line. We opted for the boardwalk trail that starts behind Old Faithful Geyser, crossing the bridge across the Firehole River, continuing up Geyser Hill, then stopping at Doublet Pool where the conjoined twins were boiling from the crusty surface. We turned around at Aurum Geyser to see Old Faithful erupt again. Today was hazy but there was no rain. The geyser's plume unfolded then collapsed back on itself, expended. It is a mesmerizing sight.

Old Faithful - 2012

Morning Glory Pool - 2012

We took the short spur to Spasmodic Geyser, an unusual formation with smooth rounded folds that reminded me of brain coral. We continued towards Morning Glory pool, stopping at each geyser and pool along the trail. Yellowstone is a land of contrast. Boiling water flows from geysers and pools into cold clear streams and hills sheathed with a fresh carpet of green new-growth trees are punctured by skeletal reminders of the 1988 fire that blackened much of the park.

The boardwalk joins a paved path near Morning Glory Pool that follows the old roadbed. The original highway bridge remains in place, now used by cyclists and walkers. The hike is a total of 3 miles round trip, every foot a sensory experience of sight and sound. Our destination achieved, I was saddened slightly by Morning Glory Pool, still beautiful, but it has lost its vibrant color.

A sign at the pool says that it is a faded glory. My memory of the pool from 1962 was of brilliant green and blue, a liquid image of its namesake flower. I do not recall the jarring ochre ring that now chokes the vibrant core of the pool, dulling the overall brightness of Morning Glory. Perhaps the image is reflective of us all: our exterior may be dulled by the years, but our inner core remains radiant.

We traced our steps back along the same path, passing geysers and pools for the second time. Previously sleeping, Grotto and Sawmill geysers awoke, gracing us with eruption displays as we passed. At Old Faithful we saw a group of Amish tourists waiting for the next eruption. It was interesting that the Amish, whose lifestyle seems to shun artificial beauty would seek the natural beauty of Yellowstone National Park.

We were low on some food basics, so we went into the small but well-stocked Yellowstone Grocery Store. It had everything we needed. Our necessities filled, we left Upper Geyser Basin to look for a lunch spot.

At Biscuit Basin we pulled into the parking area for lunch. There is a footbridge from the parking area to the basin across the Firehole River offering a great view of the flash point, hissing steam where boiling water from the thermal basin flows into the cold, fast-moving river. After crossing the bridge, we took the half-mile loop boardwalk trail. The main attraction of Biscuit Basin is Sapphire Pool, and it did not disappoint. The pool's colors were still as vibrant as I remembered from 1962.

After Biscuit Basin we stopped at the Fountain Paint Pot trail at the Lower Geyser Basin and took the loop trail. The paintpots there were similar to those at Artists paintpots but not in the same colorful palette. We then stopped at camp for a short rest.

A young family with a boy not older than three had settled in the campsite next to ours. They had a truck with a camper shell. The boy was in shorts and cowboy boots, wandering inquisitively around the unmarked perimeter of the campsite. He was watched protectively by his mother but given space to explore while they completed their camp chores. I wondered how much of this experience he will remember as an adult. I have fragments of recollections of early childhood camping. The gentle swaying of the jungle hammock as I listened to the deafening night sounds that grew louder with the darkness. The smell of wood smoke and pine. The taste of eggs fried in bacon grease. I hoped the young cowboy in the adjacent campsite was making memories for himself.

Around 4:00 p.m., we went across the Norris Road and turned south at Canyon towards the Fishing Bridge. At Hayden Valley, we found the bison herd. On the west side of the park it seems that all of the bison are solitary. I had asked a ranger at Old Faithful about it, and he said Yellowstone has the largest herd of wild bison in the United States. The solitary bison have been shunned from the herd. They are usually aged, cantankerous males. The Yellowstone River cuts through the center of the Hayden Valley. There were bison on both sides of the river, including a number of calves. One bison took a vigorous dust bath, rolling over and over, creating a thick cloud of dust. As we left the Valley we were caught in a bison jam as a group of bison were in the road with traffic restricted to one lane.

We passed a controlled burn, which gave me pause. The devastating fire of 1988 in Yellowstone was a turning point in firefighting philosophy in the national parks. Up to the late sixties, forest fires were aggressively fought and extinguished as quickly as possible. Gradually, it became recognized that fire was part of the natural process, indeed was necessary for the continuation of a healthy forest and regeneration of some species of trees that require fire to open seed pods. In the early 1970's the policy was changed to let naturally caused fires, including those due to lightning strikes, volcanic activity, sparks from falling rocks, and spontaneous combustion, to run their course; firefighting was limited to fighting man-caused fires and protecting structures. However, years of fighting every fire, natural or otherwise, had built up layers of combustible materials on the forest floor.

The 1988 Yellowstone fire was a confluence of weather, a number of small fires merging into a giant conflagration, and a hot burning fuel source of ancient detritus on the forest floor. The resulting mega-fire consumed almost one-third of the park. The initial hideous scarring appeared irreversible, but nature has proven resilient. A result of the fire is that controlled burns are now instituted to eliminate the buildup of excessive fuel on the forest floor in areas where there have not been recent fires. But there have been instances where controlled burns have surged out of control. The business of forest management is a delicate balance; too much control or too little can prove disastrous.

At Fishing Bridge, we continued to Pelican Creek and took the nature trail to the lake shore. The trail winds through thick woods then opens onto Yellowstone Lake. We stood on the shore with the wind whipping across the lake, raising whitecaps with flying foam. The sand on the shore was dark, volcanic in appearance. I thought this was the place where my father and I had followed a huge moose into a thicket to get its photograph. There was a marsh near the end of the trail that looked vaguely familiar, but there were no moose or any other animals on the trail. It was a place that had changed, or the spark of memory had dimmed too faint for clear recognition. Nonetheless, it was a beautiful walk. Yellowstone Lake is enormous, stretching almost twenty miles in length, from the Pelican Creek to the tip of the South Arm, with a depth of 410 feet. I searched the map for a dam location but found that the lake is a natural geological feature.

We returned south on the Grand Loop Road around the lake and then north past Old Faithful and back to camp at Madison. It was past 7:00 p.m. when we got back. I quickly made a fire. One difference from 1962 is that you can now buy firewood and kindling at the camp store. Then, at most campgrounds I had to forage for wood. At many sites the area had already been picked clean. Many nights on the first trip I started our campfire with wet, green twigs. It was all that was left in the woods around the campgrounds. There is nothing like setting a blaze with dry, aged firewood with precut kindling after a long day. To a camper it is almost as good as a long, hot shower. I grilled hamburgers made with local grass-fed beef and cooked beans in the cast iron skillet. Both were great.

After dinner I wrote in my journal by the light of the dying fire, then went to bed, tired but feeling I had made good use of our short time in Yellowstone. I had been able to do everything on my list. The next challenge will be the hike to Sperry Glacier. It was there that my father almost fell into a crevasse while I was filming him. I wonder if I will recognize the spot.

ELEVEN

"Crown of the Continent"

Glacier National Park

In 1900, George Bird Grinnell, owner and editor of *Forest and Stream,* gave Glacier the title, "Crown of the Continent," as part of his effort to promote the preservation and protection of this special place. Word of its natural beauty had first been passed by local ranchers and lumbermen. Then in 1892, the public gained access to the area with the construction by the Great Northern Railway of a railroad through the Marias Pass. Glacier became a national park in 1910, sparking further interest from tourists inspired by John Muir and Teddy Roosevelt to sample the wilderness experience.

The Great Northern built several hotels and chalets in the park to accommodate tourists and promote travel on its railway. It was the Gilded Age turned rustic. One of the chalets built by the Great Northern was six miles uphill by trail from Lake McDonald, situated as a bivouac for hikers and horseback riders whose destination was Sperry Glacier. It also served as a waypoint on the famed Gunsight Pass trail that weaves through the center of the park.

Taking its name from the nearby glacier, Sperry Chalet was constructed by Italian stone masons with native materials. The complex included a two-story dormitory and a combination kitchen-dining hall facility. The chalet initially had cold running water but no electricity. Toilets were fifteen gallon cans that were emptied, along with other camp garbage, by dumping the contents over the cliff behind the kitchen-dining hall. Eventually, changing environmental regulations caught up with Sperry Chalet. The cost of coming into compliance was over $1 million, seemingly an insurmountable financial hurdle. So in 1992, after eighty years in operation, the Chalet was closed.

Fortunately, a private group was established to raise the funds to reopen the Chalet. The National Park Service also recognized the historical significance of the complex. From these two sources sufficient funds were provided to make the required environmental and safety improvements. Sperry Chalet was reopened in 1999.

My father and I stayed at Sperry Chalet in 1962. It was a memorable part of our visit to Sperry Glacier, where we photographed mountain goats scampering on the trail cut into the crumbling mudstone cliffs. In planning for the return trip, I was unaware that the Chalet had been closed. Our timing for the return was serendipitous. The winter of 2010 – 2011 had been unusually harsh with a late winter avalanche roaring through the dormitory. The stone walls withstood the icy onslaught, but tons of snow and ice tore through windows and doors destroying much of the interior.

The cleanup and restoration took most of the 2011 summer, reducing the Chalet's season to only a few weeks in late August. We would have had difficulty getting a reservation for a trip in 2011. When I first called in November 2011 for a reservation, the 2012 season was completely booked, but luckily there was a cancellation that enabled Jane and me to keep this important milestone on the itinerary for the repeat trip. I was looking forward to seeing Sperry Glacier again, hoping the mountain goats are still there.

Map of
Glacier National Park

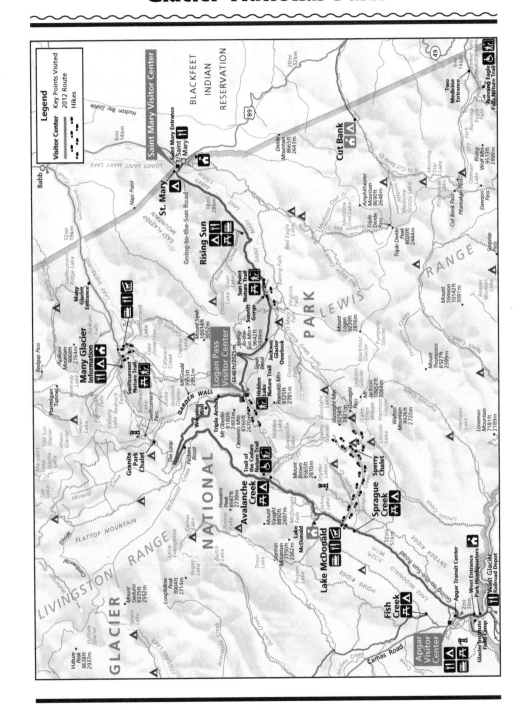

Friday • August 3, 1962

We got up early and ate in a café then headed for Glacier. At Browning we stopped at the Montana Wildlife Museum. They had a collection of very good mounted mammals, elk, bison, moose, etc. They also had a lot of dioramas that were excellent. Right next to the Wildlife Museum was the Museum of the Plains Indians. They had a lot of dioramas and exhibits of crafts and paintings.

We drove around to West Glacier and got food and ice then drove on into the park. We tried to camp at Sprague Creek but it was full and so was Avalanche Creek so we turned around and came back to Apgar and set up camp there. Then I went fishing on Lake McDonald and caught a Silver Salmon. I went back to camp and cleaned it.

Mom and Dad came back and we sat around the fire for a while then we went to the campfire program on "What to do in Glacier National Park." After the program we went back to camp and cooked steak for supper.

Saturday • August 4, 1962

I got up late and ate breakfast. We sat around camp for a while because it was raining. We invited the people next to us over for coffee. Afterwards I did the dishes. The boys, Larry and Jack, and I went down to the lake and looked around. When we got back to camp we waited until after lunch then secured the camp and I went fishing again. I fished for about two hours and caught two fish then went back to camp. I went to the woodpile and cut wood. At camp I started a fire and made coffee.

I started walking to town when they came up and we went to town together and got food and ice. We went back to camp and loafed around. I got more wood then cooked supper. After sitting around the fire we went to bed.

Sunday • August 5, 1962

We fixed breakfast then secured the camp. Our objective was Waterton National Park via Going to the Sun Highway. We

stopped first at McDonald Lodge to arrange for horses to ride to
Sperry Glacier on Tuesday then we headed up the road. The day
was very foggy and we didn't see much until we came to the Garden
Wall. It cleared up a little and we could see a few mountains.

At Logan Pass it was very cold and we put on warm clothes.
At the ranger's office we found out that a group was working on
ptarmigan in the area. We hiked to their camp and asked them a
few questions. They told us where we might be able to find some.
We hiked up a stream over boulders and through swampy patches
of ground but we didn't see anything. At the Headwall we followed
a cirque up to the trail to Hidden Lake. We hiked about a mile to
the overlook where we got a good view of the Lake then we went to
the car.

At Sunset Gorge we hiked to Baring Falls on the Water Ouzel
Nature Trail. There we got good pictures of the water ouzel. At
Sunset Point we got a view of Lake St. Mary then we drove on into
Canada. At the entrance to Waterton Lakes National Park we took
a side trip and photographed bison in a paddock.

At the park we looked around and saw a few deer and stopped
at the Prince of Wales Hotel then started back. We ate at St.
Mary's and drove straight through the campground. There we piled
out of the car and into the tents for a night's sleep.

Monday • August 6, 1962

We got up early and ate breakfast then went to McDonald Lodge
for the horses. We packed our equipment and got horses and then
started off. The trail was a gradual upgrade with shallow streams
crossing it at long intervals. The first three miles were through
dense wooded forest. At some point we lost the Leica light meter.
The next three miles were along a rocky ridge with the Chalet in
view. We went up a valley then switched back and stopped for a
half hour at the Chalet.

There was a marmot named Mike at the Chalet that was very
tame. We got coffee then got on the horses and headed up the moun-
tain to Sperry Glacier. It took quite a while to ride the four miles
to the Headwall. There we climbed the cliff and walked out on the

snow. Goats were all around us and I photographed them. We spent about an hour there then the horses left.

We were left at the Headwall after coming back from the Glacier. We photographed goats at the hitching rock. There were thirteen there from kids to old bulls. We started on the four mile hike down after we ran out of film. About half way down we took a short cut across the ridge on a goat trail. It was pretty rugged and wasn't really a short cut. We came down on the path across a rock slide. At the Chalet we got a room and rested then ate supper. After dessert we went outside and mountain goats were around the kitchen. We stayed a while in the dining room then went to bed.

Tuesday • August 7, 1962

We got up at 7:00 a.m. and ate breakfast at the Chalet. After the meal a deer came to the dining room for salt. After photographing him we started down. Just across Sprague Creek we stopped and got water then set a fast pace for the valley. We stopped one more time to rest then easily made the remaining mile and a half to the stables. There we paid the wrangler and got a drink then went back to camp. We ate a snack then took the camp down

We stopped at the park headquarters and looked at the exhibits. Then we went into Hungry Horse. We ate lunch and got a few souvenirs then drove on. At Spokane we had supper and about 60 miles outside of Spokane we stopped at a hotel.

——— DAY 22 ———

Friday • August 24, 2012

We rose and organized to leave. I saw my friend from Florida in the rest room. He was concerned about the tropical storm in the Caribbean that was predicted to hit Florida next week. He was trying to decide if he should go home to be with his family in case the storm hit them. He also was leaning towards trying to make a run for Bryce National Park and make a decision from there. I wished him luck. We dumped and filled the water tank then left Madison.

At West Yellowstone, we got fuel and I filled the diesel exhaust fluid reservoir. It was lucky for me I ran into that fellow Roadtrekker at Mammoth in Yellowstone. If not, I would probably have had the engine lock up on me at some inopportune, remote location. From now on I will be checking the diesel exhaust fluid level along with the oil level.

We then headed for Wolf Creek, Montana, on US 287. Our first stop was Quake Lake. In 1959, a major earthquake caused a landslide that buried 19 campers and created a natural dam, backing up the Madison River, forming a new lake. Even after 52 years some of the tree trunks are still standing around the edge of the lake like silent monuments to the event. I remember the place well from 1962. There is a new visitor center, but it was closed for remodeling.

We drove through Ennis, Montana, a picturesque town with upscale shops, including a Christie's Realtor office. A group of children were milling outside the library; perhaps school starts early here. At the edge of town there is a large sculpture of a fly fisherman landing a trout.

Outside of Ennis, we saw at least a dozen fishermen in dories on the Madison River. This must be prime trout country. The dories have a sharp pointed bow with a small flat stern. The boats sit high in the water with a low draft. They look like they would handle well in white water. The dories are two person boats; one person fished from an elevated stool while the other manned two long sweep oars. The current was swift and the oarsman appeared to be using the oars to steer rather than for propulsion. Barreling down the river with a chance of catching fish looked like great fun.

There were also many large ranches and farms along US 287. Each seemed to have frontage along the river and massive archway entrances adorned with western names like the Bar 7 and Long Horn Ranch.

We stopped for lunch at an overlook of Canyon Ferry Lake outside of Townsend, Montana, nothing more than a pullout with an interpretive sign and a trash can swarming with yellow jackets. We had passed a public picnic area in town with tables shaded by large trees in hope of a more scenic setting. While there were no amenities at the overlook, the view of the lake with the Big Belt Mountains to the east more than made up for the lack of facilities.

I read the interpretative sign at the lake. It had been completed in 1954 as a hydroelectric/flood control project by the Bureau of Reclamation, submerging the town of Canton in the process. After I scarfed down an almond butter-blueberry jelly tortilla, we headed to Helena for groceries. I input "grocery store" as Point of Interest in our GPS unit, following the turn-by-turn directions to an Albertsons parking lot. It felt strange being in a city with traffic, stop lights, billboards, all of the distractions of civilization, after the quiet serenity of Grand Teton and Yellowstone. I could not get back on the open highway quick enough.

Interstate 15 from Helena to Wolf Creek is a designated Scenic Byway cutting through a heavily wooded mountainous area. My parents and I had spent the night in Wolf Creek in 1962 at the A&H motel, but if it still remains it operates under another name. In planning for this trip I researched the A&H motel and found nothing operating under that name in the area of Wolf Creek. However, my search discovered a bed and breakfast lodging on the Missouri River that looked intriguing. It was located at Hardy Creek, a few miles off our route but the photographs on the website of the River's Bend Lodge showed comfortable rooms in a spectacular setting, well worth a minor detour.

We arrived at the River's Bend Lodge about 2:30 p.m., still early in the day. It's a rustic place situated on a bend of the Missouri River directly across from a high rock cliff. We had reserved the Osprey Nest Suite; it seemed like a small house compared to the confines of our RV.

After setting up for recharging our nearly depleted electrical gear, Jane took a long hot shower, steaming the bathroom with a thick fog that coated the shower door, mirror, and bathroom window with a wet opaque film. We were used to rationing water because of the limited tank capacity in the RV. An unlimited supply of hot water was a welcome luxury. Outside the clouded window I could hear warblers. Their musical song was a free concert.

I went downstairs to the Great Room to ask the owner, Soren DeTienne, for his recommendation on where to dine. He suggested the Missouri River Inn, a nondescript restaurant across the highway that looked like it catered to fishermen. He said the Inn served good food at reasonable prices. We decided to try it and found the place jammed with customers at the bar and in the restaurant. Our timing was fortunate, as a couple was leaving as we entered so we were seated without delay. At the recommendation of the waitress, we both had fish and chips that were excellent, crisp on the outside, moist on the inside.

After dinner we went back to the lodge and spoke with Soren. He built the lodge himself with the help of friends starting in 2001. He completed the project in 2009. The lodge has a deck that hangs on the river's edge. It does not take much imagination to see Lewis and Clark laboring upriver, searching for the headwaters of the Missouri.

The lodge has been a labor of love for Soren. The Great Room is a comfortable place to read, converse with friends, or simply relax in the warmth of the huge hearth. We took advantage of the Internet connectivity at the lodge to catch up on emails, then went to bed on the large, soft, comfortable queen-sized mattress in the Osprey Nest Suite.

Today was a relaxed pace; sleep came easily.

——— **DAY 23** ———

Saturday • August 25, 2012

We had a restful night. Soren, and his wife, Cindy Bania, cooked breakfast burritos and baked muffins. It was much more than the cereal we were used to for breakfast. The view from the lodge deck was beautiful. To the north is Tower Rock where the Lewis and Clark expedition camped in 1805. It is now a state park. After breakfast, we packed, thankful that all of our electronics were fully charged.

We backtracked to Wolf Creek on a service road that parallels I-15. The road runs beside the Missouri River, where many fishermen were already trying their luck. The Missouri is very shallow in places at this point. A fly fisherman was standing in the middle of the river looking like he was walking on water. A bald eagle flew overhead and there were white pelicans in the river. We were on I-15 for a short time at Wolf Creek and then turned north on US 287 towards Glacier National Park.

We fueled the RV at Choteau, notable for being the closest town to David Letterman's 2700-acre Montana ranch. There is not much else to recommend it. The road from Choteau to Browning is the epitome of why Montana is called the Big Sky country. The Rockies are a backdrop to the west with gently rolling grass hills stretching for miles to the horizon in the three other directions. The country has a stark beauty, but when we entered the Blackfeet Reservation we began to see signs of poverty. It was not as abject as in Navajo Country, but it is still evident. The difference may lie in the landscape. A rusting hulk in the barren desert that is home to the Navajo has a look of irreversible finality, while the same abandoned wreck in the grasslands of the Blackfeet's Northern Montana, cradled in shoots of greenery, seems redeemable.

At Browning, we stopped to see the Museum of the Plains Indian. Jane and I were the only visitors for the young man taking admission at $3 per person for seniors. Two Native American artists were working on crafts. The building was a non-descript brick square. It looked like it may have been constructed since my last visit, but the man at the desk told me it was the original museum building built in the 1940s.

The exhibits were interesting but looked unchanged from my last visit. There was a slide show on Indian history narrated by the actor Vincent Price. The ending was upbeat on how we are all Americans and the Plains Indians have retained their culture while assimilating into the larger society. When the credits rolled, it appeared that the film had been produced in its entirety by white men. The show reflected the political correctness of its time but seems a jarring anachronism today with a lack of sensitivity to Native Americans.

My sympathy was further aroused by the two resident artists who were excitedly talking about the fact that their Congressman and Senator were due to visit the museum in the next ten minutes.

With an empty lot at the museum, and a full one at the adjacent casino, my thought was that they were going to be disappointed. Their local Congressional delegation will likely bypass the empty museum for a place holding greater promise for potential voters. Such is political reality.

From Browning, we continued on US 89 through St. Mary along Lower Saint Mary Lake, passing the small town of Babb then into Glacier National Park by the Many Glacier Entrance. The Blackfeet Reservation was open range for cattle and horses with many wandering close to the road. We stopped at Lake Sherburne for lunch, its turquoise water surrounded by a collar of bone white small stones indicative of a man-made reservoir.

A short way past the park entrance gate there was a bear jam with cars stopped in both directions drawn by a large grizzly gorging itself in a berry patch some 200 yards from the road. The massive bear had the hump behind the neck that is characteristic of grizzlies. It paid no attention to the gathered crowd, its head buried in the patch with its maw moving side to side devouring berries. We heard talk in the crowd that two juvenile grizzlies had been wrestling in the shallow water of the lake near to shore but had moved on. We were disappointed that we had missed them, but perhaps they would be back when we passed by tomorrow.

We had a reservation for two nights at the Many Glacier Hotel, opened by the Great Northern Railway in 1915 "as one of the most noteworthy tourist hotels that has ever been erected in America." The hotel is a large five-story chalet-like structure rising abruptly above the rocky shoreline of Swift Current Lake. It is surrounded by wilderness, a charming throwback to the civilized society of the past century, blending as one with the primeval forest. As we pulled into the parking lot, our greeters were a group of big horn sheep, two ewes with four lambs, wandering between the rocks and pavement as if there were no boundary between nature and man.

We checked in at the front desk, walked the three flights of stairs to our small room, and decided this would be a pleasant change of pace from camping. It was a nod to Jane as consideration for her cold nights in the RV at campgrounds that were milestones in my 1962 journal. I had not visited the Many Glacier area in 1962 so this was new territory for me, with no memories to guide me.

The view of the lake from our window spurred us to explore the area around the hotel before dinner. There was chatter in the lobby that a grizzly had been spotted on the hillside north of the hotel. Outside, near the trailhead for the 2.6 mile loop around Swift Current Lake, we met a group of people peering through binoculars at where the bear reportedly had been sighted earlier in the afternoon, but there was no sign of it now.

Armed with a can of bear spray, which is basically self-defense pepper spray with a longer and wider spray range, our bear bells jingling with each step and making enough noise to alert the Mounties in nearby Canada of our passing, we ventured out on the trail. The air was crisp in the cool evening. The trail followed the north side of the lake then wove through the thick forest until it connected with the south lake end, hugging the east shore back to the hotel. Not surprisingly, given the ruckus we were making, no wildlife appeared, although the scenery was beautiful. It was a memorable hike.

At the hotel, we were able to get a reservation in the Ptarmigan Dining Room, a mammoth expanse with a wood truss ceiling dangling vanilla colored cylindrical lighting fixtures mixed with diffused lights that appeared to be upside down bamboo-framed umbrellas. There was a huge, unused stone fireplace, but the overall effect of the wood, stone and lighting in the massive room created a warm, comfortable, surprisingly intimate place to enjoy conversation and a good meal. We both had grilled sturgeon, and I had a cup of buffalo and venison chili. Everything was delicious.

The desert menu had an old leather cover embossed with a picture of a mountain goat and the slogan "See America First." I remember the slogan from the 1960's but apparently it originated much earlier and was used by the railroads to promote domestic tourism. Regardless of when it originated, it was a statement that I believed. I would rather visit the natural cathedrals of parks in the United States than the storied man-made edifices of Europe. At one point, I had toured every national park in the continental United States, but that was years ago. There have been many new parks established that I would like to see, a goal that will further delay my grand tour of Europe unless Jane, who spent her junior year studying in France and would love to return to the continent, exercises executive authority.

After dinner, we sat on the deck overlooking the lake, watching the sun set behind Grinnell Point, shaped like a pyramid, directly across Swift Current Lake from the hotel. The point, which appears to be a pinnacle, is actually a false peak at the east end of a long ridge leading to the summit of Mount Grinnell.

I picked up a park paper and learned that Going to the Sun Road is restricted to vehicles under 21 feet long. Our Roadtrek is just over 23 feet, so we may have to drive to St. Mary and take the park shuttle. We will have to check with the ranger at the park entrance to see if we are restricted from the highway but leave time to catch the shuttle as an alternative. If we can't drive the road we will have to make a slight deviation in the itinerary, but I should still be able to do everything I had planned for tomorrow. The shuttle stops at each of the places where I had hiked in 1962. The issue will be on Monday when we check out of the hotel and move to Apgar campground on the other side of Glacier Park. If we are unable to drive the short way through the park via the Going-to-the-Sun Road we will make a circuitous detour around the perimeter of the park, more than doubling the mileage. Apgar campground does not take reservations. We will have to arrive early to ensure that we get a campsite. Perhaps we will be fortunate, and there is some leeway in the road restriction that will allow us to squeak through. We will find out tomorrow.

——— DAY 24 ———

Sunday •August 26, 2012

The hotel alarm clock was broken, displaying the wrong time. Jane woke me up at 4:45 am thinking we had overslept our 6:00 am alarm. We got the time straight and went back to sleep for another hour. On awaking for the second time, I dressed quickly, got coffee in the hotel café, and then went outside on the deck where there was still a marked chill in the morning air. The sunrise was illuminating the top of Grinnell Point with a splash of reddish brown, bright against the dark purple of the rest of mountain still in the shadow of the ridge to the east, back-dropped by a gray sky rapidly turning blue. A mist rose from the lake. A light breeze across the water distorted the reflected image of Grinnell Point into an impressionist shadow on the lake surface.

We ate a quick breakfast in the café then left for St. Mary to try to catch the first shuttle bus if we could not take the Roadtrek

Sunrise
Grinnell Point — Swift Current Lake

on the Going-to-the-Sun Road. At the park entrance, I asked the ranger if our 23' 6" RV could ease under the 22 foot restriction but the answer was an emphatic no. It was a disappointment that we would not be able to drive the famed highway and have the same experience as I had in 1962, but at least the shuttle would take us to the points where I had hiked with my dad. Tomorrow, we would have to get an early start to make sure we got a campsite at Apgar.

We missed the first shuttle but were able to get the second bus at 8:30 a.m. and were at Logan Pass by 9:15. It was a beautiful day, far different from the cold drizzle with a swirling mist that had cloaked the pass fifty years ago. I still remember bundling into a heavy black Navy pea coat over a hooded sweat shirt tied tight, the biting wind freezing my exposed face as my dad and I clambered up a stream bed in search of ptarmigan, an elusive bird in the grouse family. The surrounding mountains would appear briefly then vanish in the fog and clouds. The sun was totally obscured by the clouds and mist; there was no trail to follow and I had a feeling of disorientation yet confidence that we were in no trouble. I had absolute trust in my father. Moreover, my own self-assurance was high. In retrospect, my self-confidence and trust in my own abilities are gifts from my father, skills obtained through experiences and tests from an early age, challenges that at the time seemed harsh but on reflection were character-building, molding a child into an independent adult. We were very different people, he was a social extrovert artist-photographer, I was an introspective button-down lawyer, but when taken out of the urban environment, placed in the wilderness without the competing stresses of civilization, we were more alike than not. I understand that now.

Jane and I took the hike to the Hidden Lake overlook, this time staying on the trail instead of bushwhacking cross country as I had on my previous visit. A red hazard sign at the start warned that the trail was closed at the 1.5 mile point due to bear activity. Apparently, young grizzlies were jumping out of huckleberry bushes along the trail scaring the wits out of unsuspecting hikers. There had been no attacks, but the park service is cautious when grizzlies get too close to trails.

When we started out the air was clear, but gradually a thin layer of haze from the Idaho fires settled in the lower elevation between the high mountains on both sides of the pass. The trail was a steady upward climb. The first part of the hike was on a boardwalk, which protects the vegetation along the trail. I thought back to my dad and I stomping across the virgin fields, no doubt leaving footprints in our path that may still remain. At that time there were sufficiently few visitors so that some off-trail excursions were tolerated. However, the influx of visitors has reached the point where the fragile environment cannot absorb the impact.

Boardwalks through sensitive areas are commonplace in the national parks, with warnings admonishing visitors to "Stay on the trails," as frequent as speed limit postings. I understand the necessity for the restriction, but I would have liked to have been able to hike across the meadow to find the place where the stream cut through the rock, forming a small gorge, and to stand on the boulder in the stream, feeling the wind through the rock opening cooled by the water; I remembered it as a treasured moment with my dad from long ago. I have a photograph of the place. I am sure I could find it again but the boardwalk constrained me.

As Jane and I continued on our hike we saw ground squirrels and hoary marmots. There was a carpet of wildflowers with yellow columbine and alpine aster. The weather was so much better than the last time I had been here. Jane had dressed for cold weather but got hot on the hike up to the overlook. She found a "dressing room" behind some trees to take off her long underwear out of sight of hikers on the trail but with a curious audience of squirrels chattering approval at the show.

The view from the overlook was spectacular with Hidden Lake curving like a crooked finger in a bowl formed by Bearhat Mountain to the west, Reynolds Mountain to the east, and Clements Mountain to the north. We spoke with a couple at the overlook who had met while working at the Tetons. The man had tried to climb the Grand Teton with a couple of friends by the Owen-Spaulding Route, but they were stopped by weather just short of the summit. They had been so disappointed because they had planned to hike down, go to Jackson for dinner and get tee shirts commemorating their climb, but since they didn't summit, they couldn't get the tee shirts. He said it was still his ambition to sum-

**Logan Pass,
1962**

mit the Grand Teton. I would have liked to continue the trail to the lake, but as the sign had indicated at the trailhead, it was closed due to bear activity so we retraced our steps back to Logan Pass.

On the way down a mountain goat suddenly rose up from beside the trail. It must have been resting in some rocks or grazing. I followed it until I got some good photographs.

Mountain Goat – Hidden Lakes Trail 2012

Farther along the trail, we noticed two young men in their mid- to late-twenties walking in front of us. They were handsome, athletic types with two attractive women walking a few yards in front of them. One said to the other, "I'm in a really good place now. I have the girl, the dog, the baby's on the way. All I need is a job and a house and I'm set." I thought to myself that it must be a generational difference, but it didn't sound like such a good place to me. I commented to Jane that priorities must be different for the younger generation, yet another change since 1962.

As we neared Logan Pass, I thought I saw in the distance the rock gorge with the creek where my dad took photographs of me. The water flow was less, but it looked like it could have been the spot. I was tempted to explore, but a "Stay on the trail" sign was an unambiguous admonition. I had already ventured off when I followed the mountain goat. I would be content with the memory of a special place, revived by a view from afar of what looked to be the same location.

Next on my itinerary was the Water Ouzel Nature Trail to Baring Falls. The water ouzel, also known as the American dipper, is unique among passerines or perching birds for an ability to dive and swim under water. We had been fortunate to see a water ouzel at Baring Falls in 1962. My dad and I had patiently waited at the base of the falls to photograph one of the birds.

Water Ouzel Baring Falls, 1962

I had been rewarded with some great footage of a water ouzel, its eyelids adapted to swimming underwater, blinking nervously while bobbing on a rock, and then turning suddenly to catch an insect that had landed behind it. My dad had ventured out on a log that extended into the pool below the falls. He got a terrific photograph of the bird with his 400 mm telephoto lens. We hoped to see a water ouzel this trip. It would make a great day even better.

From Logan Pass' we caught a shuttle to Sun Point, where we took the Sun Point Nature Trail to Baring Falls. The first part of the trail parallels Saint Mary Lake, a long, narrow, glacier-fed basin surrounded by mountains; it then turns into the woods. I realized after we had departed the shuttle at Sun Point that the Water Ouzel Nature Trail probably had started from Sunrift Gorge. However, there is no mention of a Water Ouzel Trail on the current park map.

Baring Falls was exactly as I remembered. The log that my dad inched out on to photograph the elusive bird and the boulder where I filmed the ouzel were still there. We waited a while but did not see any water ouzels. Although I was disappointed, the fact that the falls were unchanged gave me a sense of fulfillment. Once again this trip is proving that, at least in the national parks, you can go home again.

Baring Falls, 1962

Baring Falls, 2012

We hiked back to Sun Point, a roundtrip of 1.6 miles. We then caught the shuttle back to the Saint Mary Visitor Center, where we had left the RV. Originally we had planned to take a quick trip to Waterton Lakes Park in Canada, as I had in 1962, but the ease of entry into our neighbor has changed. We had left our passports at home. They were not on our lengthy list of items for the trip. It is possible that our California driver's license may have been sufficient for the crossing, but we were carrying a Smith & Wesson .357 magnum revolver for protection. I was concerned about crossing the border with a firearm and ammunition in the RV. Later I learned that you can get a permit to enter Canada with a firearm, but it must be obtained in advance. Forgoing the side trip to Waterton Lakes Park was a wise decision on my part, an unavoidable departure from my 1962 route due to regulatory changes wrought by a more dangerous world.

Instead of driving to Canada, we went back to the hotel for a rest before dinner. We dined again at the Ptarmigan Dining Room where we both had trout. The service and food were excellent. After dinner we sat on the porch watching the sunset, writing in our journals. Tomorrow we will circumnavigate the park boundary, hopefully to arrive at Apgar in time to get a campsite. Apgar was the jumping off point for the next key events of this journey, a reprise of my horseback ride to Sperry Chalet, where my dad and I had spent a memorable night, and a hike to Sperry Glacier to see if it has been diminished by global warming.

————— **DAY 25** —————

Monday • August 27, 2012

We woke to the alarm at 6:15 a.m. I showered, dressed and went downstairs to the cafe for a cup of coffee. The morning was much warmer than the day before. There was no mist rising off the lake.

We packed, checked out of the Many Glacier Hotel and hit the road for Apgar Campground. We stopped at an overlook of Lake Sherburne for breakfast, then continued on. A park ranger had recommended Duck Lake Road as a quicker way to the west side of the park. It was longer but straight and avoided the winding switchbacks between Saint Mary and East Glacier. However, Jane did not want to take a new road through unfamiliar country, so we continued on US 89 through St. Mary.

Route 89 was curvy, but at Kiowa we turned on to State Road 49, and the windy road became a snake with a steep drop-off on one side. The view was beautiful, but the road was awful. Parts of the road were gravel with cave-ins in the outer lane. But once committed there was no turning back. We arrived at East Glacier, white-knuckled but safe.

Being off the grid did not unbind us from the monthly obligations for mortgage, power and light, and sundry credit cards. Jane is the family banker. She has embraced much of what the computer age has to offer—email, Facebook, Internet surfing—but on-line banking is a bridge too far as yet. Some of our obligations she paid in advance, while others we must pay on the road. We found a post office in East Glacier to mail our bill payments for September.

It made me wonder what my parents did in 1962 to address the monthly bills while we were on our six-week trip. I suppose that they tried to pay the obligations in advance. It must have been difficult. My father's fishing tournament business peaked in June to early July. As soon as the tournaments were over, he would immerse himself in the darkroom, making the photo albums that were his livelihood. The albums would be sent to clients in mid-July with revenue coming in after they were received. Much of his revenue for 1962 must have been received after we left on the trip. In some ways the trip must have been taken as a matter of faith, a knowing certainty that the money for it would be waiting in envelopes to be opened when he returned.

We were not wealthy but my father's business provided him the resources to purchase the best photographic equipment available, and to do essentially whatever he wanted to do. He was his own man, supporting himself and his family with his own skill, talent, and creativity. For all of the issues that I had with him in my later adolescence and early adulthood, he never displayed any of the pressure he must have confronted from the high-risk nature of his livelihood, dependent solely on himself. However, I think alcohol became his escape. A tumbler of Canadian Club and water were as much a part of his later character as the ever-present tobacco pipe. He was a classic product of an age when the three martini lunch was a business model. But I do not remember him having a single drop of alcohol on our 1962 camping trip.

From East Glacier we turned onto US 2. The scenery was beautiful but the haze was much more evident than in the east side of the park. We reentered the park at West Glacier, quickly found Apgar Campground and searched for a campsite. We were early. There were several good sites. We picked one (A-27) that we could drive through. It was sufficiently flat so that the leveling blocks were not required.

As we passed through West Glacier, we saw a sign for a laundromat. It had been two weeks since we had last been able to do laundry. We were in desperate need of clean clothes. We checked in for our campsite, then went back into town to the laundromat. It was a barracks-type building with rows of coin operated washers and dryers. We stuffed several machines with our laundry and stacks of quarters then explored West Glacier, returning to feed additional piles of quarters into the huge rotating dryers. I don't think I had been in a genuine laundromat since my college days when a once a week trip to one was something of a ritual.

Watching the large dryers turning reminded me of two of my fraternity brothers who were slightly crazy. They would take their dates on Saturday night to a seedy laundromat on Main Street in Lexington to ride the dryers. They called themselves "Laundronauts," competing to see who could stay in the spinning dryer the longest time as the temperature became hotter. The girls were usually unimpressed. The centrifugal force under heat on their hirsute craniums apparently did no permanent damage. They both survived; one becoming an attorney in Washington State specializing in health care and insurance regulation, the other a newscaster in Pennsylvania and author of childrens' books.

While waiting for our laundry to finish, we looked around the well-stocked grocery store in West Glacier. I bought several small nylon sacks that looked like they might be useful. It turned out they were perfect stuff bags for packing the items we would need for our trip to Sperry. Everything of ours in the East Glacier laundromat came out clean and dry.

We then drove to Lake McDonald to check in with Swan Mountain Outfitters and confirm how much we could bring on the ride to Sperry Chalet. Our limit was what we could stuff in the saddlebag and pommel bag they would provide. We could also carry our camelback hydration packs, but they had to be empty. I was told that we were not permitted to wear cameras around our necks while on the horses. That is a new rule. I had been looking forward to getting a photograph of Jane on the trail at the bend where my dad took a picture of me. Alas 'twas not to be.

Armed with information for the next day's ride, we returned to camp where I walked the short path to Apgar Center. There I bought two slices of freshly made huckleberry pie to go. We organized ourselves for the ride, packing our bags with clothes, headlights, personal items, including the requisite medications that are my one acknowledgement to age. Then I built a fire. I grilled pork chops and cooked baked beans in the can on the fire. The food was good, but the dessert was better.

We watched the fire slowly burn to faint embers, as I thought about the ride tomorrow. I kept thinking how fortunate we were to have two nights at the Chalet. Originally, only one night was available. When my dad and I made the ride in 1962 we rode all the way to the Headwall, only a mile and a half from Sperry Glacier. Today, the horses stop at Sperry Chalet; the glacier is an additional four-mile hike with a 1,500 feet elevation rise, a total of eight miles round trip. The morning riders arrive at the Chalet about noon. The family-style dinner at the Chalet is served promptly at six pm, which does not give much time to hike to the glacier, spend some time exploring, and return for dinner. In the afternoon the horses leave for Lake McDonald by 1:00 p.m. To try a morning hike to the glacier and return in time for the afternoon ride down the mountain would be a challenge. Having the extra night at Sperry Chalet gave me a full day to hike to Sperry Glacier without the stress of having to rush back.

As I went to sleep, I was trying to remember the last time I was on a horse. It may well have been the ride to Sperry Glacier. I eased into sleep confident that although that was a long time ago, riding a horse would be like riding a bicycle—you never forget how to do it. However, in my case, I had been on a horse no more than a half dozen times, enjoying the experience but never really mastering the skill.

One of last my last experiences had been near Cloudcroft, New Mexico, on an earlier trip with my parents. I rented a horse at a corral intending to ride him back to our campground several miles away. The livery owner sternly admonished me not to run the horse, cautioning that I was responsible for any injuries to the animal. The horse plodded along the trail until out of sight of the corral, then it veered off through the woods at a gallop with me hanging desperately on the pommel to stay on. I narrowly ducked tree branches as the horse madly ran on, seemingly trying to scrape me off the saddle. At a meadow, the animal suddenly collapsed with its legs flaying and eyes wild. I jumped from the saddle as the horse fell. I thought it was dying but after a few minutes it rose up. The owner's warning still fresh, I was afraid to get back in the saddle for fear the horse was injured and I might do more damage. I held the reins and walked it back to the trail and then to the corral. When I explained what happened, the owner muttered, "Damn horse. He hasn't been ridden for a week. Sometimes he has to be shown who's boss or he rolls around a bit. I should have warned you. Hope you had a good ride." Well, it was not much of a ride, but I had a good walk.

Trail to Sperry Chalet 1962

Jane, on the other hand, had taken riding lessons as a young girl. I anticipated some good tips on horsemanship.

DAY 26

Tuesday • August 28, 2012

We rose at 6:00 a.m. I showered, ate my usual breakfast, and then organized the RV. We left the campground for the Lake McDonald Lodge parking area at 7:30 a.m. There were not many cars in the parking lot, and we found a good spot to leave the RV for the three days we would be on the trip to Sperry. We got our gear together, restricting what we carried to fit into our two-saddlebag limit. Small items - headlights, toiletries, GPS, SPOT, and bear spray – were carefully packed in the newly purchased stuff bags.

We walked across the road carrying our bags, proceeding down the Sperry trail approximately 100 yards to the corral. The Swan Mountain Outfitter wranglers were organizing the morning riders. We signed our liability waivers and Jane elected to wear a helmet. Fortunately, all of our stuff fit in the two saddlebags and the pommel bags. For safety reasons, the wranglers were very strict. You could not have anything around your waist or neck that might snag on a branch, so cameras had to be packed; photographs on the trail were not a possibility. We had a short demonstration on horse-handling and safety then it was time to get on our horses.

My horse was named Suede. He was the boss of the corral, tall, russet-colored, and feisty. Jane's horse was Nick. As instructed, I grabbed Suede's mane and the side of the saddle, swung my right leg over the saddle bags, and easily mounted my horse. I sat straight backed, tall in the saddle, ready to ride. Then I turned to watch Jane.

Her mounting was a bit more difficult. Her camelback was tied to the back of her saddle, which made the height to clear with her right leg a little higher. She also had a difficult time reaching the stirrup with her left foot so she had the wrangler lower the stirrup, which made it an even longer stretch to clear the back of the saddle with her right leg. She tried but could not get her right leg over the saddle. She was stuck with her left foot in the stirrup and her right leg extended parallel to the ground. In this awkward position she panicked, insisting that she could not do it. She pleaded to be helped off the stirrup. In a millisecond, Plans B, C, and D flashed through my mind. Was there a vacancy at McDonald Lodge? Could I hike up to the Chalet later after getting Jane settled? Would I have to scratch Sperry Glacier from the itinerary list? Fortunately, another wrangler pushed, while the first wrangler pulled, and Jane got properly seated on Nick. My first thought was relief that alternative plans need not be pursued; my second thought was apprehension at the realization we would have to do this again for the return ride down from Sperry. Well, we had two days before we had to face that crisis.

Mounted on Suede and Nick, we rode up the trail to the Chalet behind the wrangler. The six-mile-ride took a little over three hours, most of it in dense forest. The trail paralleled Sprague Creek for a while, and we passed a beautiful waterfall. There were two spots where the horses watered in the stream. I thought I recognized the turn in the trail where my dad took my photograph.

Suede rode beautifully. Nick gave Jane trouble all along the way to the Chalet. He constantly turned to eat shrubs bordering the trail, which the wrangler emphasized we should not let the horses do. Jane tried pulling up on Nick's reins, but he was too strong. As Nick was sauntering up the trail with half a tree in his mouth, Lisa, our wrangler, kept telling Jane to control Nick, to not let him eat. Jane kept explaining that she learned to ride English-style with a light touch on the reins. Lisa finally lost patience and said that if Jane could not control Nick, she would take the reins and lead him the rest of way. Jane got the message, yanking hard on the opposite rein to jerk Nick's head away from his snack.

It was a battle of wills, but Jane finally gained control over the recalcitrant Nick. It may have been that Nick was simply stuffed, having partially denuded the forest along the trail for the first two-thirds of the ride. Jane, feeling abused by Nick and reprimanded by Lisa, was not excited to learn that Lisa was also going to be our wrangler for the return ride. She had a full day and a half to think about the ride down the mountain, possibly on Nick again under the stern guidance of Lisa. And she had to accomplish that tricky mounting exercise again. Jane's lobbying to hike down from Sperry instead of ride was bound to start soon.

We first saw the Chalet from the trail below, about a half mile away, perched on a high cliff overlooking the Sprague Creek Canyon. It looked the same as I remembered it from 1962.

At the Chalet, we got off the horses, our first dismount since we left the corral some three hours earlier. Jane's legs wobbled after dismounting. She took some time to get her land legs, but was thankful to be off of her nemesis, Nick. When she recovered we went into the stone dining building, which doubles as the office, checked in and were assigned Room 11, which had a double bed, on the second floor of the dormitory.

A year ago the dormitory sustained avalanche damage, snow crashing through windows, gutting the interior partitions but leaving the basic stone structure unscathed. The Chalet had been closed for repairs for the first two months of the summer, reopening at the end of August for a shortened season. The building's survival in this harsh environment of wind and snow is a testament to the skill of the Italian stonemasons who built the structures from native stone found on the site.

We ate the sack lunch provided by the Chalet, then took a brief rest. It was still early afternoon, and I wanted to see some of the area before dinner. My father and I had taken the trail to Sperry Glacier, but we had not gone beyond the Chalet on the Gunsight Pass Trail that runs from Lake McDonald to Jackson Glacier Overlook on the Going-to-the-Sun Road. I took the trail east over Lincoln Pass to the Lake Ellen Wilson Overlook. It was beautiful with spectacular vistas. There was still snow on the mountains, but it was a lot less than I remember from my last trip. The hike was almost four miles to the overlook and back, a good warm-up for the hike tomorrow to Sperry Glacier. I did not see anyone else on the trail. There was complete solitude except for an occasional ground squirrel. The only sound was my breathing, labored by the steady uphill climb from the Chalet, the crunch of my hiking boots on the trail, and the wind, invisible yet omnipresent, whistling around my clothes, shaking the needles on the fir trees, scouring the rocks smooth in its path. I was alone but not lonely.

At the Chalet Jane had pulled the chair out of our room, placing it on the deck, catching the rays of the sun as it coursed to the west. I joined her when I returned from my hike. We watched the afternoon riders depart for Lake McDonald, then wrote in our journals. Lounging around the Chalet, we met a couple from Boston. He is a doctor. She grew up in Miami, but we had no common acquaintances. However, we chatted about our remembrances of Miami; swimming off South Beach, cruising Collins Avenue on

Miami Beach on Saturday night, exploring the Seminole Indian villages off the Tamiami Trail, watching the Miami Marlins from the Class AAA International League play the Havana Sugar Kings before the revolution. Good memories, but it had been a long time since either of us had been back to Miami.

At dinner we had assigned seating. At our table was a couple from Gaithersburg, Maryland. He works for the National Institute of Health. Jane and I lived in Northern Virginia the first years of our marriage. We shared fond memories of the Washington, D.C. area with our tablemates. When we worked in nation's capital we felt that it was the center of the universe. After we moved to the San Francisco Bay Area in 1983 we found that what was front page news in the Washington Post was barely mentioned in the San Francisco Chronicle. There is a different perspective outside the Beltway.

A diverse group of people had traveled a far distance to visit Sperry Chalet. It is interesting how being in a remote place with a

Sunset at Sperry Chalet with view of Lake McDonald

small group provides a common experience that makes people at ease with each other, an instant friendship based on the shared love of the outdoors and a bond formed by the effort it took to get to this special site. Dinner was pot roast, and it was very good.

Afterwards we watched the sunset from the rock ledge that provides an unobstructed view west to Lake McDonald. There is no electricity or running water in the dormitory. We climbed the stairs to our room on the second floor, guided by the yellow beam of our headlights, then went to bed.

------ **DAY 27** ------

Wednesday • August 29, 2012

The walls of the Chalet are only eight feet high and do not extend to the ceiling. The staff warned that anything said or done in the Chalet can be heard everywhere in the building. Earplugs are provided in each room. I used the complimentary earplugs, but I had a fitful sleep with loud snoring in the room below, periodically jolting me awake. We got up around 7:00 am, splashed cold water on our faces, and then went to breakfast. I had a hearty breakfast of eggs and ham. We saw our new friend Tom, the doctor from Boston, and his wife, who had decided not to hike to the glacier today because the weather looked threatening.

I packed my gloves, thermal underwear, and the lunch provided by the Chalet staff. The hike to Sperry Glacier from the Chalet is four miles with a 2000-foot-elevation climb. It was very cold with an overcast sky. The wind was biting, whipping through my sweater and pants as if they were thin gauze. The first part of the trail crossed several streams with two waterfalls bridged with rough-hewn boards. The flowers were in full bloom. I passed a woman coming down the trail who said the trail was too steep for her. She said she was getting vertigo and had turned back.

The marmots were whistling an alarm as I passed, but they kept out of sight. At about the mile-and-a-half mark I decided to visit the "Marmot Changing Room" and put on my thermal underwear. I also tied my hat under my chin. Both were good moves.

With my head down against the wind I noticed fresh bear scat in the middle of the trail. Alone in grizzly country, I felt for the can of bear spray attached to my belt. It was still there but my best protection was to stay alert and make noise. I didn't want to startle a bear or be surprised by one.

As the trail climbed to the Headwall, the wind increased and the temperature plunged further. I put on my gloves. In 1962, we rode all the way to the Headwall. The trail has become so narrow that it would be dangerous to ride to the Headwall today. Below the Headwall there are two lakes, Akalyan and Feather Woman, fed with glacier runoff. The lakes looked little changed from my last visit.

The Headwall is climbed by narrow stairs cut into the granite. At its top, the trail to the glacier goes over several snow packs and is marked by cairns. I met up with a couple and followed them across the snow pack to the final cairn that marks the main Sperry Glacier. It has a plaque. I photographed the glacier and ate my lunch in the cover of some rocks out of the wind.

Sperry Glacier is noticeably smaller than when my father and I walked on it, but it seemed familiar even though I had only been here for a short time a half century earlier. I scrambled over rubble rocks, snow and ice to a good vantage point where I took a photograph looking towards Gunsight Mountain. Eerily, when I later compared my photograph with one my father took in 1962, they were taken from virtually the same location. There was no trail on the glacier but I had ended at the identical spot. It was another sign that my journey to find my youth and perhaps to repair the connection with my father that had been lost over the years was on the right path. I had been to this same place before; I could sense the arc of time was accelerating to close a circle where my age and youth connect.

I started back after lunch. When I re-crossed the snow field, I thought of my father's mishap where he had sunk into the snow to his knees. As I was filming him in this predicament, a crevasse opened, swallowing him to his waist as he braced his fall with outflung arms. I pulled him out and we laughed about it, but as I gingerly made my way across the snow I realized that a misstep here could send me sliding down the steep slope into either an icy glacial lake, an unforgiving rock pile, or, as with my father, a fall into a crevasse of unknown depth. I moved carefully, following the footprints I had made in my earlier crossing.

At the Headwall, the wind was howling up the narrow stairs like a furnace chimney. I felt I could lean into the blast and the

Akalyan Lake, 1962

Akalyan Lake, 2012

force would keep me from falling off the Headwall ledge. Instead, I cautiously made my way down the rock-hewn stairs with the wind inflating my jacket into a parachute that tugged me backwards as I made my descent.

Sperry Glacier in 1962

Sperry Glacier in 2012

From the base of the Headwall, I hiked down slowly, taking time to wait for the sun to come out from behind clouds so I could get good light for photographs. Two mountain goats approached me on the trail. We were at a standoff, but they moved

**View of
Sperry Glacier,
1962**

**View of
Sperry Glacier,
2012**

off the trail and passed to one side. They were within 10 feet of me when they passed.

I also played hopscotch on the trail with an ewe and her lamb. Whenever I would get between them, the ewe would stare at me. I went off the trail to urinate behind some boulders. The ewe and lamb quickly were at the spot, treating it as a salt lick.

Impasse on the trail - 2012

The bottom part of the trail was a blaze of flowers with water flowing from every pore in the rocks. It was a spectacular sight.

Back at the Chalet Jane and I took a rest and then organized our things. I sat on the rock, looking at Lake McDonald and writing in my journal while waiting for dinner. At dinner we were served by Renee, an attractive young woman with a gorgeous smile. Renee had worked at the Chalet the previously year helping with the repairs after the avalanche. She had carried a 100-pound propane tank the 6 miles up the trail to the Chalet before the trail was open for pack animals. The rest of the staff was equally engaging. During their daytime off-hours, they spent their time hiking the trails around the chalet, taking full advantage of the unparalleled setting where they worked.

Sperry Glacier Trail

After dinner, we talked with other guests on the rock ledge while watching the spectacular sunset, before going to bed.

——— DAY 28 ———

Thursday •August 30, 2012

We slept a little late, arriving for breakfast at 8:00 am. I had eggs and ham again. They were a delicious change to my standard fare of cereal. The morning was crisp but cloudless with no wind. It was a contrast to the blustery conditions of yesterday. Our friends, who had delayed their hike to Sperry Glacier in hope of better weather, had been rewarded. I wished them well as they started off for the glacier.

Jane and I packed the belongings in the dormitory then left our gear in the dining room. As I was leaving the building, I noticed a park ranger with a rifle slung over his shoulder. He was in a conversation with a hiker. I overhead the ranger tell him that two juvenile grizzlies had been entering the Sperry campground, a short distance from the Chalet, and were staying on the trail even when confronted by hikers. They had become pests, and he was going to look for them. Seeing the rifle, my thought was that those grizzlies were toast. It is unfortunate, but I guess that wildlife is the collateral damage when civilization intrudes on a wilderness setting.

The weather was so beautiful that I convinced Jane to hike to Lincoln Pass to get a feel for the area. We were only a short way on the Gunsight Pass Trail when we ran into a mountain goat ewe and her lamb. The lamb was feeding on something and would not move. Eventually they sauntered down the trail in front of us. We saw them again at the pond next to the Sperry campground. We also heard marmots whistling our passage. One was sunning itself on a rock beside the trail. There were also pika in abundance.

The views of Lake McDonald from the trail were spectacular. We took a slow walk up to the pass, then stayed there for about a half hour watching the pika, soaking in the view. The hike back down to the Chalet was an easy downhill grade. At the Chalet we ate our sack lunches on the bench in front of the dining building, enjoying the warmth of the sun on our faces as we watched the staff off-load supplies from the pack mules that arrived from Lake McDonald. Everything at the Chalet has to be packed in on animals, including the propane for cooking and running the generator that provides lights in the dining room.

As we were finishing our sandwiches, the park ranger with the rifle appeared from the direction of Lincoln Pass. The resident Sperry ranger asked him if he had any success. The ranger said he had found the two juveniles at the switchback on the trail at Lake Ellen Wilson. He explained that when he yelled at them they moved off the trail but only to the side. I immediately assumed the delinquent grizzlies had been dispatched. Pointing his arm as though aiming at an imaginary target he explained that he shot one bear with a rubber bullet, then fired off several cracker shots that sent both bears running up the hill. He thought they would stay there for a while out of trouble. Curious about the ranger's responsibilities, I asked him about his role. He said, "I haze the bears to make them associate pain with using the trails. These particular grizzlies are losing their fear of people. That's not good for them or the hikers that use these trails. Grizzlies and people don't mix. Part of my job is to keep them separated."

After we talked, the ranger posted a "Bear Warning" sign at Sperry Chalet for the area between Lake Ellen Wilson and Lincoln Pass, the same trail section I hiked the first day we arrived at Sperry. He said another ranger would make a patrol in the next couple of days to see if the bears were still in the vicinity of the trail. The bear warning would stay in effect until there were two consecutive patrols without a bear sighting. I was glad to hear that these grizzlies were being "re-educated" instead of summarily dispatched. The long rifle was not as lethal as it looked.

The horses arrived around noon with Lisa, our wrangler from the previous ride, at the head of the string. Jane was still concerned about being able to get on her horse. She was also concerned about the ride down with some of the severe drop-offs along the trail. The previous day an eighty-year-old woman had been bucked off her horse. The woman was not seriously injured, but she was not in any shape to ride or walk down the mountain. Jane wanted desperately to hike down instead of ride, but we did not have packs to carry our gear. She was going to have to dance with the one who brought her.

After Lisa had her lunch, we were ready to start down on our horses. Lisa had brought Jane a new horse, Tuff, with a feedbag that would prevent him from eating on the trail. Tuff looked like he was only hours from the glue factory. Jane had a bit of difficulty getting on the horse, but Lisa gave her a big shove with Jane flying up and almost over the other side before wrapping her arms around Tuff's neck and holding on tightly. Jane finally settled in the saddle looking as if she had ridden all her life. My horse was Henry. He was not as frisky as Suede, but he was a fine horse.

The ride down was much quicker than the ride up, but the trail was very dusty. For most of the ride the horses kicked up clouds of fine dust that swirled up their legs and withers, hanging suspended at saddle level, coating our jeans but leaving the air we breathed relatively clean. Tuff had a hitch in his gait, seeming to trip and stumble as he made his way downhill. There is a section of the trail where there is a steep drop-off on one side with a vertical cliff on the inboard side. Horses have worn a rut in the trail leaving a narrow semi-flat ridge on the drop-off side. All of the horses except Tuff walked downhill following the rutted path. For some reason Tuff insisted on following the narrow ridge next to the drop-off. Riding behind them, they formed quite a sight, Tuff stumbling along the precipice with Jane leaning as far to her right as she could extend. I was amazed that she was that flexible to be able to bend almost 90 degrees sideways at the waist. She looked like an outrigger beam on an ocean canoe. She later told me that she kept her eyes closed and prayed on the narrow parts of the trail. I don't blame her, but she made it down without incident.

At the corral we thanked Lisa, then carried our gear back to the RV in the Lake McDonald Lodge parking lot where we had left it two days earlier. We settled into the captains' seats, far more comfortable than the hard saddles we had been on for the last several hours, then drove to Apgar Campground to find a campsite for the night. Our previous site had been taken so we chose A11. We checked in for the site, then drove to West Glacier.

At first Jane did not want to go to anyplace nice for dinner because we were so grubby from the horseback rides, and two nights at Sperry with only cold water at an outside sink to wash up. However, the Belton Chalet, which had been recommended to us as a terrific place to dine, had outside tables. Belton Chalet was opened for business in 1910, the first of the Great Northern Railway's Glacier facilities that also included Sperry Chalet. We took a table on the deck and enjoyed a wonderful meal. I had Montana meatloaf made with bison meat. Jane had ravioli and shrimp. Both entrees were excellent.

We drove back to the campground and put away our gear from the Sperry trip. I wrote in my journal, then we listened to Mitt Romney's convention speech on the satellite radio in the RV. Normally I am a close follower of politics, but being "off the grid" while in the national parks has been a welcome respite from the presidential campaign. Finding the parks essentially unchanged after fifty years gave me hope that whatever the result of the 2012 election, our foundation will survive. I trust that I will not encounter changes on the remainder of this journey that undermine my expectation.

TWELVE

It May Not Be Global Warming, But the Glaciers Are Melting

Mount Rainier National Park

We started the hike in relatively clear weather, with broken clouds but good visibility. At the first snowfield, the trail became a faint indentation flattened by the boots of previous hikers, barely visible in the slanted light of the afternoon sun but marked with rock cairns at sight line intervals. As we struggled to follow the trail up the steep slope, a cold white fog rolled across the mountain obscuring the path, and limiting our vision short of the next marker. The temperature dropped precipitously with the chill penetrating my thick black Navy surplus pea coat and wool gloves. The whiteout was total, eliminating all reference points except the slope of the mountain. We could continue blindly upslope or retreat downhill, hopefully in the direction where we had started. Light was fading, and we were not equipped for a night on the mountain. Foolishly perhaps, we continued upwards, squinting with eyes straining to see any dark shadow on the white snow that might be a distant cairn.

Blindly, we stumbled upwards in the gathering dusk, intermittently shouting thankfully, "There's one to the left," or "Straight ahead, keep going, we're on the trail." Finally, out of the fog it appeared before us, a dark opening in the snow. We could hear it before we could see it, the water rushing down from the glacier over the smooth rocks, a musical sound muffled by the fog.

Paradise Ice Cave was world famous, one of the most popular destinations in Mount Rainier National Park, carved from the snowmelt of Paradise Glacier, at its peak a cave labyrinth over eight miles in length. That day in early August 1962 when my father, mother, and I stood in the cave, marveling at its beauty, wondering what it would look like with full sunlight shining through the blue ice of the thick cave walls, Paradise Ice Cave looked as immortal as Mount Rainier. By the early 1990s it was gone; the only remnant left was the rushing water that created it. Paradise Glacier remains but has withdrawn higher up the slope. Each year it is smaller than the previous.

In 1962, there was no talk of global warming. In fact, we were at the beginning of a period when concern about the coming of a new ice age was first generating interest. In the early '70s, there was significant press about the imminent danger of global cooling. There was some suggestion that a solution might be to melt the arctic ice cap by covering it with soot. In time, the fear of freezing to death was overtaken by hysteria over global warming, supposedly caused by man's use of fossil fuel and the greenhouse effect.

As temperature patterns seem to vary as to whether we are warming or cooling, the activist mantra has changed from "global warming" to "climate change." The debate still rages as to whether "change" is man-caused, and thus can we humans affect its course? Or it is an immutable force of nature, a natural climatic cycle, or perhaps due to increased sun spot activity? I lean towards the latter. We can, and should, be good stewards of our environment, but it is foolish narcissism to believe we can significantly change our climate on a global level.

But whether one believes that climate change is man-caused or not, there is no denying that the glaciers are dying, and I lament their passing. At Glacier National Park there were 150 glaciers in 1850; today there are 25, and at the current rate of decline they will all be gone by 2020. I shall pay my respects to the late Paradise Ice Cave. I hope I have not seen Sperry Glacier for the last time.

Map of
Mt. Rainier National Park

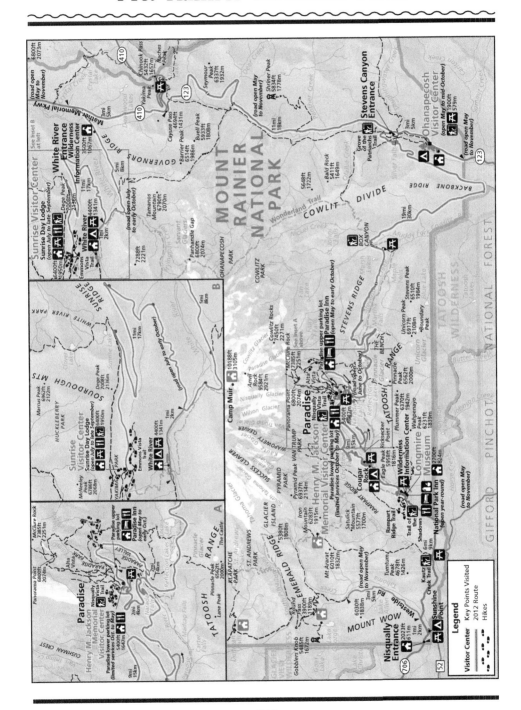

Wednesday • August 8, 1962

We got up early and drove through some of the orchards. We had breakfast and got some fruit. Just across the Columbia River was a small museum called the Gibbs Petrified Forest. In it was a really good collection of wood. After seeing the museum we drove on through the Snoqualmie National Forest. After crossing White Pass we entered Mt. Rainier National Park.

At Ohanapecosh we drove to the campground and the museum. There we ate lunch and got some books on the park. We decided to camp there that night. We quickly set up a basic camp then drove towards Paradise. At the canyon we photographed the scenery but Mt. Rainier was obscured by clouds.

At Paradise we got our camera equipment ready and started up the 2.5 mile trail to the Paradise Ice Caves. It was a gradual climb up the ridge then over the top and along another ridge... we got beautiful views of snowcapped mountains. Slowly the fog rolled in making a weird effect on the hike. Two miles up we encountered the first snow field we had to cross of any size. The snow was completely covering the ridge and blended into the Paradise Glacier.

The thick fog made it impossible to see more than 50 feet in front of you so the cairns marking the trail were hidden from view. We finally made it to the Ice Caves and the fog lifted enough to photograph them but not in the blue color of sunlight through the ice. The hike back was much shorter and easier as most of it was downhill. At the Paradise Lodge we bought some souvenirs then we went back to camp and fixed supper then went to bed.

Thursday • August 9, 1962

We got up early and ate breakfast. The sky was beautiful so we decided to drive to Sunrise Point and photograph the mountain. We went to the visitor center then took the Emmons Glacier Vista Nature Trail. It was a real short walk but very enjoyable. We started back on the loop road and stopped at several overlooks for pictures. At Paradise we saw four black bears in the valley. We ate lunch. At Narada Falls we walked to the bottom and got a beautiful view. At Nisqually Glacier Bridge we hiked two miles up to the glacier over boulders and ice. The ice was crevassed extensively and the ground kept caving in. We hurried back down and left. At Longmire we took the Trail of the Shadows Nature Trail. It was beautiful walk through a gigantic Douglas fir forest. We saw the museum there then drove back to camp. There we ate supper and went to bed.

Friday • August 10, 1962

We got up early, ate breakfast and broke camp. We made a couple of stops for pictures then drove on to Seattle. There we searched for a motel and finally found a vacancy at the Hotel Cambridge. There we got showers and changed clothes then gathered up some camera gear and headed for the monorail terminal. On the way we got film and a few accessories at a camera store. We also tried to have Dad's Minolta fixed. At the monorail we got tickets and rode to the Fair. At the Fair we got a snack to eat then went to the US Science Pavilion. It was very crowded and you couldn't see much. After that we got on a tour and went to the foreign exhibits. The Denmark and Indian exhibits were especially good. At the domestic exhibits we saw the Railroad of the Future and the GE Modern House. Those exhibits were excellent and ingenious. We ate supper at a seafood bar then I went on the rides. They were a lot of fun and some had been imported from Europe for the Fair. At 12:30 everything closed and I caught the last monorail and walked the five blocks to the hotel.

—— **DAY 29** ——

Friday • August 31, 2012

The night was cold but we had a good sleep in the RV. We had our morning drill down to a practiced routine. While still half asleep, I reached up to turn on the electric heater, located on the side wall above the window. I could reach it without getting completely out of the Havasack. When the heater had cut the chill on the floor, I would jump out of bed, turn on the hot water heater and pump then pop back into the warm sack for a few more minutes. The water heater was efficient, and within a few minutes I could take a hot shower. I cleaned the bathroom, dressed, lit the stove to boil water for coffee, and then it was Jane's turn to get up. We would glide past each other, she to the front to dress, me to the rear to convert our bed back to a sofa and table for breakfast. There was not much room but we managed to make the morning transition efficiently, without knocking each other over, setting the RV on fire, or spilling any coffee. Practice had made us good if not perfect.

In West Glacier, we stopped at the Historical Society to buy a copy of *View with a Room,* a book about the lodges and chalets of Glacier National Park. They were out of stock in West Glacier but had a copy at their St. Mary store, so we purchased a book and had it mailed home.

The ride from West Glacier to Kalispell was through thick forest. The wilderness setting was broken by Glacier Park Airport, a huge complex of long concrete runways with taxiways lined with sleek corporate jets and large commercial airliners. Modernity had been dropped into the midst of the forest primeval.

We drove along the west edge of Flathead Lake, huge, circled by dense forest interspersed with small log cottages. In the Flathead Indian Reservation on Montana Highway 28, a truck stopped abruptly in front of us as a bear leisurely crossed the road, then disappeared into the woods. After we turned on to Montana Highway 200 the road ran parallel to Clark Fork, a wide river that looks like it would be teeming with trout. There were a number of fishermen in dories floating downstream.

At St. Regis we picked up Interstate 90 and sped into the Idaho panhandle. We passed through Coeur d' Alene, taking a quick view south down the lake and then we were in Washington State. That section of Idaho is so narrow it seemed as if we could have held our breath across the state, like a bored kid in a long tunnel. Our destination for the night was the Residence Inn in East Spokane, located just off the Interstate. Although we were early, the room was ready when we arrived. We were back in the Pacific Time Zone and gained an hour. As usual when we stopped at a hotel watering hole, we plugged in all our electronics and washed a load of laundry.

We were planning to meet Peter Tooker, a fraternity brother of mine from Washington & Lee, and his wife, Sandy, when we visited Olympic National Park. After college Peter had worked as a river guide on the Green and Colorado Rivers, a mine safety inspector in Utah, and at The American Mining Congress in DC, before moving to Washington State. I hadn't seen Peter for a number of years. So the trip was a great opportunity to reconnect with an old friend. When we were settled in the hotel room, I called Peter to let him know we were on schedule and looking forward to seeing him and Sandy at Kalaloch on the Olympic seashore.

We asked the desk clerk for a recommendation as to where to eat. She suggested Twiggs, a local bistro, and gave us a 20% discount coupon. The recommendation was right on the mark. I had salmon and Jane had a salad. Both were terrific. We went back to the hotel, checked our email then went to bed. I looked forward to seeing Mount Rainier tomorrow. The weather on the mountain is notoriously fickle. In 1962, we had been blessed with clear skies that afforded great views of the magnificent peak. I hoped that we would be fortunate tomorrow with another unobstructed view of the mountain.

——— DAY 30 ———

Saturday • September 1, 2012

We ate breakfast at the Residence Inn and Jane checked our emails. We thought it might be the last chance we would have for several days. Interstate 90 wove through wide open areas. Grant County pronounced itself, "The Potato Growing Capital of the US." Outside of Moses Lake, we caught a glimpse of a snow-capped mountain that I first thought might be Mt. Rainier but more likely was Mt. Adams, another dormant volcano in the Ring of Fire located south of Rainier.

On the west side of the Columbia River, we pulled off the Interstate to stop at the Ginkgo Petrified Forest State Park. I asked the ranger about the Gibbs Petrified Forest Museum that I had visited in 1962. She was not familiar with it but said that the current museum had been part of the state park since the 1940's. The museum building had been built before 1962, so it must have been the one I previously visited. Over the past fifty years there has been an unexplained name change.

We viewed the exhibits and watched the movie. It was interesting that this area has more different types of petrified wood than any other petrified forest in the world.

We ate lunch and drove on toward Mt. Rainier. On the drive we listened to the Syracuse – Northwestern football game, won by Northwestern in the final minutes. We then listened to the Miami – Boston College game, which was won handily by Miami. Satellite radio is a blessing for the long distance traveler. The variety of programming and the convenience of not losing the station signal when you travel out of range is an enormous convenience. I can remember listening to the static of an AM station fade in and out on the fringes of its range while turning the tuning knob in an endless circle, a futile effort to find another station carrying the same program. Sirius/XM is a great service.

We stopped in Naches, Washington, at a small food mart for groceries. The meat looked awful, a greenish-gray color, so we only bought a pack of bratwurst. We drove around Naches in search of a larger, brand-name grocery but could not find one. For the size of the town it seemed as if there should be another food store. If one was there, it was well hidden as we crisscrossed the main highway and side streets of Naches in our search without success.

US Highway 12 from Naches to White Pass parallels the Tieton River with white water propelling scores of thrill-seeking rafters along its entire length. At one break in the trees where we could see a stretch of the river, we counted six rafts, each with six paddlers. Today was the first day the floodgates were opened on Rimrock Lake, a large body of water formed by a dam on the Tieton, running east-west along US 12. Earlier in the year, the Tieton has too little flow for rafting. With water gushing from the lake, the Tieton provides 19 miles of Class III rapids with a 600-foot drop in elevation. It is the fastest river in the state. We were fortunate to see it in full flow. A day earlier and the river would have been a ghost stream with little water and no people.

Further down the highway, we saw the vehicles in front of us slow, then turn into an overlook. The sign read "Rainier Overlook." We followed the lead car, fortunate to find a space for the RV. In the distance, Mount Rainier rose above the trees, looking like the alien spaceship from *Close Encounters of the Third Kind,* stark white against the blue sky, poised for launch on a dark green base, a thin layer of clouds hanging below the nosecone. I remember being awed by this view the first time I was here. The mountain has lost none of its majesty over the years.

Past the overlook, we turned on to Washington State 123 then drove into Mount Rainier National Park. Ohanapecosh Campground is just inside the Park. At the entrance to the campground was a sign that it was full, but we had a reservation. Our campsite was F005, a heavily wooded site with large 100-foot tall trees. The configuration of the site was unusual in that the campfire and picnic table were separated from the parking site for the RV. In fact they were closer to the next campsite than they were to our RV but, overall, the site was satisfactory. We put out our chairs then went to the Ohanapecosh Visitor Center where we obtained information on the park. Paradise is 21 miles away, too far to try to hike to Paradise Glacier today. Labor Day weekend will bring crowds to the park so we will need an early start to ensure parking at Paradise.

Back at the campsite I quickly made a fire. Bratwursts were soon sizzling on the grill with baked beans bubbling beside them in an opened can. It was an easy but satisfying camp dinner. After wards we walked around the campground loops. There were several spectacular sites backing on the Ohanapecosh River that

Mount Rainer from Rainier Overlook - 2012

were marked "reserved" starting yesterday but as yet were not occupied. We briefly entertained the thought of moving to one of these preferable campsites but thought that the people who reserved them may eventually arrive. We reluctantly returned to our own nondescript site.

—— **DAY 31** ——

Sunday • September 2, 2012

The early morning light filtered through the tall trees like thin white fingers reaching to touch the soft dark earth. I opened the windows a crack to feel the brace of a chill then turned on the heater to warm the RV before venturing out from the warm comfort of the bed. I looked at the park map and our itinerary. As we had deferred the hike to Paradise Glacier yesterday, we needed to make some schedule adjustments. Today, we were supposed to go to Sunrise in the morning but from the map it looked to be on our route to Seattle tomorrow. We decided to spend the day at Paradise and Longmire and visit Sunrise as we departed the park. To make all of our objectives we had to be flexible.

We were on the road to Paradise by 7:55 a.m. At the first overlook we stopped to photograph Mt. Rainier. There were a few clouds on the mountain but the sky was a brilliant blue with the glaciers standing out as if they were magnified.

Further up the road we stopped at Reflection Lake. It was dead still with no wind. The reflection of Mt. Rainier in the lake was perfect. There were several serious photographers at the site lamenting that the conditions were perfect except for a single jet contrail that wafted across the mountain like a smeared chalk line. One optimistically commented that he could Photoshop the contrail to digitally remove the imperfection.

Digital photography with its ability to manipulate the image to correct a flaw of nature, or a fault of the photographer, was something my father and I never imagined in 1962. He was an artist who embraced technology, experimenting with fisheye lenses, infra-red film, and the latest film formats. With his black and white photographs, he had some latitude in the darkroom to compensate for exposure, lightening or darkening areas of a photograph print by using his hand to shade the projector light from the photographic paper. He could also crop the image to eliminate clutter or emphasize the subject. But back then, the view through the lens was essentially the limit of the ultimate photograph. A great photographer had to be successful at the point of attack, the scene in the field. Digital photography moves the skill point from the lens to the computer. When I look at an outdoor photograph today, I frequently ask myself, how much of it is real? At some point trying to improve upon nature is a form of narcissism. To be honest, I much prefer my father's simple black and white Ansel Adams-like landscapes to my own saturated color, digitally mastered photographs, although I still connect to place and time through both.

When we arrived at Paradise we drove to the lower lot. Our angst had been for naught as there were plenty of open spaces. We parked then walked to the Henry M. Jackson Memorial Visitor Center, but it was 9:30 a.m. and it did not open until 10. I had planned to take the shuttle to Longmire and start the day at Trail of the Shadows, but Jane decided she wanted to try the hike to

Reflection Lake - 2012

Paradise Glacier. We got our gear and started up the trail. It was steep from the start. Jane quickly decided that she had made a bad decision. I suggested she hike with me to Myrtle Falls, about a half mile away, then return and I would double-time up the trail to the Paradise Glacier. She agreed.

After Myrtle Falls Jane went back to the RV and I picked up the pace. The route initially followed the Skyline trail. It ran uphill through meadows of wildflowers. The views of Mt. Rainier were stunning. I passed three people packing skis who were hiking up to a point where they could ski down.

At about 1.5 miles a branch off the Skyline Trail leads to Paradise Glacier. At first the trail was rocky, then it was marked by cairns just as I remembered from 1962 except then the cairns were on snow. At 2.5 miles the trail continued on to a snowfield. I could hear water running down from the glacier. I stopped to get my bearings. Nothing looked familiar. The roar of the rushing water, however, was the same sound I remember when standing in the Paradise Ice Cave. The cave is gone, but I believe I was near the spot where it had been located. There is nothing left but the rushing water and my vivid memory of the blue ice dome fifty years ago, seeming as immortal as myself at fifteen, a sobering thought.

I continued on the snowpack until I got a good view of Paradise Glacier, then I headed back down at a fast clip. I averaged about three miles per hour and the total hike was 6.1 miles. As I neared the end, I could see that cars were now parked on the side of the road around the curve from Paradise. It was a busy Labor Day weekend.

I walked back to the RV and saw that the parking lots were now full. It was 12:10 p.m. We ate lunch and then went to the main lot to catch the shuttle for Longmire. The park has five shuttle buses but three were out of service, so on a crowded Labor Day Sunday, one of the busiest days of the year for the park, there were only two shuttle buses operating. Jane and I got on the first shuttle we could, and it wove through the lower loop parking and on to Longmire. By the time we got to Longmire, it was obvious that there were long waits for a return shuttle and more people waiting than could be accommodated on each bus. We decided to stay on the shuttle and return to Paradise.

At Paradise, we took the mile-long Nisqually Vista Loop Trail that originated at the lower parking lot. I remember the Nisqually

Paradise Ice Cave, 1962

Former site of Ice Cave, 2012

Glacier well from the 1962 trip. As we were walking on the trail, we heard a loud crack that sounded like thunder. There was not a cloud in the sky. It had to be ice breaking in the glacier. It reminded me that my dad and I had hiked out on the glacier without knowing it. The foot of the glacier was brown, the ice covered with soil and rock. We thought we were on solid ground until we heard the sound of rocks falling beneath us, echoing in the melting chambers, with ice cracking like gunshots under our feet. We got our photographs of Nisqually and then gingerly made our way off the glacier. On this day, I was taking a long view of Nisqually. I had no desire to repeat my adventure on the glacier.

We then drove the RV to Longmire where we found a parking spot without a problem. We walked the three-quarter-mile Trail of the Shadows. The trail circled a meadow that bubbled with carbon dioxide. There was also a hot spring that Longmire had turned into a resort in the late 1800s. After the walk we ate dinner at the National Park Inn in Longmire. Once again the food in the parks was remarkably good. We both had trout.

After dinner we drove back to the campground, stopping first at Narada Falls where we walked to the view point. We got back to camp just at dusk, a full day. But we accomplished everything on the itinerary.

─────── **DAY 32** ───────

Monday • September 3, 2012

We got up early to make sure we got a parking space at Sunrise. We ate breakfast and dumped the tanks on the way out of the campground. It was a gorgeous day. The moon was still visible in the morning sky.

We got to Sunrise at 9:00 a.m. then took the trail to the Emmons Glacier Vista. It was a short hike with a great view. I took a photograph from the same location as in 1962.

We continued on the trail for a short while through a flower-strewn meadow. After the hike, we gulped a cup of hot chocolate at the snack shop and bought some gifts. By the time we finished, the visitor center was open and we took a tour. Jane asked some questions about flowers, and the ranger gave us a flower guide.

Emmons Glacier Vista – 1962

Emmons Glacier Vista - 2012

I then took the 1.5 mile Sunrise Nature Trail that winds up the hill and loops along the ridge above the parking area. The trail offers some great views to the west and also crosses meadows of flowers. The day was crystal clear with people looking for climbers on Mt. Rainier through binoculars. I took out my binoculars and caught a glimpse of two climbers coming down from the summit.

We then drove out of the park and on to Seattle. The GPS took us through the middle of downtown Seattle where we promptly lost the signal among the tall buildings. I didn't have a map open. We were relying exclusively on the GPS for directions to our hotel. Eventually we found an open area near the waterfront where we reacquired the elusive GPS signal.

After a circuitous blind ride through the maze of Seattle, we finally found the Lake Union Residence Inn. From the entrance, I could see the Space Needle, a reminder of the 1962 World's Fair. Our RV was too tall for the hotel garage. I checked with the desk, and they let me park it in the delivery van space. We checked in early and as usual powered up our electronics, checked our email, and took the opportunity to do a load of laundry.

We had planned to have dinner at the restaurant on top of the Space Needle, but we didn't have the energy to tackle the logistics of getting there. Instead, we walked a few blocks to the docks on Lake Union where we had dinner at Duke's, a seafood restaurant. The crab cakes were delicious. After dinner we went back to the hotel and went to bed early. We were ready to get out of the city and back to the woods.

THIRTEEN

A Peninsula Apart

Olympic National Park

The Olympic Peninsula is bounded on the west by the Pacific Ocean, the north by the Strait of Juan de Fuca, and the east by the Hood Canal that separates the peninsula from neighboring Bainbridge Island. Although only a short distance from Seattle as the crow flies, the peninsula is a trek. The shortest and most scenic option is a ferry from one of several terminals on the east side of Puget Sound to Bainbridge Island and from there to Washington State 101 Bridge at Port Gamble across to the peninsula.

For those who want to avoid the water, or the toll, the route is Interstate 5 south to Tacoma then Washington State 3 north to Bremerton on Bainbridge Island, then further north to Port Gamble. Alternatively, one could continue south from Tacoma to Olympia, the state capital of Washington, then north on US 101, avoiding Bainbridge Island altogether. These land routes circumnavigate Puget Sound but add considerable time to an otherwise short trip due west by water. By any route, it is apparent to a traveler that the peninsula is isolated.

Virtually the entire north portion of the Olympic Peninsula is occupied by the Olympic National Park and the adjacent Olympic National Forest and Bart Cole State Forest. There is narrow band of private land along the northeast and north shores with a small wedge between the Olympic Seashore and the National and State Forest lands; the remainder of the peninsula is public land.

In 1988, Congress designated 95 percent of Olympic National Park as "Wilderness," the highest level of protection that can be afforded to public lands, ensuring that it will be maintained in its current pristine, undeveloped state, prohibiting motorized transportation or equipment. Only four percent of the public lands in the United States have been designated as Wilderness Areas.

Apart from being untouched wilderness, Olympic is perhaps the most diverse biosphere of any national park. It encompasses mountains, topped by Mount Olympus at 7,980 feet, a variety of subalpine and lowland forests that merge into the Hoh Rain Forest with more than 240 inches of precipitation a year, and a coastal swath on the Pacific Ocean; glacier peak to ocean water with all the variety of flora and fauna that such an isolated and diverse environment produces.

When you stand on Hurricane Ridge looking over the unbroken expanse of wilderness towards Mount Olympus, it is easy to believe that Sasquatch is alive and well, living undisturbed in the Olmpic interior, a short ferry ride and drive from Seattle, yet a world apart.

Map of
Olympic National Park

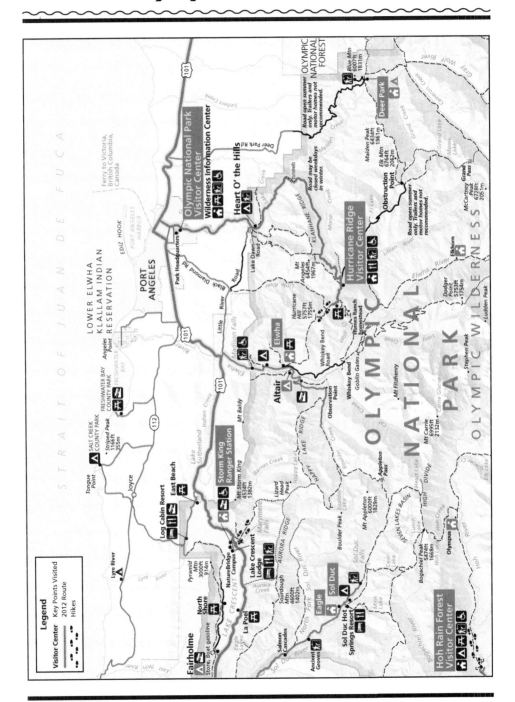

Saturday • August 11, 1962.

We got up and left the hotel after packing. The ferry from Edmunds to Kingston was a half hour trip across Puget Sound. On the ferry, we had a snack and we ate a big lunch of crab outside Port Angeles. We drove to the visitor center and looked around then went on to the Olympic Hot Springs road. Elwha Campground was not very nice so we camped at Altair on the banks of the Elwha River. We set up camp and looked around then I went fishing. I didn't catch anything.

We ate supper then went to the naturalist program. It was the Walt Disney film, "The Olympic Elk." The film was very good and after it was over we talked to the naturalist about the wildlife. We then went back to camp, built a fire then went to bed.

Sunday • August 12, 1962

We had breakfast then went into Port Angeles. We stopped at a Chevron dealer and had the car overhauled. We spent 4 hours in town looking around and waiting for the car to get finished. We had lunch at a small café then picked up the car.

There was time to drive to Hurricane so we started up. It was very foggy and we didn't see much at all. At Hurricane Ridge we saw deer and we went into a really good gift shop and bought a few bird carvings. We also had a bite to eat.

We drove back down to Altair and I went fishing again. I didn't catch anything. Back at camp we ate supper and had a campfire then went to bed.

Monday • August 13, 1962

In the morning we left for Hurricane Ridge. There we stopped at the visitor center and shot a few scenics then drove on to the end of the road. There we took the one mile hike up Hurricane Hill. On the trail we found many beetles – mostly long horned, with a few green tiger beetles. Up on the rocks, the Olympic marmots were abundant and we got terrific pictures of them. A deer crossed the meadow below us as Dad photographed a sooty grouse. Up on the hill was the Hurricane Self Guiding Nature Trail. It was .3 miles in length and was very fine. A wonderful panorama of the Strait of Juan de Fuca spread out before us. The hike down was leisurely and we exchanged one carving at the gift shop for a totem pole.

We drove back to Altair and then up Olympic Hot Springs. There I went swimming in the pool. At camp we ate supper then went to bed.

Tuesday • August 14, 1962

We broke camp, packed and headed towards Kalaloch. We passed Crescent Lake and hiked the Marymere Falls Nature Trail. It was a delightful 1 ½ mile trail. We got to Kalaloch about 2:00 pm and found the last vacant campsite and set up. Then we ate lunch. While Mother slept, Dad and I hiked along the beach then up to the lodge and down the Kalaloch Nature Trail. This took us through a dense forest with moss and lichen then over Kalaloch Creek. At camp we built a fire and had supper then I washed the dishes while Mom and Dad took a walk. It started raining and the chores were done so we went to bed.

Wednesday • August 15, 1962

We got up early and went clam digging. Mother got into it and we got 15 clams. We had them for breakfast then we went to Lapish. There we had a flat tire and I changed it. We ate lunch there then left.

At the Hoh Rain Forest we took the nature trail. It was raining the whole time. The sky was overcast so we went back to Kalaloch. On the way we bought a new tire and a clam shovel.

At camp we relaxed and got wood for a big fire. After supper we sat around for a while then went to bed.

Thursday • August 16, 1962

We got up early again and dug clams. This time I dug and finally got the hang of it. We got 23 and had them for breakfast. We took down the camp.

We went down the road to Queets Rain Forest and shot a few pictures there. The road was awful. We drove along the Washing-

ton coast and went across on the ferry to Astoria to Oregon. We stopped at Cobra Gardens and looked at the snakes. The Oregon coast at night was beautiful. We ate supper at Wheeler then went to bed.

———— **DAY 33** ————

Tuesday • September 4, 2012

We had a good night's sleep at the Residence Inn. The directions back to I-5 were simple, although the construction had changed the access in front of the hotel. I got a photograph of the Space Needle to mark the 50th anniversary of the World's Fair. It was a relatively short ride out of Seattle to the ferry at Edmonds, but the morning traffic was heavy.

At the ferry landing, we took the senior discount but were assessed a surcharge for the height of the RV, making our fare $52.00. Our timing was perfect. As soon as I paid the fare, we drove on to the *Spokane* without any wait.

After parking, we climbed the steel stairs to the upper outside deck where we could see Mt. Rainier in the distance beyond the skyline of Seattle with the Olympic mountain range capped with patches of snow in front of us. The breeze was cool, so we went inside the cabin where it was warm. The steel deck plates vibrated with the hum of the ferry's engines, providing a low-pitched background rumble that echoed inside the closed cabin. I got a cup of hot chocolate and Jane had a diet Pepsi as we watched the landing at Kingston draw closer. The smooth crossing of Puget Sound to Kingston took about 30 minutes. By the time we had finished our beverages we were there.

We drove on Washington 104 through some quaint towns. Port Gamble reminded Jane of the towns on outer Long Island. The houses were small but immaculately maintained. In Port Angeles, we stopped for groceries at a Safeway. We then went into the Olympic National Park Visitor Center in Port Angeles. Afterwards we drove to the Elwha Valley. The park service has removed the Elwha River dam to restore the river's original flow and return salmon to their spawning grounds. The river is turquoise, still laden with silt, the sediment from the dam reservoir not yet flushed downstream.

The road is closed just past the Altair campground, so we were unable to go the old Hot Springs site. My understanding is that the pool where I swam in 1962 served as the burial site for the remains of the complex; debris from the site was bulldozed into the pit then covered with topsoil and replanted. Apparently nothing remains of the popular resort that opened in 1909 and closed in 1966 after its lease with the park service expired.

We drove around the Altair campground and selected campsite #6, which was across the road from the Elwha River but sufficiently near that we could hear the water moving swiftly downstream. The campground was much wooded. It was more overgrown than I remembered. The river, however, looked the same. We took a rest in the afternoon with the river and wind providing soothing sounds in the background.

In the late afternoon, we walked around the campground to see if there were any vestiges of the woodpile with the huge log from 1962, where I cut firewood. I thought I saw where it probably had been located, but it was only a guess; there were no traces of the woodpile. In the past 50 years either the massive log that was the centerpiece of the pile had been hauled away or the natural decay process in the wet Olympic environment had been complete. I made a campfire, grilling salmon and asparagus. We had an early night.

—— **DAY 34** ——

Wednesday • September 5, 2012

I woke to the sound of the river gently drawing me from sleep into consciousness. Wood smoke curled upward from a stove pipe sticking out of the roof of a small trailer parked in the campsite across the road next to the river. I thought that with a fire, such a confined space must be extremely hot. The trailer was plastered with an eclectic collection of bumper stickers that offered no clue as to the political persuasion of the owner, although it seemed to be from one extreme to the other. I hoped to catch a glimpse of our neighbor before we left, but he was a recluse and never left his trailer.

We drove back through Port Angeles to the Hurricane Ridge visitor center where I obtained a trail map and asked the ranger about the Hurricane Hill Nature Trail. The ranger was a young woman who told us that there wasn't a Hurricane Hill Nature Trail. I asked about the map plaque I remembered at the top of the hill that showed Port Angeles, Ediz Hook and the Straits of San Juan de Fuca. She said that there was a short quarter-mile trail through the meadow from the visitor center to a point with a great view. I told her that I had been here 50 years earlier and had taken a mile hike up Hurricane Hill. In a condescending tone, as if I had drool running off my chin, she said the trail up Hurricane Hill was 1.6 miles and had a 700 foot elevation gain. She advised that the meadow trail would be much easier and had the same view. I wanted to say that I'd give her a 15 minute headstart and we'd see who made it to the top of Hurricane Hill first, but I kept quiet and politely thanked her for the information. I left shaking my head. Did I look like a meadow stroller? I was a mountain man and had already proven it.

Still steaming from the ranger's implied insult, I drove to the end of the Hurricane Hill Road and parked. The trail up Hurricane Ridge to Hurricane Hill was as I remembered it, starting in the trees then emerging onto the open windswept ridge with views of Mount Olympus rising beyond an unbroken carpet of dark green trees. The view was the very definition of "wilderness." The Olympic seaside sparrows flitted along the trailside. In an open area by a marmot interpretive sign, Jane spotted an Olympic marmot busily grazing by the trail. I got some great photographs. The marmot looked like a stand-in for the furry nemesis of Carl, the grounds-keeper, in *Caddyshack*.

**Olympic Marmot on
Hurricane Ridge Trail**

It was a beautiful day for the hike, clear without a breath of wind. The trail was 1.6 miles to the top. At the top were the two plaques I remembered. The first was a map of the Strait of San Juan de Fuca, and the second showed the peaks of the Olympic Range. We could also see Mt. Adams to the north. We lingered at the top for a while then hiked down in 45 minutes. We saw plenty of mountain goat tracks but no goats. Two years earlier, a hiker had been gored to death by an aggressive mountain goat near Hurricane Ridge. Wild animals can be unpredictable. We grow up in a Walt Disney culture that ascribes human-like qualities to wildlife, making them seem docile, capable of understanding our good intentions. However, they are wild, usually with horns, claws or fangs, capable of doing great bodily harm, not through malice but instinct. We must treat them with respect and maintain a reasonable distance.

On the way back to the campground we stopped at the visitor center in Port Angeles to get directions to the fudge store. We found it, and Jane bought some freshly made fudge. Back at Altair campground we turned on the generator and watched the movie of the 1962 trip. It brought back great memories. That night I made chili in the cast iron skillet, browning ground beef then adding black beans, corn and chili sauce. It was tasty.

DAY 35

Thursday • September 6, 2012

We rose and cleaned the RV. We looked for water ouzels at the bridge on the way out of the campground but we didn't see any. Crescent Lake is very large. At the west end of the lake is a ranger station with the trailhead to Marymere Falls. We took the 1-and-a-half-mile round-trip hike to the falls. The trail wove through a dense rain forest with tall trees. The slant light of early morning filtered through the forest like long yellow fingers. There were two bridges spanning a creek. The first was a steel bridge and the second was constructed of half logs. The final part of the trail was a steep loop. Marymere Falls is a tall ribbon-shaped falls. It was in shadow. We completed the hike in an hour.

At Sol Duc we turned down the road to take the trail, but the ranger at the park entrance said that all the campsites at Kalaloch were reserved. Since we didn't have a reservation, we turned around and hurried on to Kalaloch to try to get a campsite. We ate lunch on the road. At Kalaloch, we found a campsite (A-22) overlooking the beach. The sky was clear and there was a light sea breeze. We checked our cell service to call the Tookers, but we had no reception. As we sat in our chairs watching the ocean, Peter and Sandy drove up.

We talked for a while then they went to check in at the Kalaloch Lodge. Jane and I tried to walk along the beach to the lodge but the way was blocked by a broad inlet. Peter and Sandy had seen us on the beach from their cottage through binoculars and drove back to our campsite. Peter and I took the Kalaloch Nature Trail that my dad and I had hiked. It ran through a dense forest, and the sunlight was filtered through the thick branches. I didn't remember anything specific about the trail, but the mood of the place was familiar, a melancholy mixture of light and shadow, damp and dry. On the way back we saw the trail to the Kalaloch Lodge. We walked to the store and looked around. There was a mercantile section with groceries, beer and wine, snacks, firewood, and ice. An adjoining area had a wide assortment of camping gear and Olympic-related gifts. Our curiosity satisfied we left.

Back at the campsite we met up with the women. Peter and Sandy then went back to the lodge, where we joined them for dinner. I asked the desk clerk why there weren't any people clamming, and she told me that it was out of season. She said that the clam population had been depleted and some years the National Park Service closed the beaches to clamming for the entire season. The dinner was very good. We each had the shrimp and crab risotto. It was late when we got back to camp. I sent off the SPOT signal that we had arrived at our campground then went to bed.

–––––––– **DAY 36** ––––––––

Friday • September 7, 2012

We slept in, but we were ready when the Tookers arrived at 9:00 am. We had reorganized the RV so that the two rear captain's chairs could be used. Our destination was the Hoh Rain Forest. The day was bright and clear. There was not a cloud in the sky. The Hoh

Rain Forest visitor center is 12 miles from the main highway. The road is lined with a thick canopy of trees. The foliage is so thick that satellite radio reception was intermittently interrupted.

At the visitor center, we got our hiking gear and took the 1 ½ mile Spruce Trail which winds through the rain forest and along the Hoh River. It was quite different from 50 years ago, a day that was overcast with a continuous drizzle. Now the sun streamed through the trees with beams of bright light. The only sign that we were in a rain forest was the abundance of ferns and lichen.

The Hoh River was aqua blue and silver, typical of a glacial-fed river. The river bed was wide with smooth stones on the outer edges, reminding me of the famous photograph of Bigfoot. It looks like the same place the photograph was taken. I kept expecting Bigfoot to emerge from the underbrush on the far bank but the only movement was Peter Tooker. He may have been D.B. Cooper reincarnate, but he wasn't Bigfoot.

The walk along the river trail was leisurely. We then took the three-quarter-mile Hall of Mosses Trail. That trail has some slight elevation changes, rising about 100 feet. The trail weaves through the forest and around many weird-shaped trees, including nurse trees that grow out of dead and fallen trees. When we finished the hike we had lunch in the RV. On the way to the visitor center we had seen an Olympic elk with a huge antler rack, but the herd was not around.

In the afternoon we went back to main road and drove to Forks for fuel and groceries. I hadn't noticed it when we first passed through on our way to Kalaloch, but Peter said that Forks was the place where the *Twilight* vampire series had been filmed. As we drove through town, I could see that the residents were capitalizing on its claim to fame. There were signs, "Native to *Twilight*" and *"Twilight* Firewood." There were *"Twilight* Tours." Everything was *"Twilight"* related. We purchased groceries then drove back to Kalaloch.

We rested in the afternoon, then I made a campfire and grilled bratwurst and asparagus. We watched the sun set over the Pacific.

The campsite was beautiful. We showed Peter and Sandy the photographs we had taken so far on our trip. They then said good-bye and went back to the lodge. It had been good to spend some time with Peter and Sandy, even if it was short. Friendships born of the shared stress and excitement of college are enduring. They

Sunset at Kalaloch Beach – Olympic Seashore

may lie dormant for many years but when reengaged they are as strong as they were on commencement day.

The stars were out and it was a dark night. The roar of the ocean was a welcome sound in the background.

—— **DAY 37** ——

Saturday • September 8, 2012

The morning was overcast and there was a mist flowing in from the ocean. The breakers were pounding in steady waves. We packed the RV and dumped the tanks. The day was much cooler than yesterday. We drove US 101 to Oregon through a series of small fishing and logging towns. Weyerhaeuser had logged and replanted large stretches of the land along the highway. We ate lunch at a rest stop on the Washington side of the Columbia River. The river is now crossed by a bridge to Astoria instead of the ferry we took in 1962.

The Oregon coast was beautiful. At Tillamook we stopped at a cheese factory but decided not to go in. I called the Pt. Lookout Bed & Breakfast for directions. We got there around 3:00 p.m. and relaxed. We went to dinner at Roseanna's Café in Oceanside. The razor clams were delicious as was the huckleberry pie.

After dinner we got groceries at the Safeway in Tillamook, then drove back to Pt. Lookout. As I flopped in bed it dawned on me that we had made the turn south. The trip was almost over; we were headed home. I had accomplished everything I had wanted on this journey but a sadness came over me. I did not want the trip to end.

FOURTEEN

A Blue Like No Other

Crater Lake National Park

Mount Mazama was a towering 12,000 foot mountain. Native American tribes dwelled within the shadow of its forested slopes when 7,700 years ago in a massive volcanic eruption, the top half of the mountain exploded in a cloud of pumice and ash, propelled by hot gas released from the magma rising from the bowels of the mountain. The hollowed out cavity of the magma chamber collapsed under its own weight, creating a giant caldera. Over the centuries the deep basin filled with snow and rainwater and, with no incoming stream or river source carrying suspended mud and soil, formed an immense lake of pure sediment-free water.

Sagebrush sandals and other human artifacts have been found beneath the ash of Mount Mazama's eruption, establishing that Klamath Indians observed the catastrophic event. Tribal legend describes the formation of the lake as a battle of the spirits. Llao, spirit of the underworld, fell in love with a Klamath chief's daughter, but she rejected him. He swore revenge on the tribe, so they sought the help of Skell, spirit of the above-world. Llao and Skell engaged in a tremendous battle, hurling molten rocks amid thunder and lightning. Eventually, Skell drove Llao deep into the underworld below the mountain. To imprison him there Skell collapsed the mountain and filled the void with blue water.

Llao's blue prison remained unseen by white men until June 12, 1853, when John Wesley Hillman, Henry Klippel, and Isaac Skeeters, members of a group searching for the "Lost Cabin gold mine," stumbled over the rim and stood awe-struck at the sight of the bluest lake they had ever seen.

When they got back to civilization the three described the lake's incredible beauty, but they could not accurately identify its location to allow a return visit. The lake was rediscovered in 1865 by hunters. Its beauty was becoming legendary, but no one name for the lake seemed to fit its unique and special character. It was called "Blue Lake" and "Lake Majesty" before newspaper editor Jim Sutton finally named it "Crater Lake" in 1869.

Crater Lake became our sixth national park in 1902, another of President Teddy Roosevelt's wilderness legacies. At 1,943 feet it is the nation's deepest lake and one of the clearest in the world with visibility to over 100 feet. The crystal clear water absorbs all the colors of the spectrum except for the dazzling blue which is scattered and seen by those who gaze into the caldera as awe-struck as the first party of gold seekers who looked over the rim in 1853. It is a blue like no other.

Map of
Crater Lake National Park

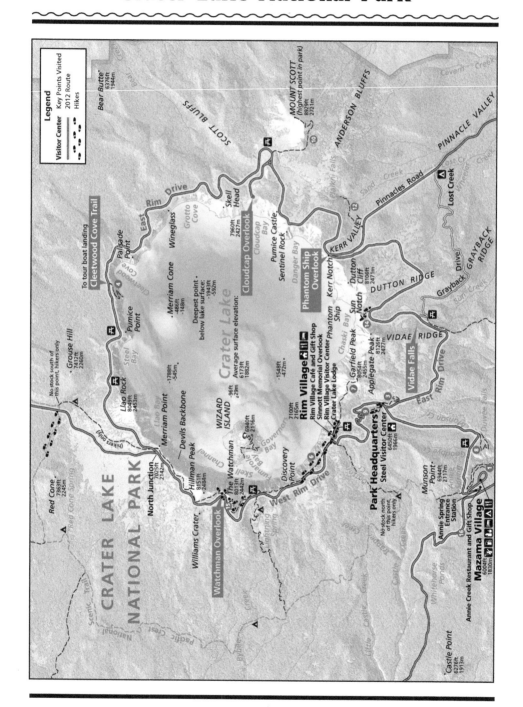

Friday • August 17, 1962

The Oregon coast was dotted with state parks, small but beautiful. We stopped at several of these parks and shot pictures.

At the sea lion caves we got our gear and went down to the overlook. Three hundred sea lions were playing on the rocks. We photographed them and then went to the Cove. The caves were dark and the photographs weren't too good but the sea lions were there.

We drove down the coast and ate lunch then turned inland towards Crater Lake. Along the way we got fruit and crossed the park boundary just at dark. First we drove to the Rim Campground. There we found a note saying Uncle Carl and Aunt Alice were at the Rim Campground. We quickly found them. The campsite was very nice and we set up almost everything there. After talking for a while we went to bed.

Saturday • August 18, 1962

All of us went up to the lake and heard the geologist talk. Afterwards we hiked to Discovery Point, then hiked to Watchman. There we got a very good view of the lake and surrounding peaks. After we climbed down we drove to Diamond Lake. We had a picnic lunch then Uncle Carl, Dad, Wayne, Carl, Jr., and I went down to the docks and rented equipment and a boat to go fishing. We rode across the lake then started fishing. Uncle Carl caught a small one quickly then little Carl quickly caught a 15 inch rainbow trout. We fished for a few more hours without catching anything. We drove back to camp and went to the campfire program. After the program we ate supper and talked then went to bed.

Sunday • August 19, 1962

We started out on the Rim Road. We stopped and got pumice at the Pumice Desert. We traveled the Rim Drive and stopped at all the overlooks. We ate lunch at a picnic table. We continued along the drive stopping to hike down to the water at the boat dock. We hiked the Castle Crest Nature Trail and the Sunset Trail to the Phantom Ship overlook. We also took a short hike to see the Lady of the Woods. At camp we rode around the loops on the top of the car. After that we had a campfire and sang. We then ate supper and went to bed.

—————— **DAY 38** ——————

Sunday • September 9, 2012

I got up at 7:30 am to call my mother. It was the first time I had cell service on Sunday in the past three weeks. I described the trip and she seemed to understand and remember. Katie and Jim, our hosts, cooked a fantastic breakfast of Florentine eggs with zucchini bread and fresh fruit. The Pt. Lookout Bed and Breakfast was a good find. We left around 9:45 and headed south on 101.

The trip down the Oregon coast was beautiful. As my 1962 journal had indicated, the coast was dotted with small state parks. At Neskowin, we could see people digging for clams on the beach. We were never far from water. The road crossed numerous bays, inlets and rivers that were lined with small boats, some moored at docks or buoys, others moving on the water headed to a fishing spot or returning home. The scene was bustling yet tranquil, an animated painting.

We stopped at the Sea Lion Cave which has been operating as a private attraction since 1934. We paid the admission of $11 each for seniors. The sea lions were not in the cave but were lounging on the rocks below the cliff. There were not as many as in 1962, but others may have been in the surf searching for food. Except for the slight reduction in the number of sea lions on the rocks, the view was unchanged from 50 years ago; the lighthouse still stands vigil on the point to the north.

In planning for the trip, I had researched the Internet for Cobra Gardens in Oregon, but the only reference I found was a posting from someone lamenting that it had passed, a remembered relic of his childhood that he and his family used to visit in the early 1960s. I wonder how much longer the Sea Lion Cave will survive. The roadside attractions of my youth, heralded by billboards for a 100 miles in both directions, like the Sea Lion Cave, have surrendered to destination theme parks comparable to Disneyland and Six Flags. Travelers are in a hurry to get from point A to point B, with no time for the diversion of a roadside attraction. I fear that someday the Sea Lion Cave, as has Cobra Gardens, will disappear, a piece of Americana lost to future generations. But for now it is still alive and well.

We then continued on to Gardiner, passing by the Oregon Dunes.

At Gardiner we turned inland along the Umpqua River. The road along the Umpqua River Valley was one of the most scenic drives on the entire trip. Outside of Roseburg there were elk viewing spots overlooking a large meadow, with two elk herds. We were tempted to stop but drove on, as we wanted to get to Crater Lake before dark.

We got to Crater Lake about 6:00 pm. The sun was setting and the colors were very warm. We saw the lake as we drove by, but it was late so we did not stop. We drove directly to Mazama Village campground and picked out a site. It was grilled steak for dinner. We wrote in our journals and had an early evening.

--------- **DAY 39** ---------

Monday • September 10, 2012

The night had been extremely cold. The temperature had been expected to reach a low of 32 degrees. It certainly felt like it. I wore my Columbia thermal top and it worked well. The water for shaving was frigid, and never reached more than a tepid temperature for my shower.

After breakfast, we headed for the Rim Road. We stopped at Discovery Point then took the 1.1 mile trail back to the Rim Village. The view from Discovery Point was great. It was the same view of Wizard Island as in 1962 photographs: the island was a cone rising out of the blue lake, circled by the high rim wall.

The Rim Trail afforded great views of the lake. There were only a couple of hikers on the trail. At the Rim Village, we had hot chocolate at the store before retracing the trail.

We finished the Discovery Point Trail, a total of 2.2 miles, then drove to the Watchman parking lot. The Watchman trail was 1.6 miles roundtrip but had an elevation gain of over 700 feet. Jane decided to pass on the hike and I went up alone. The trail marker

Wizard Island, 1962

 Wizard Island, 2012

indicated that the average time was 30 minutes up and 15 minutes down. I made the hike in 16 minutes up and 13 minutes down. Not bad for a senior.

The trail starts with a steep boulder slope to the left. My 1962 film shows Wayne and me pointing to a small sign stating, "Stay on the Trail," while Carl scampered up the boulder slope. At about the place in the trail that looked like the spot where we filmed this caper, there was a short wood post with rusted nails. The cross piece that had been attached to the post was gone but it could have been the "Stay on the Trail" sign from 50 years ago. Further up the trail, Wayne, Carl and I had pelted John with snowballs, but on this day the rocks were bare; there was no snow, not even a patch from which to make a missile for a fight.

I wished that my cousins could have shared this trip with me. On each of my family's trips west to visit national parks in 1960 and 1962, we had rendezvoused at some point with the Bryans, who had moved to California from Miami in 1956. Wayne, Carl and I were roughly the same age, while John was a few years younger. We had a great time together for those few days in 1962. I look back now at the four of us, three driven teenagers and John a preteen following the big boys. Each of us became Eagle Scouts and earned law degrees. Carl is now a retired California Superior Court Judge. Wayne is a World Team Tennis coach, tennis commentator, and father of Mike and Bob Bryan, the world's No. 1 doubles team. John is an attorney is San Diego. I think you could see the ambition and motivation in us even in the summer of 1962.

There is a fire lookout at the top of the Watchman. In my 1962 film there's a segment of Wayne looking at a bas relief map of Crater Lake with the lake in the background. I thought that we filmed the clip at the lookout on Watchman. I tried to open the door to the lookout to check for the map but it was locked. The lookout is active and only open when staffed. I peered through the window. It was dark inside but I didn't see the table with the bas relief map. I thought they may have moved it.

I set up my camera for time delay and shot several photographs of myself along the wall where we had taken family photographs with the lake in the background.

I chatted with a couple about my trip and then made a quick hike down to rejoin Jane for lunch in the Watchman parking lot. We then drove around the lake, looking for the right spot to park the RV and have a rest. We finally found a good place at the Phantom Ship Overlook. We next drove around the Rim to the Rim Village and went into the Crater Lake Lodge, which was built in the early 1900s and had been in danger of being razed but was restored in 1988. The outside of the lodge is plain. The bottom is stone with wood shingle siding. The inside, however, is very warm with an exhibit room that documents the lodge's history and its near demise. We walked to the rim and saw the plaque honoring Stephen Mather, the first superintendent of the National Park Service.

Watchman – 1962

We then drove to Discovery Point, where we took photographs of the lake in the late afternoon light. We continued to Mazama Village and Annie Creek Gift Shop, where I bought the book, *Great Lodges of the National Parks*. The weather forecast for the night was for a low of 26 degrees. We would be cold in the RV. The salesperson at the gift shop informed us that 2000 bicyclists were due to arrive in the park tomorrow from Klamath Falls. We would need to get out in front of them. We went back to camp, and I made a campfire. I grilled chicken and sautéed zucchini in the cast iron skillet. We enjoyed the warmth of the fire until the night's chill overcame the fading embers.

----------- **DAY 40** -----------

Tuesday • September 11, 2012

It was another frigid night. Jane took the Woolrich blanket in the middle of the night. The Columbia omni-heat top kept my torso warm but my legs and feet were cold. During the night I dreamed

Watchman 2012

about the Grand Teton climb. I was sleeping in the hut on the Lower Saddle and had to use the outside privy. It was cold. I braced myself against the wind as I made my way in the dark over the crest to the primitive john. As I sat down, looking up at the stars, I felt something warm and wet on my leg. Jolted from my dream, I leapt out of bed and dashed to the RV toilet. It was the senior equivalent of a wet dream. In searching for my youth I had over-shot my teenage years target to land somewhere in my infancy. A time recalibration was in order.

After breakfast we started up the road to Crater Lake. The bicyclists had already arrived and were climbing the road. We decided to take the East Rim Drive to avoid the congestion. Our first stop was Sun Notch where a trail crew was working on a new loop trail. The old trail went straight through a meadow to the Rim Overlook. The new trail circles the meadow. The work is part of a meadow restoration project. I asked one of the workers if he was permanent with Crater Lake and he said he was seasonal—May through November. When the first snowflakes appear, he said he heads to Mexico. The morning was beautiful. The air was crisp and clear with a good view of the Phantom Ship from the Sun Notch Trail.

We then turned down the Pinnacles Road and took the Pinnacles Trail. It was a one-and-a-half-mile trail along the edge of a canyon with good views of the Pinnacles that were formed by hot fumaroles. The trail continues to the park boundary. There is a stone monument, built in the 1930s, that was the original east gate entrance to the park. When the main road was rerouted, the east entrance was essentially abandoned.

On the way back to the rim from Pinnacles, we tried to take the hike to Plaikni Falls, but the trailhead parking lot was full. We drove up to the Cloudcap Overlook, the highest point on the rim. In the parking area were a number of antique cars that were part of a group circling the lake. We then headed counterclockwise around the lake. The bicyclists were circling the lake in the opposite direction. Just before Cleetwood Cove, one of the cyclists hit a pothole and had a spill. An ambulance was already there, and other cyclists had stopped to render aid. The cycle was damaged, but the cyclist didn't appear to be seriously injured.

We stopped for lunch at Grouse Hill picnic area, later walking to the rim for some good views of the lake. On the rim there were rock overhangs, where we could look straight down to Steel Bay. With the sun almost directly overhead, the water color was an incredible azure blue. The richness of the color was accentuated by the definition provided by wind generated wavelets, giving the bay the appearance of a colorful washboard.

From the rim road, we turned north to the Pumice Desert. Pumice is volcanic rock that has rapidly cooled, trapping gasses and creating material that is extremely light for its size. The larger pumice rocks look much heavier than they are. There were not as many pumice boulders as I remember, but out into the desert we found some good-sized rocks for photographs.

We drove to the Pacific Coast Trailhead where I took a short one-and-a-half-mile hike on the trail while Jane rested. Next stop was the Steel Visitor Center, which featured a small bas relief model of Crater Lake, and I asked the ranger if one had been at Watchman. This one was much smaller than the one I remember from the film. He said there was another model at the Rim Visitor Center. My search for the model was becoming a treasure hunt.

We watched the orientation movie on the park at the Steel

Steel Bay – Crater Lake

Visitor Center, then drove to the Rim Visitor Center, which has a model of the lake, but it also was smaller than the one I remembered. I asked the ranger there about whether there had been one at the Watchman fire lookout. He said there was a larger model at the Sinnott Memorial Overlook. We walked to the Overlook and finally found the elusive model I remembered with the view of the Lake in the background. I had been wrong. It had not been on Watchman; it was on the Sinnott Memorial Overlook, unmoved and unchanged after 50 years. There is something comforting about finding a touchstone in the place it is supposed to be; it gives you a feeling of permanence, of solidity. Change may be good, but I believe in the adage, "If it ain't broke, don't fix it." Being able to go back to a spot years later and find it unchanged recalibrates one's internal compass, an important step to take every 50 years or so.

We drove back to Mazama Village and rested. At about six o'clock p.m., we went back to the Crater Lake Lodge for dinner but the dining room was booked until nine. Disappointed, we drove back to Mazama but stopped at the Steel Visitor Center and took the Lady of the Woods Trail. The Lady of the Woods is a sculpture in a rock completed in 1919. The trail also tells the story of the architecture of the buildings in the main park area.

I have absolutely no recollection of the Lady of Woods, although my 1962 journal mentions that I hiked the trail. Much of the 1962 trip I remember in vivid detail. On reflection, however, those memories have been reinforced by my film and my father's photographs, which I have viewed frequently over the years, each time renewing the memories. I have no photographs or film of the Lady of the Woods, only the singular reference in my journal that does not include a description of the rock or the trail.

The only part of the 1962 trip that remains fresh in my mind without the prompt of photographs and film is the Grand Teton climb. I have only the photograph of me on rappel, but the memory of each step of the hike to the Saddle and the climb to the summit is as intense as the day I made them, notwithstanding the lack of visual reinforcement over the years. When you are in a state of high excitement, life on the edge, the experience must burn deep into the neurons of your brain, making it impervious to the dulling effect of time and age.

A herd of deer scattered in the woods as we approached. The trail rises 100 feet above Munson Creek and was a great appetizer for dinner. At Mazama Village we went to Annie Creek Restaurant. Their computers had broken and there was a jam at the cashier. It took a while to get seated, but eventually we got in. The food was fairly good. I had fried cod and Jane had a large salad. After dinner we went back to camp, wrote in our journals before sleep. Tomorrow would be the last leg of this incredible journey. I had one more mountain to climb.

FIFTEEN

An Undiscovered Jewel

Lassen Volcanic National Park

The Pacific Coast of the United States lies along the intersection of two major tectonic plates of the earth's crust, the Pacific Plate and North American Plate that slowly move in opposite directions, creating friction, the edges thrusting, grinding, and fighting against the other. This is a seismic zone with nearly continual earthquakes of some lesser magnitude and an occasional "big one" that reorients the landscape. It is also part of the Pacific Ring of Fire, a string of dormant and active volcanoes that encircle the ocean where the plates meet.

The United States portion of the Ring of Fire begins north at Mount Baker and continues along the Cascades with outlets at Mount St. Helens, Mount Hood, the former Mount Mazama, which is now Crater Lake, and Mount Shasta. At the southern terminus of this volatile string of fire breathers is Mount Lassen, which last erupted in 1915, although steam still vents from the crater on its summit.

Mt. Lassen was the first major volcanic eruption in the lower 48 states in the last century. It was a prelude to the later explosion of Mount St. Helens in 1980. Lassen demonstrated that, despite the devastation of ash, pumice and lava flow, nature slowly but inexorably heals itself. Eventually the forest returned, a lesson repeated on the blasted slopes of Mount St. Helens.

In California, Yosemite is the magnet for visitors. They are drawn to its storied valley with its towering granite walls and waterfalls that seem to flow from the sky. For variety, some travelers also include Sequoia and Kings Canyon, with their giant trees and Sierra vistas. But few visit, or even have heard of, the small park in Northern California that rivals any of those three more popular designations in sheer beauty, and far exceeds them in the wilderness experience, with uncrowded parking lots and trails that can be hiked in quiet solitude.

Lassen Volcanic is a park of incredible beauty and diversity. It even has a thermal area at Bumpass Hell with boiling pools and mud pots reminiscent of Yellowstone. The view of Lassen Peak in early morning and at dusk when the alpine glow is present is not to be missed. This undiscovered jewel was a fitting place to conclude our journey.

Map of
Lassen Volcanic National Park

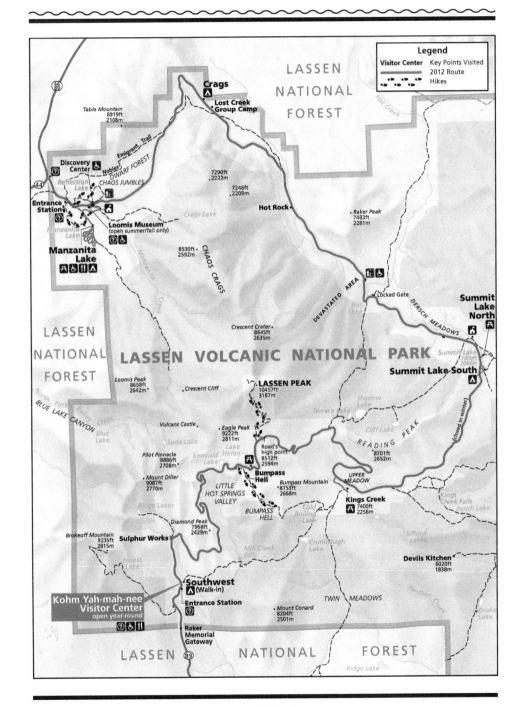

Monday • *August 20, 1962*

We packed the camp after eating. We all got into our cars and took off for Lassen Volcanic National Park. Wayne, Carl, Dad and I were in one car. The rest rode in Uncle Carl's jalopy. We drove to Klamath and separated. They went to get groceries and we were to meet them for lunch at Burney Falls. We went on and stopped at Mt Shasta to look for climbing supplies. I finally found my ice axe, Klettershoes, pitons, carabineers, and all the other mountaineering equipment. I bought $30 worth of equipment.

At Burney Falls we ate lunch, left a message for the other car, then left for Lassen Volcanic. There we went to Manzanita Lake campground and set up camp. After about 3 hours Uncle Carl finally came. We ate supper then set up a few more tents and had a campfire then went to bed.

Tuesday • *August 21, 1962*

We all got up early and ate breakfast then Dad, Wayne, Carl and I went down to the museum and looked at the exhibits. While our tire was being changed we headed down towards Lassen Peak reading all the signs. We ate lunch at Kings Meadow then went to the parking lot for the Lassen Peak trail. Before going on the trail, Dad and I got a picture of us climbing and rappelling on a small rock face. Carrying our climbing equipment we started up the trail. It was a 15% grade. The trail was very easy and Wayne, Carl and I made the 2 ½ miles to the top quickly. While waiting for Dad to come we climbed the 200 foot summit roped in. At the summit there was barely enough room for all of us but the view was magnificent. Shasta looms up on the horizon 75 miles away.
We took pictures then came down and went to camp. There we had another campfire then ate supper and went to bed.

Wednesday • *August 22, 1962*

We got up early at six a.m. and went down to Kings Meadow to photograph deer. Dad's last Minolta jammed and we came back to camp. After breakfast Mom and Dad left, then the rest of us

went swimming. *After an hour we went back to camp for lunch
then decided to go fishing. We drove about 25 miles to a crystal
clear stream stocked with trout. We fished for quite a while then
I climbed a cliff behind the stream. Coming down we saw a fish
across the bank eating gnats. We gave Carl, who still had a bathing suit on, the rod. He went downstream and after a while came
back with the fish. He didn't want to carry the rod across the
stream, so he asked Uncle Carl to catch it when he threw it across.
Uncle Carl spent about 5 minutes showing him how to throw it.
Then Carl threw it like a javelin and hit Uncle Carl square in the
mouth. The blood spurted from a jagged laceration an inch-and-
half long in his upper lip. We went back to camp and had supper
then went to bed.*

Thursday • August 23, 1962

*Dad and I got up at 5:30 am and went to photograph a marten.
We saw him but it was too dark to get a picture. Back at camp we
ate breakfast then took down everything and packed. While we
were packing, Uncle Carl drove on down to Bumpass Hell where
we were going to meet him for lunch. After stopping at a few places
for pictures we met them for lunch. We also stopped at the Sulphur
Works. It is the heart of a fallen volcano, Mt. Tehama. We then
left Lassen and headed for Reno.*

*In Reno we got left in a park while Mom, Dad, Uncle Carl and
Aunt Alice went gambling. But then we said goodbye to them and
we went gambling. After breaking even we left Reno.*

──── **DAY 41** ────

Wednesday • September 12, 2012

We slept late after another cold night then organized the RV and left Crater Lake. The drive to Klamath Falls was through cattle country with broad wide valleys of lush grass. Outside of MacDoel on US 97, the fuel gauge went from three bars to one, then the low fuel light came on. It was 38 miles to Weed, and there was nothing on the map that looked like a town where there might be fuel. We were stopped for road work after Hebron Pass. The flagman said that if we could not get the RV started again he could declare us stranded and send a truck for fuel. However, when the pilot car came our direction, the RV started cleanly. We coasted downhill when possible and made it to a station three miles outside of Weed. It took 21.522 gallons to fill the tank. The fuel capacity is 25 gallons so we had a couple of gallons to spare, but it was a harrowing experience.

We stopped in Mt. Shasta for groceries. The view of Mt. Shasta was terrific. There was some snow but it was significantly less than in previous years. We picked up Highway 89 and drove towards Lassen, stopping on 89 at a viewpoint of Shasta for lunch. We passed Burney Falls, and I recognized the stream where Carl, Jr. caught the trout. I hadn't realized that it was Hat Creek, perhaps the most famous fly fishing trout stream in California.

At the Lassen Volcanic National Park entrance, we stopped at the Loomis Museum to look around. The ranger told me that the trail to the summit of Mt. Lassen was closed for repairs. It was open for the first 1.3 miles only. I would have an abbreviated summit climb of Lassen.

At the campground entrance we were behind a group that had a reservation but had failed to print a copy. They were relying on the email confirmation on their IPad but there was no Internet service in the park. The group couldn't remember their campsite number. The ranger told them the campsite had a slip with their name on it. All they had to do was drive around the campground until they found the site with their name on the post. However, there are 179 campsites dispersed over four loops. They might be looking for a while.

Fortunately, I had prepared in advance. I printed out the reservations for each campground and hotel. We had campsite C-35. As we were setting up camp, I saw the group that had been ahead of us still cruising the campground loops looking in vain for their site. Relying on computers in the wilderness is a fool's choice – hard copy paper is the only option in the woods.

At 5:00 p.m., we checked out the camp store and hiked around Manzanita Lake and Reflection Lake, a total of 3 miles. We got some great photographs of Lassen reflected in the two lakes. We also saw several does with fawns on the Manzanita Lake Trail.

Back at camp, I made a fire and cooked beef Rice-a-Roni. We then wrote in our journals.

——— **DAY 42** ———

Thursday • September 13, 2012

The night had not been that cold, but I turned on the heat to warm up the RV. After breakfast, we headed for Bumpass Hell. Although there had been predictions of smoke from the fires in Lassen, the sky was clear and the day was beautiful. Between the Devastated Area and Summit Lake we saw a recently burned over area. There were several park service trucks at turnouts with rangers looking for hot spots. Signs warned of smoke, but we didn't have a problem.

We stopped at the Devastated Area to take the interpretive trail, which was set up to accommodate visitors with disabilities and incorporated the latest technology. The path was crushed rock with a gentle grade that could accommodate wheelchair access. Along the trail were interpretive stations and the usual illustrated signs, but each also had a motion activated speaker powered by a solar panel that provided a narration of the interpretive sign. When we approached the first station, a voice started explaining the view. It was a bit startling. This type of trail only works where the stations are in sunlight and can be solar-powered. A forest trail does not get enough light to power the solar panels.

The Devastated Area was where the photograph of Lassen in my journal was taken. The trees have grown substantially in the past 50 years.

Mt. Lassen – 1962

Mt. Lassen - 2012

After completing the trail we drove past Kings Meadow and on to the Bumpass Hell Trailhead. The trail is 3 miles roundtrip. The first part is gradually uphill and the last ½ mile is a descent into the thermal area. At the start of the trail is a sign explaining that Mt. Tehama imploded after an eruption, leaving Brokeoff Mountain as a remnant.

Bumpass Hell is stark but beautiful. It has steam vents and boiling mud pots as well as sapphire blue pools. The only feature missing from those at Yellowstone are geysers. While photographing the steaming cauldron, I accidently dropped my Nikon lens cap. I had already lost one lens cap and was determined not to lose my last one. The black plastic cap rolled off the boardwalk and bounced down a bare slope towards a mud pot, stopping a few feet short of being lost forever in the gray bubbling mud. I gingerly tested the ground with my trekking poles to make sure it would support my weight, then slowly inched my way about 20 feet down the slope to a point where I could fully extend one arm to grasp my lens cap with my fingertips while leaning on a trekking pole with the other arm. I made a successful, and thankfully uneventful, retrieval. Do not try this at home.

After the Bumpass Hell hike we drove to Lake Helen and had lunch on a picnic table overlooking the lake. When we finished we drove to the Mt. Lassen Trail parking area. I turned on the generator for Jane so she could charge her phone and Nook. I then hustled up the trail. The first two hundred yards were deep soft sand and very steep. At the first turn there was a narrow path straight up the side of the mountain. A sign indicated that the worn path was an unauthorized shortcut route used by hikers on the return and it was a scar on the landscape that would take years to heal. The sign also said that if shortcutting did not stop, the trail would be closed except for guided parties. That would be a tragedy.

The day was hot and the trail was steep. I had a good recollection of the trail from the first hike in 1962 and also a second climb in 1992. The footpath was closed at a point .9 miles from the summit. I took some photographs and turned around. The closure point was just short of the rocks where the photographs of Wayne, Carl and I rock climbing were taken.

It had taken me 40 minutes to make the 1.6 miles up the mountain. On the way down I met a party of four going up. I told them this was the last day of a 43-day trip. They seemed interested

Climbing Mt. Lassen in 1962

On the Mt. Lassen Trail in 2012

in the concept of a book on what had changed over the past 50 years. I made it down the trail in 30 minutes.

We drove back to the campground and took a break. At five p.m., we followed the Lily Pond Nature Trail that starts at the Loomis Museum. The trail winds through the forest with markers at significant trees, identifying their name – white fir - and some information on species, such as, "One of the most common trees at this elevation." It was a good way to end the day.

We went back to camp and I built a fire for grilled bratwurst and beans. After dinner we wrote in our journals by the fire, waiting until it burned out before going to bed.

——— DAY 43 ———

Friday • September 14, 2012

We got up early to organize the RV for the drive home. The last day felt strange. I knew I had to get back to work, but if the option were open, I'd head for Yosemite. I wasn't ready for the journey to end.

Kings Meadow, Lassen Volcanic National Park

At Lost Creek, we stopped and looked at the "Hot Rock" that is so large ten people stood in front of it for a photograph after the 1915 eruption. The 300 ton rock was blown five miles from the Mount Lassen crater to its final resting spot at Lost Creek.

The sky was not as clear as yesterday. There was some smoke as we drove through the fire area, stopping at King's Meadow for a photograph. The view of the meadow with the creek in the foreground and Mt. Lassen in the background is one of the most beautiful spots in the park.

We stopped briefly at the Sulphur Works then drove out of the park to Red Bluff and on to I-5. As we got closer to the Bay Area the heavier the traffic became. We reached the East Bay at 3:00 p.m., the front end of the Friday rush hour. It was a rude initiation back into civilization after more than 40 days on back roads.

SIXTEEN

Reflections

We pulled into our driveway in Santa Clara, having driven 6715 miles through nine states and visiting eleven National Parks. This was a trip to recapture my youth, but along the way it was an unexpected reconciliation of a long estranged relationship with my late father. The journey brought back memories of shared experiences of father and son that on reflection were more meaningful and important than the friction that grated between us in later years. My father was a unique individual with admirable qualities and many talents. I had developed my own identity. No longer smothered by his outsized personality, I was able to sift the good from the bad, weighing both and finding that the positive measure overwhelmed the scale. It was not a surprise, but it was an assessment that I had avoided making until this trip. He was a talented artist, generous with his friends, a man who had contributed much to the conservation of parks and wildlife.

As I read my 1962 journal in preparing for the trip, I was struck by the number of friends my dad had made in the park service, their generosity with their time in sharing their intimate knowledge of the parks where they now served. They were rangers and naturalists he had met at Everglades National Park. His infectious personality had held him in good stead. He made friends easily and kept them. The 1962 journal and reprise trip reminded me that the relationships my father had with his good friends were not one-sided. He received as much as he gave.

While at times I felt smothered by my father, feeling pushed towards a path in his image, his greatest gift to me was giving me the freedom to be independent. In 1960, when I was 13 years old, my best friend, Berk Scott, and I flew by ourselves to Washington, DC, then caught a bus to Centreville, Virginia, to attend the centennial reenactment of the battle of Bull Run, spending the night at the home of strangers who were renting rooms to visitors for the reenactment. The next day we hitchhiked the five miles from Centreville to the battlefield with me carrying my heavy Bolex movie camera. For two young civil war buffs the reenactment was thrilling, living history. Similarly, I made the Grand Teton climb without parental supervision, heading off for the climb after my mother and father had already left for the day. Accomplishing those life events by myself at a young age gave me self-confidence as an adult. It was a priceless gift.

It was a paradox that he tried so hard to mold me in his image yet gave me such independence. At some point years ago I disengaged from the relationship, letting my father be himself and I making a life for myself on a different path. On this reprise trip I found that, although I had strived to break from my father's image and had achieved my own identity, we were in many ways the same, both driven individuals, independent, and instilled with a deep love of nature and the serenity of the wilderness.

At one point, I mentally calculated how old my father was when we made the trip in 1962. There is always the generational spatial relationship between parent and child; the parent older, the child younger. As I was repeating the activities of the 1962 trip and thinking about my father, he always seemed older than I. It was a shock when I realized he had been 39 years old when we made the trip in 1962. I was now 26 years older than he was at the time. It was a calculus that made my head spin. I felt disoriented, as if in a time warp. He was the younger, I was the older.

There were other, less introspective, observations on this journey that were related more to the travel than the traveler. Much has changed in the fifty years between my two journeys. The roads are better. The interstate highway system that was in its infancy then is now complete, shortening the travel time between parks, if not improving the view.

The mode of transportation has improved. Other than the addition of fuel and fluids, our Roadtrek Mercedes Sprinter required nothing but a firm hand on the wheel and some duct tape to repair a minor fender-bender. In contrast, our 1962 Corvair 95 threw a fan belt outside of Denver, had major engine work in Estes Park and Port Angeles, and at least two flat tires. The reliability of our ride improved substantially even though the fuel mileage remained the same at about 15-18 miles per gallon.

The Electronic Age has changed travel. GPS has replaced paper maps. Everything runs on a rechargeable battery—cameras, phones, even books. Recharging appliances has become a problem in logistics with the search for available electrical outlets as important as finding potable water.

Park visitor demographics has also changed. The typical American family of five in a station wagon with a tent has been replaced by a tour bus of Asian visitors and rented RVs with couples from Germany, France, the UK and Australia. Our most popular attractions are our parks.

Park visitation has exploded. With the increased number of visitors, the park service has changed its approach to park access. Instead of bringing visitors to a sensitive area, the park service has routed visitors away from such sites, making it more difficult but not impossible to visit. Now visitors have to walk to some areas we drove to in 1962.

While there have been changes in how we travel, and modifications to park infrastructure, the basic landscape, except for the glaciers, is no different today than in 1962. When I compare my father's photographs with mine from this last trip, there are differences in vegetation, but remarkably little else has changed.

I had searched for the Fountain of Youth and found it hiking the trails and climbing the mountains of the national parks. While, I, like the parks, have changed some over the past fifty years, there are new lines and some surface weathering, I still have the same joy at the "strange wonders" I beheld fifty years earlier. I may be a sixty-five-year-old man in body but my spirit remains youthful, much unchanged from the fifteen-year-old who made the journey in 1962. May it ever be so.

Afterword

As I'm feeling energized, I realize that I have
four more journals from my youth, each describing
a summer's adventure. There are many more
strange wonders in other parks
waiting to be revisited.

Acknowledgements

I carried the idea for this book in my head for twenty years before embarking on the 2012 journey that started the writing process. Over the years I would describe my goal of repeating the trip I took as a fifteen-year-old and writing about the changes I encountered. Friends and acquaintances provided encouragement that the project was something that might be of interest to others besides myself. For those people who gave me support I thank you.

Friends and family have been generous with their time in reading manuscript drafts and providing helpful suggestions. My Pi Kappa Phi fraternity brothers, Peter Tooker, Jim Desouza, and Steven Haughney, made the book immeasurably better. They read early drafts and provided cogent suggestions. My cousin, Carl Bryan and his wife, Shelley, also were helpful with their comments, urging me to dig deeper into my relationship with my dad. Jane's good friend Hilma Mortell provided a critical read and perspective from someone who would not normally have read a book like this one. Patricia Saunders, the wife of a Lockheed Martin colleague, and professional editor, had offered some years earlier to edit the book when I wrote it. Unfortunately for me, Pat retired before it was completed but she generously read a draft and gave me great comments. I thank M.L. Stein for his fine final edit of the manuscript. The detailed park maps were prepared by Mike Woodard at Mapping Specialists. A special thanks goes to the talented Rebecca Byrd Bretz Arthur for the hours she spent on the cover and book design, translating my rough ideas into a work of art.

A special thanks to my children, Bryan, Elizabeth, and Virginia. I hope you have some childhood memories of your own that will provide you joy in your later life.

The most important acknowledgement, however, is for my wife, Jane. We met in college when I was nineteen, four years after the 1962 trip. She experienced the tension with my dad, relived the 1962 trip in reading my journal and looking at photos and film, and encouraged my quest to repeat the journey. She was the co-pilot on the trip and made most of the hikes with me. On those she passed on, she was there to meet me each time I returned, eager to hear what wonders I had seen. Jane was the first to read the manuscript and was my sounding board for passages I wrote late into the night. This book is as much hers as mine. Without her it would not have been written. Thank you, Jane.

About the Author

Whit Thornton is retired after 43 years practicing government contract law in government, private practice, and with Lockheed Martin. He received his undergraduate and law degrees from Washington & Lee University. With an interest in history and thirst for adventure, he and his wife, Jane, split their time between homes in the Low Country of South Carolina and in the Sierra Nevada Mountains north of Lake Tahoe. The author of numerous legal articles, this is his first book.

CPSIA information can be obtained
at www.ICGtesting.com
Printed in the USA
LVOW05s2046101115
461855LV00009B/15/P